W9-BCT-166

LIBERTARIANS
ON THE
PRAIRIE

Center Point
Large Print

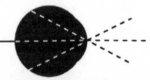

**This Large Print Book carries the
Seal of Approval of N.A.V.H.**

LIBERTARIANS
ON THE
PRAIRIE

Laura Ingalls Wilder, Rose Wilder Lane,
and the Making of the Little House Books

Christine Woodside

CENTER POINT LARGE PRINT
THORNDIKE, MAINE

Library of Congress Cataloging-in-Publication Data

Names: Woodside, Christine, 1959- author.
Title: Libertarians on the prairie : Laura Ingalls Wilder, Rose Wilder
Lane, and the making of the Little House Books / Christine Woodside.
Description: Center Point Large Print edition. | Thorndike, Maine :
     Center Point Large Print, 2018.
Identifiers: LCCN 2018001387 | ISBN 9781683247425
     (hardcover : alk. paper)
Subjects: LCSH: Wilder, Laura Ingalls, 1867-1957. |
     Wilder, Laura Ingalls, 1867-1957. Little house books. |
     Lane, Rose Wilder, 1886-1968. | Ingalls family. | Authors, American—
     20th century—Biography. | Women pioneers—United States—
     Biography. | Frontier and pioneer life—United States. |
     Frontier and pioneer life—United States. | Libertarianism—
     United States—History—20th century. | Large type books. |
     BISAC: BIOGRAPHY & AUTOBIOGRAPHY / Literary. |
     LITERARY CRITICISM / Children's Literature.
Classification: LCC PS3545.I342 Z976 2018 | DDC 813/.52 [B]—dc23
LC record available at https://lccn.loc.gov/2018001387

For Nat, who steered my proverbial wagon on this literal and drawn-out journey

CONTENTS

FOREWORD

The email from Christine Woodside landed in my inbox like a lot of story pitches: She'd been given my name by a colleague of mine in her writers' group; she had a research project that she wanted to turn into a book. She thought we might be interested for the Ideas section of the *Boston Globe*, even though she hadn't written an article on the topic before.

Normally these are red flags, especially the last: everyone thinks their pet project is a book waiting to be written. But it wasn't hard to see that this was the real thing. Over the course of years poring through the Laura Ingalls Wilder archives, Christine had been marinating in the backstory of one of the most beloved icons of American literature, and she started telling me the kinds of details about the Little House books that every editor is thrilled to hear. What Christine was offering readers was that rare crackle of discovery: the ability to see a beloved cultural artifact in a totally new light.

Many fans of the Little House series know that Rose Wilder Lane was heavily involved in writing her mother's books; some even know that Rose had strong anti-government politics. But what Christine had found in these letters and drafts was a tug-of-war that shaped the books in deeply ideological ways.

These books weren't just entertainment. They were an entry into one of the most profound political conversations in America, all the more powerful for being cloaked in charming pioneer garb. Christine was right: her research did become a good article and an even better book. Since her book was published, she has followed it with a fascinating article in *POLITICO Magazine*, tracing Rose's wider influence on twentieth-century conservatism, and it's hard not to keep seeing fingerprints of the ideas in Little House, and Rose's ambitious politics, on the nation today.

Much as we might bemoan the intrusion of politics into literature, a clear moral stance has always been part of the power of great stories. In the case of the Little House books, their politics was part of their power all along, whether readers realize it or not. Christine's work helps give the creative tension between mother and daughter its rightful place in an American argument that is still playing out.

Stephen Heuser
Editor, *POLITICO Magazine*

PREFACE TO THE
LARGE PRINT EDITION

This book has surprised many admirers of Laura Ingalls Wilder who thought they knew her. In it, I reveal the extent and nature of her daughter Rose Wilder Lane's collaboration on the Little House Books and how their shared disgust at the New Deal politics of the 1930s shaped Laura's pioneer stories for children. I've heard from all sort of readers, ranging from American West buffs to followers of American conservatism. Journalists and scholars have discussed my analysis in news outlets, blogs, and academic journals. I've been invited to speak at history conferences and libraries, including the Herbert Hoover Presidential Library, where most of the Wilder family papers are housed. The public dialogue I've started, even when it turns critical of me, has been heartening. Odd though this may sound, I believe I first learned persistence in seeking the whole truth from reading the Little House books when I was growing up.

Many of the facts of Laura and Rose's collaboration on the books have been publicly available since the early 1980s, yet the wider public has only slowly become aware of them. Laura and Rose never talked about Rose's part in the making of the books. The Little House books and their inspiring stories of the American frontier are children's stories, and so digging into the often unpleasant part of their creation sometimes felt like a betrayal of innocence. I'm sure that Laura and Rose themselves would have at the very least felt uncomfortable in dissecting their collaboration the way I do. And yet, once my desire to know the whole story of the Little House books had fully gripped me, I felt I owed it to myself and all others who shared my fascination with the Wilder family to write this book.

Some reviewers have asserted that I believe Rose Wilder Lane ghostwrote the Little House books. That is not my belief at all. Ghostwriters do all the writing. Rose and Laura worked as full partners telling Laura's story. Rose wrote in scenes, changed structure, added dialogue, and removed stories. So did Laura. The only person who called Rose a ghostwriter in her time was Rose herself, and she most likely was not referring to her work on her mother's books. She was talking about books she wrote for Lowell Thomas, Frederick O'Brien, and others. On this subject, Rose's biographer, William Holtz, quoted the following statement from Rose's January 24, 1933 journal entry in his appendix to *The Ghost in the Little House*: "I have written and ghosted seventeen books." She wrote this at the time she was revising Laura's second book.

It's difficult if not impossible to know which volumes Rose meant by this statement or even what her definition of ghosting was.

We know enough from the available papers and documented recollections that we don't have to ask who really wrote the Little House books. That we sometimes do still doubt the shared authorship shows how closely Rose and Laura held their secret about Rose's role and how powerful the popular myth of pioneer authenticity that has grown around Laura.

I hope this book will inspire others to explore the political and economic ideas that influenced ordinary Americans in Laura and Rose's time— and that do in all times. In today's volatile political climate, we will benefit from looking back on all the ways our deepest beliefs came of age and understanding how those beliefs still guide us at the polls.

June 2017

NOTE TO THE READER

Laura Ingalls Wilder's Little House books include:

Little House in the Big Woods, published by Harper and Brothers (which published all of the books on this list) in 1932, about the Ingalls family's life in a log cabin in the early 1870s in Wisconsin.

Farmer Boy, published in 1933, about Almanzo Wilder's childhood on a prosperous farm outside Malone, New York, in the 1860s.

Little House on the Prairie, published in 1935, about the Ingalls family's year living in Native American territory that later became Kansas.

On the Banks of Plum Creek, published in 1937, about the Ingalls family's migration to Minnesota in the 1870s, and their farm and town life.

By the Shores of Silver Lake, published in 1939, about the family's last migration to work on the new railroad and file a homestead claim in Dakota Territory in 1879 and 1880.

The Long Winter, published in 1940, about the 'Hard Winter' of 1880–81 in Dakota Territory.

Little Town on the Prairie, published in 1941, about Laura's social life and studying to be a teacher in De Smet, South Dakota.

These Happy Golden Years, published in 1943, about Laura's coming of age and Almanzo Wilder's courtship near De Smet, South Dakota.

Not part of the original series but included with it is *The First Four Years*, which is an unedited manuscript about Laura and Almanzo's disastrous attempt to farm in Dakota Territory's drought years in 1885–1889. This book was published in 1971, after the death of her daughter, Rose Wilder Lane.

Pioneer Girl, Laura's memoir that provided the framework for the series, was published eighty-four years after Laura wrote it—in 2014. It tells the factual story of Laura's life from age three in 1870 through her marriage to Almanzo Wilder in 1885. Laura drafted it by pencil on tablets at the request of Rose, who revised it twice but was unable to find a magazine that would serialize it. Pamela Smith Hill edited and annotated *Pioneer Girl* with a group called the Pioneer Girl Project; the publisher was the South Dakota Historical Society Press.

INTRODUCTION

IRENE LICHTY TURNS ME DOWN

In 1976 I wrote a letter to the curator of the Laura Ingalls Wilder Home and Museum in Mansfield, Missouri, and asked for a summer job—any job. I was seventeen and lived with my large family in a split-level house in Princeton, New Jersey. I wrote her that I would go alone to Missouri. I would lead tours, file letters, sweep floors—whatever she asked. The curator, Irene V. Lichty, had actually known Laura, the pioneer author of the inspiring Little House books, which told about her self-sufficient childhood in the late nineteenth century. Laura had traveled by covered wagon across the Midwest with Pa, Ma, and her sisters Mary, Carrie, and Grace, from cabins to sod house to shanties, making farms on wild lands.

Soon a light-pink envelope came in the mail. On thin stationery, the note went something like this: "Dear Christine, I cannot offer you a job at the Home. We do sometimes hire girls from the area." Mrs. Lichty's ballpoint pen had made channels in the thin paper. "But there is nowhere you could stay. I am sorry, but there is nothing for a girl your age to do in this town."

I was crushed, not because she had turned me down but because she seemed so brusque. I was embarrassed to think that she sensed I had no idea what I was asking. Yet, much as I pictured myself standing inside the Wilder home, leading others through the rooms, I lived in Princeton, New Jersey—what might be called the quintessential settled Northeastern town. I knew nothing of farm or pioneer life: going for the cows, keeping watch for wolves and bears, harvesting potatoes. I ranged free on my bicycle and watched sparrows struggle when a neighbor kid hit them with a BB gun, and my harvesting amounted to going to the produce aisle with my mom.

The introduction to Laura's last book had urged readers to visit and promised that the curators would be excited to hear from us. Mrs. Lichty's note, though, seemed like a reprimand. I felt that somehow Laura's legacy of optimism had, in the nineteen years since her death, faded from her friend's attitude. Of course, I had no way to dig deeper then. I put aside my hopes for my dream job and spent the summer making sandwiches in a restaurant.

After my brief correspondence with Mrs. Lichty, an urge to know the real Laura gripped me. From that day on, for the next four decades, through college and adult life of work and family, I read everything I could about Laura. I read the books over and over, noticing more of the themes of independence and wilderness in them each time. In college I wrote a paper for my American West course about the difference between Laura and Mary in *By the Shores of Silver Lake*. I studied articles, biographies, the columns Laura had written for a farm newspaper, her diary for the trip when she moved to Missouri in 1894 (published in 1962 as *On the Way Home*), and, finally, letters, diaries, and manuscripts from the Wilder family—all except those the family had evidently thrown away.

I steeped myself in Laura's philosophy of life. In my thirties, I wrote a newspaper tribute to Laura's energy and temperament as a housewife. It ended with that great scene from one of her farm columns, when she got so sick of cutting her hand on the so-called easier modern butter churn that she kicked it down the hill. But my admiration, I realized, was built on a foundation of selectively positive stories about her. I was ready for more, so I sought every trace of Laura Ingalls Wilder and the American pioneer experience wherever I could find them. I traveled to study the surviving Wilder family papers in Iowa, Missouri, Michigan, and a few other places.

I had once believed that the simple yet poetic Little House books told Laura's true story and outlined America's frontier history. In my pursuit of the full story, though, I've collided with the surprising reality that the Little House books idealized Laura's life, creating a parable that was easy to take for true history.

This book tells the story of two women who lived on Rocky Ridge Farm: Laura Ingalls Wilder, a farmer's wife and occasional journalist who became the beloved heroine and author of the Little House books, and her daughter, Rose Wilder Lane, who tutored Laura in the art of writing for a mass audience, and who left Missouri bitter and estranged. The chapters that follow tell what I learned during a quest that, by now, has stretched over more than half my life.

It began as a desire to know the real Laura. But the Wilder family papers showed me clearly that Laura's daughter, the bestselling writer Rose Wilder Lane, had helped write the Little House books. Rose had worked in secret. The documents that were left underscored her participation, yet for half a century it never came up in public so far as I could see. Rose had hidden her role and kept it hidden, even after Laura died in 1957. This revelation stunned me. I discovered as I wound my way deep into the details that Rose didn't just help; she created an idea and, editing and revising, led Laura in realizing it. She shaped their tone, ideals, and politics. She built them around certain themes—freedom, respect for free markets, and love of nature and the natural order—and she removed many stories Laura had told that did not fit those themes.

Rose was a novelist, a biographer of Herbert Hoover, and a writer of national prominence known for her stories and articles in the popular magazines of the day. She was one of three women who inspired the libertarian political movement, and she took under her wing Roger Lea MacBride, the man who cast the first Electoral College vote for a Libertarian candidate in 1972. MacBride called Rose "Gramma" and inherited the royalty income of the Little House books. He said the Wilder family's strong pioneer ways inspired him when he ran for president on the Libertarian Party ticket in 1976.

The shared project that became the Little House books started in 1930, soon after the stock market crash that launched the Great Depression. Laura was sixty-five years old and was fulfilling an ambition she'd held for years. She wrote down the story of a childhood spent traveling in covered wagons and starting new farms across the western prairies. She had been one of the early pioneers on a now-disappeared frontier. She had watched her parents fight fires, blizzards, and drought. She went after the cows and gathered firewood beginning in her toddler years. She listened for the howls of wolves and rejoiced when her father did not kill them. She helped load hay onto wagons and twist the dead grasses into fuel for the stove.

In Laura's drafts, the family withstood the frontier staunchly, jaws set. Laura told Rose she *had* to write the tales this way because the Ingallses *were* stoic by nature. "I wish I could explain how I mean about the stoicism of the people," Laura said in a 1938 letter to Rose. "You know a person can not live at a high pitch of emotion. The feelings become dulled by a natural, unconscious effort at self-preservation." The family had never, Laura said, reacted to anything emotionally. As Rose crafted later drafts in the quest for publication, she added stories, and those details from Laura's life that remained were framed differently, so that the Ingallses faced hardships with genial hope expressed in cheerful dialogue. Rose's revisions allowed for plenty of optimism and self-expression— and no bitterness, resentment, or remorse—as the family migrated from place to place. Rose created a new pioneer myth—one that eschewed the violence of Daniel Boone and the then-wildly popular Western novels of Zane Grey. This new pioneer story, told through young Laura's eyes, extolled the power of ordinary people to make their own destinies. The books became primers for authentic, simple living. They underscored self-reliance.

And they did more than that. The divergence between the Little House narrative and Laura

Ingalls Wilder's real life story explains why the pioneer myth is more than the stuff of great literature. It is a political ideal. This message was formed through the confluence of three forces: First, the two women's shared determination to sell the stories and earn desperately needed cash as the Depression bore down on their farm. Second, the complicated dynamic of their relationship as mother and daughter as well as co-creators, which included competition to control the family's narrative. Third, their political beliefs.

As they witnessed the struggles of those around them during the Great Depression, Laura and Rose expressed horror at social changes like controls on farm production and the reduction in the workweek brought about by Roosevelt's New Deal. The women came to admire and espouse conservative, anti-government ideals. Laura thought people were complaining too much; it irritated her, a self-sufficient woman who'd been through hard times over and over. Rose took this view in an ideological direction. She thought the country, in its policies and government, was broken. She infused her mother's children's stories with examples of a set of zealous free-market principles she devised over several years of reading, thinking, and reasoning with like-minded friends. The ideals run deep now in certain parts of American culture.

• • •

In studying the papers they left behind, I pieced together the nature of Rose and Laura's collaboration. I've come to believe their partnership deepened the original story. The message of the books became broader and more universal. The ideas that shaped the Little House books would inspire the libertarian political movement, which began as a crusade during World War II against communism, taxation, and Social Security and for property rights and individual freedom. Only a few years after Rose and Laura finished the last of the Little House books, Rose was at the forefront of the libertarian movement, along with her friend the writer Isabel Paterson, author of *God of the Machine*, and her acquaintance Ayn Rand, famous for having written *The Fountainhead*.

As she helped her mother, Rose, for the first time in her life, found herself admiring the courage her pioneer parents had mustered in migrating around the prairie. At the same time, Laura, as Rose's literary partner, realized that she, like Rose, mistrusted Roosevelt's New Deal relief programs. And so self-reliance became the Wilder family business.

Rose probably had no idea what she was in for when Laura brought her the first of her handwritten pages. She set herself to work on the story. Rose knew that stark truths about poverty, illness, and natural disasters alone would hardly make the books appealing to readers, whether young or old. She applied her keen narrative skills to Laura's experiences. She arranged and transformed them into cheerful tales of American strength and ingenuity. Some writers and fans have said that Rose did little more than lightly edit as she typed her mother's stories, encouraging Laura to find themes and a storyline. My examination of the family papers shows that Rose did far more than this. She transformed the whole of her mother's life by removing many parts and changing details where necessary to suit an idealized version of the pioneer story.

During the five years they lived a half-mile's walk apart on Rocky Ridge Farm in Missouri and the eight years they exchanged drafts by mail, Laura and Rose persevered in a tense partnership. Laura would hand over her handwritten stories; Rose would rewrite. The women intended the first two books to stand alone, but readers wrote glowing letters asking for more.

Laura and her husband, Almanzo (also a character in the Little House books), had always believed in hard work and making their own way, even though Almanzo suffered from a crippled leg most of his adult years. They'd made little more than a life of subsistence out of their farm in Missouri. They bought the land in 1894, but during most of Rose's childhood they actually worked and lived in town while they built up the farm. Making slow progress in establishing their fruit and dairy enterprise was largely fine with them. Not so with Rose. As a child, she was ashamed of the family's poverty and hated farming. She left home at fifteen in the hope of freeing herself from that existence, and she built an impressive career.

Laura and Almanzo stopped full-time farming in 1928, just when Rose returned home from abroad announcing that she would support them. Rose's feelings about going back to Missouri ranged from misery—as she complained to her diary—to exaggerated enthusiasm: she told friends the place was "cool and remote." During the nearly nine years that Rose lived mostly on her parents' farm, she welcomed writers and friends, some of whom stayed for years with her in the farmhouse. She brought electricity, central heating, and refrigeration to the farm and built and moved her parents into a separate house on the land.

Rose and Laura's relationship had never been warm, and while Rose lived on the farm their ongoing tension carried into their writing collaboration. They persevered through the strain of it because readers kept asking for more books. The books became their greatest source of income. But as they worked on the series, something greater arose, guided by their fervent beliefs. By joining their different strengths, they created literature.

The enterprise broke them, and they tried to hide that. Living near Laura, Rose seemed outwardly happy. But privately, something dark— even if it was just that they lived too close— persistently marred the love they proclaimed in public and in letters. Money fears haunted them even when they had enough. Rose overspent, prompting her parents' ire. During their years of collaboration, Rose wrote in her diary of "miserable" feelings toward her mother. We can't know exactly what incidents she was referring to, but surviving letters reveal that those feelings started early. For her part, Laura had been an exasperated mother during Rose's childhood. Almanzo's difficulty walking and using his hands had followed a bout of illness early in their marriage, and it put excessive strain on Laura from then on. The family endured drought and poverty, moving six times in seven years.

Rose's anxiety and Laura's strong personality clashed, but also fed the books' success. Laura confidently left major rewriting to Rose. Rose did the work but seemed to chafe under the obligation. In the drafting Rose exerted power to which Laura reluctantly yielded. They both wanted the books to be Laura's, and Laura would enjoy the fame. Nevertheless, for Rose, this could not have been a happy secret.

Laura and Rose did not tell anyone—not their agent, editor, or house guests—what Rose was doing. Some of Rose's friends guessed, but they, too, kept silent.

Had they not believed urgently that they must sell Laura's story, Rose would not have felt obligated to work so hard on them. Doomed (as she might have put it) to helping Laura, Rose advanced a revolution in individualistic thought and the principle of freedom inspired by Thomas Paine and the framers of the Constitution—libertarianism—with a small "l." In the Little House books she tried out many of the theories about freedom and what being American really means that became the central ideas of her libertarian treatise, *The Discovery of Freedom*, published in 1943—the year the last Little House book came out. In this way, the Little House books foreshadowed and underscored the libertarian movement. Incidents Rose retold about the hard-working members of the Ingalls and Wilder families outlined the basic tenets of libertarianism: freedom, property rights, "spontaneous order" (which means that left alone people make ethical choices), limited government, and free markets. As young Almanzo's father says in *Farmer Boy:* "You work hard, but you work as you please, and no man can tell you to go or come. You'll be free and independent, son, on a farm."

Free market ideals play out in many scenes. For example, in *The Long Winter*, the storekeeper tries to overcharge starving neighbors who want to buy the last stock of wheat available. A riot seems imminent until Pa speaks up: "This is a free country, and every man's got a right to do as he pleases with his own property. . . . Don't forget that every one of us is free and independent, Loftus. This winter won't last forever, and maybe you want to go on doing business after it's over." It's an appealing distillation of the idea that a free market can regulate itself. Laura rarely wrote extended dialogue in her own recollections, the manuscripts show; her daughter most likely invented this long exchange.

Within their simple, cheerful tales of self-sufficiency, the Little House stories advance ideals of maximum personal freedom and the limited need for the government. In their essence they illustrate libertarian ideals, and in this they reflect the attitudes of both women at the time they were writing the books. Laura's descriptive abilities and masterful memory for the details of daily living in marginal circumstances mix with Rose's plotting and thematic genius, and made them beautiful pieces of literature, too. But make no mistake: these stories deliver a political ethic. They say that "we'll weather the blast" and come out happy. Laura herself did not believe that to be true in all situations. She believed in weathering the blast, for sure. She knew, though, that the blast might win at times. Her early drafts occasionally said this, but her finished books did not.

As a teenager, I studied Rose's introduction and editorial comments in Laura's 1894 travel diary *On the Way Home.* I puzzled over her terse portrayal of Laura as a short-tempered young mother. So I read Donald Zochert's biography of Laura. He was the first to state, plainly, that many intermediate drafts of the Little House books seemed to be missing and that the full extent of Laura's revision process was unknown.

Later, I admired the columns for the *Missouri Ruralist,* where she wrote: "Now it isn't enough in any garden to cut down the weeds . . . cultivating the garden plants is just as important" (January 1920). And: "So much depends upon the homemakers. I sometimes wonder if they are so busy now with other things that they are forgetting this important work" (August 1923). I read these words when I was a newspaper reporter with two very young daughters. I believed deeply that homemaking creates a stable and happy family life, and Laura's reminder inspired me during my most exhausted times. And also:

"It would be much better for us all if we could be more interested in the work of our hands, if we could get back more of the attitude of our mothers toward their handmade garments and of our fathers' pride in their own workmanship" (January 1920). My city-bred parents did not know most of these pre-industrial skills, but I'd taken on Laura's family as my second one. My mother and I had sewn clothes since I was twelve years old, and Laura underscored the value of this skill.

In 1993, early one morning, I awoke to the sound of a National Public Radio host interviewing William Holtz, an English professor from the University of Missouri who had written a biography of Rose, *The Ghost in the Little House.* The host asked why readers of the Little House books were upset to know that Rose had been involved in the writing. Shouldn't the fact—one more insight into the life of a woman we admire—grab us?

Yet I knew, lying in bed, that this fact exploded our innocence. At the time, it was almost too much to handle. I realized that, if Rose had helped to write the books, then they didn't represent the pure memory of their main character. The writing of the books was a more complicated story. I already knew that real-life frontier history was less glorious and more tedious than the Little House books portrayed, but now Holtz had documented that Laura was not the person I'd imagined. At first I mourned my new knowledge. And then my disappointment led me into the stirring, real-life story that I want to share here: that of two strong women creating literature and crusading for their fervent beliefs.

PART I
OUTSIDERS

1

LAURA

(1867-1885)

> We were on our way again and going in the direction which always brought the happiest changes.
> —*Laura Ingalls Wilder, describing the train ride from Minnesota to Dakota Territory, in her first draft of the autobiography, "Pioneer Girl"*

The factual details of Laura Ingalls Wilder's life seem harsh when held up against the atmosphere of her autobiographical Little House novels. Between Laura's third and thirteenth years, the Ingalls family moved six times. Her father, Charles "Pa" Ingalls, was a fiddle-playing, poetry-reading adventurer. He and Laura's mother, Caroline or "Ma," took Laura and her sisters by covered wagon on a multistage pilgrimage seeking fertile land, good hunting, and wide-open spaces. What reality brought were natural disasters, crop failures, and hunted-out regions. Each time they decided to leave a place, Charles and Caroline loaded the wagon with the most basic supplies—cornmeal, live chickens, a few dishes, iron pots, and blankets—and set off, camping on the prairie or in creek bottoms each night. Until they were big enough to sit up, Laura and the other children sat in their mother's lap; once they were older (she wrote), they perched on a board placed across the wagon's sideboards.

In fall 1869, Ma and Pa loaded her and her older sister, Mary, into the wagon. They left their log cabin in Wisconsin—their "little house in the big woods"—and made their way, along with possibly thousands of other settlers, onto a small band of land that the federal government had kept closed to all but some thirty-one tribes of Plains Indians in the future state of Kansas, near the Oklahoma border. The region was called the Osage Diminished Reserve because the Osage had been there the longest and lost the most. The Osage had signed a treaty to relinquish the land just before the Ingallses headed there, but the treaty had never been ratified. In *Little House on the Prairie*, Laura would call this land Indian Territory, although it lay just north of the actual Indian Territory (another region also closed to non-Indians at that time).

Laura recalled little from the year they tried to farm there, but she and Rose combined family stories with best guesses and some invention in writing *Little House on the Prairie*. We do know that Pa built a house of logs from the creek bottoms and the family began breaking land for crops and planted a garden. Their third daughter, Carrie (Caroline), was born there. With the tending of the vegetables and livestock and the planting of crops, daily life settled in, but tensions rose between the settlers and the Osage Indians. Later, in a letter to Rose, Laura would remind her daughter that the family had had no right to be there, since the treaty hadn't been ratified. She called Pa a squatter, and he was one of many.

It seems likely they left in 1871, in part because of mounting worry about conflict between the settlers, the Osage, and the federal government. But as Laura wrote in the manuscript of her life story, which she called "Pioneer Girl," the family left when they did because the man to whom they had sold their Wisconsin farm couldn't continue paying them for it. Both reasons probably influenced Charles and Caroline. So they went back to Wisconsin to the welcoming embrace of grandparents, aunts, uncles, and cousins. They resumed living on the produce from their garden and livestock, fresh game, and the proceeds from fur trading in the town of Pepin. In the spring of 1873, when Laura was six—with economic recession setting in—the Ingallses sold their property to a town merchant, giving them some capital. They bought it back from him in the fall and prepared to resell it for $1,000 to another man. They lived with relatives through the winter of 1874. In the early spring, they loaded up the wagon again and rattled away onto the prairies of Minnesota, traveling part of the way with Pa's brother Peter Ingalls. They settled near the town that would become Walnut Grove, where land was cheap, supposedly due to infestation by the Rocky Mountain locust. Pa bought a dugout house and 172 acres and traded a pair of horses for a pair of oxen. He planted wheat and, in the second year, built a house using lumber apparently acquired on credit against his future wheat crop. Great trials ensued. During their second farming season, the grasshoppers came. Actually, what came was the largest locust swarm in history—a flying cloud of roughly 3.5 trillion Rocky Mountain locusts. The swarm measured 1,800 miles long, 110 miles wide, and up to a half-mile deep. They landed like hail, as Laura later wrote, eating the Ingalls's crops and every living plant. The loss of their crops left the family in debt. The next spring, in 1876, the locust eggs hatched, and the insects resumed crunching. "The crops were ruined again," Laura wrote in her early draft, "and Pa said he'd had enough. He wouldn't stay in such 'a blasted country!' "

Pa had his way. They left that blasted Plum Creek for a year and tried running a hotel in Burr Oak, Iowa. The story of that year jarred with the hopeful pioneer themes in the Little

House books and so remained an unpublished interlude. (Today, Laura Ingalls Wilder fans visit the restored hotel when they make the rounds of all of the houses where the Ingallses lived.) On that journey, Laura rode with her older sister, Mary, her younger sister, Carrie, and her new baby brother Freddie, who'd been born back in Minnesota. Freddie died of a mysterious illness during the trip, and the baby does not appear as a character in the Little House books. Laura wrote in "Pioneer Girl": "Little Brother was not well and the Dr. came. I thought that would cure him as it had Ma when the Dr. came to see her. But little Brother got worse instead of better and one awful day he straightened out his little body and was dead." The following May, the Ingallses had another daughter, Grace.

The family found the relatively urban life of Burr Oak depressing (a saloon operated next to the hotel) and, in the fall of that year, with them owing money to a landlord Pa had decided not to pay, the covers went back on the wagon and the family packed up and drove away in the middle of the night. They headed back to Walnut Grove, Minnesota, where the difficult times continued. Ever since the locusts had come, the weather had been dry, so crops withered. In the winter of 1879, when Laura was twelve, Mary became ill. "She was dilierous [sic] with an awful fever," Laura wrote in a section of "Pioneer Girl" that also did not make it into the Little House books. "We feared for several days that she would not get well, and one morning when I looked at her I saw one side of her face drawn out of shape. Ma said Mary had had a stroke, and as I looked at her, I remembered her oak tree away back in Wisconsin that had been struck by lightening [sic] all down one side." Mary recovered, but she'd been blinded. "The last thing Mary ever saw was the bright blue of Grace's eyes as Grace stood holding by her chair, looking up at her." This scene, Mary seeing the last sight in her baby sister's eyes, appears in *By the Shores of Silver Lake*, the fifth Little House book. Mary's blindness became an important plot point in the later Little House books, providing Laura's character the chance to mature and help Mary "see" what was around her by hearing Laura's descriptive words.

Laura reported in "Pioneer Girl" that she had a job that summer, and that she also helped care for Grace while Mary recuperated. She would tell her daughter Rose that her parents had never been the same after their daughter's illness and loss of her sight.

Following their return to Walnut Grove, the Ingalls family stayed for less than two years in a house Charles built behind the town's hotel. He worked as justice of the peace. In 1879, the family again went west, this time to Dakota

40

Territory, a move covered in *By the Shores of Silver Lake*. Pa worked first as a paymaster and timekeeper for the expanding railroad. The family lived at the railroad camp in fall 1879. Through the winter of 1879 and 1880 they house-sat for a surveyor who was away. In the spring, Pa filed with the government for a 154.25-acre homestead near a new town site, De Smet, in the future South Dakota.

Dakota, with its giant sky, incessant winds, and waving grasslands, appeared wild and uninhabited when the Ingallses first went there. Yet massive change had molded this landscape's lonely beauty. The United States government's policies toward the various bands of the Dakota tribe, its treaties and wars with them, and the mass killing of the buffalo that had once ranged there had left the land the way it looked when the Ingalls family arrived.

Clashes between settlers and Indians had begun in the 1850s, when the federal government pushed Indian tribes onto arid prairies and away from the upper Minnesota River Valley following the First Sioux War. As Norman K. Risjord writes in *Dakota: The Story of the Northern Plains*, the unrest between new settlers and natives slowed migration to Dakota for a while. But in February 1861, one week before Abraham Lincoln's inauguration, Dakota was organized as a territory (as were Colorado and Nevada). Yankton, east of where the Ingallses headed, was named the capital. From then until the late 1870s, with the encouragement and financial support of Congress, at least a half dozen railroad companies built tracks west through the upper Midwest. The Union Pacific Railroad went first, laying tracks west of Omaha, where before only tribes and gold miners had lived. Like the other railroad companies, it owned huge pieces of land around the tracks that crews slowly put down. Railroad expansion continued until the financial panic of 1893.

The Dakota Southern Railroad laid tracks in the northern part of Dakota Territory. The Chicago and North Western Railway expanded west across Minnesota and into southern Dakota, with the financial help of towns and cities whose residents were tired of waiting for Washington. By 1871, the Dakota Southern Railway Company formed and began laying track between Chicago and Dakota. The Panic of 1873 halted some of these routes, but by the late 1870s, when Laura's family migrated to Dakota, competing firms were building boomtowns along the new tracks. Among them was De Smet, where Laura's father went as paymaster for the Great Northern Railway.

Trains seemed grand and modern, but the companies struggled for cash. At one point in the mid-1870s Northern Pacific railroad land agent James B. Power announced that the company would give investors large tracts of its government allotment of land in exchange for company bonds the investors held. The bonds were worth almost nothing, but the investors snapped up the land and then quickly resold huge tracts in the Red River Valley called "bonanza farms," where farmers used migrant labor and newly available machinery, such as steam-powered threshers, to run large-scale factory farms.

In southern Dakota, where the Ingallses home-steaded, the land was offered to settlers in tracts of 160 acres, more or less, under the tenets of the Homestead Act. The largest numbers of settlers to date followed the railroad construction in 1879, the year the Ingallses went, and they remained to claim homesteads. By then, the buffalo (American bison) were gone, and with them large mammals like the wolves and grizzly bears that preyed upon them.

Native tribes had disappeared, too. The land of promise had become so because the government had pushed the Indians to the north and west of the territory. Dakota was a bit like an empty stage set by 1879. Photographs from the 1870s and 1880s of government officials posing after meetings with Indian leaders who'd agreed to vacate those lands are haunting. They show stoic, proud people who look supremely uncomfortable and heartbroken. In one of the photos, a government man actually poses with his arm raised and finger pointing; the caption explains he's told the Indians it would be better for them to go elsewhere.

The next winter, 1880–81, was "the Hard Winter" portrayed in Laura's 1940 volume *The Long Winter*—seven months of blizzard after blizzard. The Ingallses retreated into town, living in a store building Pa had built to sell. They took in a young couple who'd begged them for shelter and whose child Ma delivered in an upstairs room. The couple, George and Maggie Masters, did not show up in *The Long Winter*—the family is portrayed as surviving stoically alone—and this couple proved themselves burdensome. George did little work and always grabbed his food first, once burning his mouth eating his potato too quickly. The family made a joke for years, Laura later remembered: whenever they wanted to comment that someone was selfish, they would repeat George's remark, "Potatoes do hold the heat!"

The blizzards blocked trains and overwhelmed the town; the only food they had after the first few months was seed wheat, which they ground in a coffee mill for bread. With young Almanzo Wilder, who'd moved to De Smet the previous year, Charles hauled hay from his stacks back on his homestead into town for the livestock. And, as Laura told, late in the winter, when the supply trains had not been running for months, Almanzo and Laura's schoolmate Cap Garland risked a trip by horse-drawn sleigh, between blizzards, out to a homesteader who had seed wheat. They persuaded him to sell it so that the starving townspeople would have something to eat. Back in the store building, the stalwart Laura helped her family make fuel by twisting hay into sticks. A photo of Laura taken just after that winter shows a serious, pretty girl in a gingham dress. As she stands next to her sisters, she gazes to the side, looking determined. Her long wavy brown hair is pulled partly back. Her hands are curled into loose fists as she poses for the photographer, jaw set.

In the spring, the Ingallses moved back to their homestead, but they would spend most winters in town from then on. Laura studied hard at school and earned a teacher's certificate, even though she was sixteen, not eighteen as a new Dakota law required. Laura would teach at three schools: the Bouchie School in winter 1883, the Perry School in spring 1884, and the Wilkin School in spring 1885. She wrote that she gave her earnings from the first two schools to her parents, who still were struggling to get started in farming and wanted to pay for travel and buy an organ for Mary, who now was at a school for the blind in Iowa. The first years in Dakota were unusually rainy, so farming went well. They grew corn, oats, and vegetables and raised a cow and chickens. These were happy years, chronicled in the last two books of the series.

Drought would settle in later.

In the fact-filled earliest draft of her "Pioneer Girl" memoir, Laura portrays her parents as carefree and optimistic. This affect probably described them often enough. But the struggle to feed themselves and secure permanent shelter was a slog. We know from Laura's fond memories of the many people and situations she witnessed on the frontier that the strain of life eased whenever Pa pulled out the wagon cover while Ma packed the dishes and they took off again, camping as they went. They chased a new start, the way many families in their time and place did, and they were determined to make the best of it. No one now knows how well Pa and Ma's crops grew when the weather moderated and tragedies slowed. Probably they farmed adequately and dreamed well.

The Ingallses were typical in another sense, too. They changed their farming practices between the time they were first married in the 1860s and the mid-1870s—from subsistence farming, which provided most of their food and clothing in Wisconsin, to relying on selling crops to buy food and clothing while on the open plains. In Dakota, the treeless, drier land did not lend itself to subsistence farming, but the change found the Ingallses in the middle of a trend in the 1870s toward making farms cash businesses. "The driving civilization of the country has banished the loom, the spinning wheel, and the shoemaker's bench from the farm houses," the *Kansas Farmer* reported in 1875. Farmers needed cash, the journal said, and farming "depends for its progress upon profit. Profit schools the children, provides for the family, pays taxes, builds and furnishes good homes."

Pa and Ma's migration and farming years coincided with this change. The evolution of farming in America in the 1870s made the whole attempt at agriculture on the open prairies possible; the railroad meant they could use farming methods they'd learned back east. After they left the "Big Woods" of Wisconsin and they no longer could build a house with trees from their own land—for the open prairies provided no wood—they set their hopes on selling crops for lumber and provisions. They don't seem to have ever accumulated much savings.

Ma was a stoic, hard worker who ran efficient households through the horrible ups and downs of bad weather, crop losses, and economic panics. She made homes inside rough shelters where wind screamed through the wall cracks. Pa was an eternal optimist who supplemented the family income with carpentry, clerk work, and shopkeeping. As readers well know, Pa played the fiddle and sang songs.

In the late 1880s, Charles abandoned farming for good, only a few years after he had received title to his Dakota homestead. (He earned this because the family had lived there for at least half the year over five years and made improvements. Harvests were not required.) As soon as Pa owned the homestead, he rented it out and moved the family into De Smet, where they'd lived most winters since arriving anyway. That final move to town came in 1885. Charles built a house on Third Street, and Caroline, Mary, Carrie, and Grace all lived there. The house still stands and is owned by the Laura Ingalls Wilder Memorial Society, which gives charming tours of the only extant structure built by Charles Ingalls's hands and tools.

Laura and Almanzo—or "Bess" and "Manly," as they called each other—continued Laura's parents' quest for the right farm. They married August 25, 1885, in a quiet ceremony at the Reverend Edward Brown's homestead claim and then drove over to Almanzo's tree claim three miles north of town. The new house there must have been appealing and sturdy, with its extensive cabinets and shelves and its carpeted bedroom. On the first morning, as Laura later wrote, she cooked midday dinner for a pack of wheat threshers who were harvesting on the close-by farm Almanzo had owned since late 1884, having "proved up" and earned his title from the government.

The next spring, Almanzo planted wheat and borrowed against the crop for a binder, but just before the harvest, when Laura was five months pregnant, a hailstorm destroyed the wheat. Laura wrote: "The storm had lasted only twenty minutes but it left a desolate, rain-drenched and hail-battered world. Unscreened windows were broken. . . . Leaves and branches were stripped off the young trees and the sun shone with a feeble, watery light over the wreck."

Drought threatened the cottonwoods, maples, and box elder trees that Almanzo was supposed to grow in order to prove up on the tree claim. To raise money, they rented the house and moved a short distance to the first farm, where Almanzo hurriedly built an extra room onto the low shanty that stood there. Weeks before Laura was due to deliver their first child, they moved to the top of a low hill north of town.

2

ROSE AND LAURA

(1886–1920)

Laura thought the trouble was all over
now. But that was not to be for many a
day yet.

—*The First Four Years*

Rose was born in the shanty on the low hill
north of De Smet on December 5, 1886. She was
weaned on farming and migration. Between her
birth and the summer of 1894, when she was
seven, Rose and her parents moved six times. The
first move came when she was not yet a year old.
To raise badly needed funds, Laura and Almanzo
sold the farm he'd worked before he married
Laura and moved back to the tree claim.

During Rose's earliest years she spent much
time sitting in baskets while her parents farmed,
or riding in a horse-drawn cart when they visited
the kinfolks. In 1888, both Laura and Almanzo
contracted diphtheria during an epidemic. The
bacterial disease, which had been identified
only a few years earlier, at first seems like a bad
cold, but it attacks the mucous membranes or

tonsils and can cause heart damage. The disease is rare today because a vaccine was developed in the 1920s. Laura apparently had the worst of the disease, but neither she nor Almanzo could work and, fearing for Rose's health, they let the Ingallses care for her for several weeks.

Another misfortune followed. Almanzo collapsed after what the doctor diagnosed as a stroke, apparently caused by his working too hard too soon. He got out of bed one morning, fell, and only after Laura rubbed his legs and hands could he move about at all. That attack, whatever it was, would leave Almanzo nearly crippled. He limped for the rest of his life. He was never tall, but he had been strong, with broad shoulders. As the years went by, his body took on a twisted look; his legs thinned out—one looked shorter than the other—and he leaned on a cane. The impact of his impaired ability on Laura and Rose was huge: Laura bore more of the burden of farming from then on. Years later in her farm columns she advocated the philosophy that men and women should be partners on a farm. She'd learned the hard way.

Diphtheria profoundly affected the entire Wilder family. As Rose grew up, the overworked Laura's short temper would frequently leave her upset. Both Laura and Rose relegated Almanzo to a protected status. On the one hand, they adored and doted on him. On the other, Laura seemed to assume responsibility for the major decisions about farming and life. Rose felt that her parents fought a lot. Almanzo himself believed that it was Dakota Territory that had robbed him of his health and livelihood.

In 1889, Laura gave birth to a second child, a boy, but he died ten days later, still unnamed. A few weeks after that, their house caught fire from the stove. Rose, who was then only two years old, blamed herself for the blaze, recalling many years later that Laura had allowed her to feed hay sticks into the stove and she'd missed the mark. The house quickly burned to the ground.

Drought again parched the crops, and the family could not repay bank loans for equipment and supplies. They mortgaged the tree claim but were unable to repay and eventually the bank took possession of their lands.

It was a mournful time. Laura could not have believed farming was a good occupation and would lead to happiness. Years later, she wrote a book about this period, which wasn't published until three years after Rose's death in 1968 as *The First Four Years*. She ended the manuscript with this verse: "But for our blunders, Lord in shame/ Before the face of Heaven we fall./Oh Lord, be merciful to me/A fool." But when the book was prepared for publication in 1970, that epitaph for the Dakota farming effort was left out. (Those lines on the last manuscript page were circled and a note next to them read, "Jan, don't type.")

Needing respite from their struggles in Dakota, the Almanzo Wilder family moved to Spring Valley, Minnesota, where Almanzo's parents were living on what seems to have been a prosperous farm. His parents had moved there from Malone, New York, the site of Almanzo's early childhood, which Laura recounted in her book *Farmer Boy*. While living at his parents' farm, they had Rose pose for a photograph. She later remembered that she kept switching her pose so that her left hand, with a ring, would show, and finally the photographer gave in. Rose had light brown hair and her mouth is turned down a little at the corners. In the photo she looks as if she is humoring the photographer.

One mystery I've never solved is why Rose, Laura, and Almanzo never posed together for a photograph. Perhaps they did at some point, but none have survived.

In October 1891, Laura, Almanzo, and Rose took a train south to try homesteading in Westville, in the Florida Panhandle. They stayed for an ill-fated ten months. Laura suffered in the heat and humidity. Indeed, she looks flushed and uncomfortable in a posed photo as she stands with her hand on the seated Almanzo's shoulder before a backdrop of tropical plants. All three of them seemed to suffer culture shock. Many years later, an article under Laura's byline in *The*

Junior Book of Authors explained, "We went to live in the piney woods of Florida, where the trees always murmur, where the butterflies are enormous, where plants that eat insects grow in moist places, and alligators inhabit the slowly moving waters of the rivers. But at the time and in that place, a Yankee woman was more of a curiosity than any of these." Rose's take on that period appeared in her sinister short story titled "Innocence," published in *Harper's* in 1922. The story is narrated by a horrified child whose backwoods aunt tries to poison her. Its darkness likely reflects the whole family's lingering attitude toward their Florida experience.

They returned to De Smet in August 1892 for the sole purpose of working in town and saving money so they could get away again. Rose recalled well this last stage in Dakota, when she was five and started school. In her preface to *On the Way Home*—an edited version of a diary Laura wrote during their 1894 journey from Dakota to Mansfield, Missouri, which was published in 1962—Rose writes: "The prairies [in Dakota] were dust," and a financial panic had set in. The Wilders rented a house in De Smet but owned no furniture. "We were camping, my mother said; Wasn't it fun?" Rose didn't think so. "To me, everything was simply what it was." Rose's narrative here crisply attacks facts; she doesn't mention homey details like her nickname for Laura, "Mama Bess," or father, "Papa."

Actually, "camping" in the empty rented house marked a momentous turning point for them. They were saving money and packing for the last of the Ingalls-Wilder wanderings—the last, at least, until Rose herself would grow up and wander the globe by train, ship, car, and airplane. Between fall 1892 and spring 1894 they enjoyed daily contact with Laura's parents and sisters, but that would never happen again.

Rose wrote a charming story, never published, that detailed the homey routines of a family who were obviously the Ingallses in De Smet during that period. The typed lines on yellow copy paper of this draft, entitled "Grandpa's Fiddle," hint at the future Little House project. The story's narrator is a child—Rose herself was age seven then. She knows she's about to leave Dakota with her parents, but before they leave, they have one more dinner with the "Clayton" family. In this passage, the narrator knows about the family's past troubles and idealizes their cozy, simple living:

> It sounds, to tell it, as if they'd known nothing but calamities, but the truth is they didn't expect much in this world and they just shed thankfulness around them for what they had. You'll never see a more cheerful home. There they had that snug

house, two little bedrooms and the lean-to kitchen and that sunny sitting room with a rag carpet and lace curtains, and they'd been the first settlers in that town and had helped to found the church; everybody respected them. Grandpa was a Justice of the Peace and made a little something from fees, and besides he was hired to do most of the carpenter work that was hired in town. With the garden and the hens and what little he made, they didn't, to say, really want for anything.

Seems to me I can hear Grandma saying now, when she was lighting the lamp to get supper by, and a wild stormy night was starting outside, "My," she'd say, "I am thankful for a good roof over our heads." And when she was chopping the warmed-up potatoes in the frying pan and they'd begin to brown, Aunt Mary's face would light up and she'd say, "Mm, that smells good!"

In the story, Rose also wrote of the contrasting despair of her own parents, Laura and Almanzo:

That was after we lost the homestead and even the tree claim on the mortgages, and Papa was not able to work. [His diphtheria had] left him partially paralyzed for some years, so all he could do was hunt for little odd jobs. Mama was working at the dressmaker's, she worked from six in the morning to six at night and she was getting a dollar a day and saving up to make a fresh start.

The Wilders set their sights south, to Mansfield, Missouri. A friend had visited there and brought back glossy pamphlets calling it "The Land of the Big Red Apple."

Just as Laura's parents had made a deliberate decision to stop moving after they reached Dakota in 1879, Laura and Almanzo resolved to end their wandering once they'd arrived in Missouri. They would buy land and build a farm. But when they got there, as Rose recounts in the epilogue to *On the Way Home*, their entire savings, a hundred-dollar bill, was found to be missing. Laura and Almanzo had planned to use it to buy an unimproved farm, and Laura had stored it in a wooden writing desk for the ride. Rose watched in horror as Laura and Almanzo searched for the money and then canceled their meeting with a bank officer. A few days later, Laura discovered it in a crack in the desk, hope returned, and the bank granted the Wilders a mortgage. Rose's description of Laura as she combed out her hair to meet the banker reminds us what a striking young woman she was that year, at the age of only twenty-eight. Although suffering from his lame leg, Almanzo, too, was still strong and broad-shouldered, with a thick head of hair and an easygoing demeanor.

The Wilders began slowly clearing their wooded property. For four years, they lived in a rough cabin on the land. So Rose's early memories of Mansfield are of farm life. In 1898, they moved to a rented house in town, where Laura sold meals to travelers and railroad workers and Almanzo delivered oil for a company. Almanzo's father bought them the rented house as a surprise gift on a visit. They stayed in town about twelve years, moving back to Rocky Ridge full-time in 1910, after Rose had left home. This sequence of facts matters because it underscores that Rose was a struggling farmer's daughter only until age eleven. She lived in a small town rather than on the farm from age eleven until she left home. The farmhouse on Rocky Ridge, now the Wilder shrine, was a place she would live in only as an adult.

Like Pa and Ma Ingalls, Laura and Almanzo had to face the fact that prosperity would look a lot different from what they'd expected on the farm where they settled for life, the farm that represented their decision to stop moving. Neither generation would achieve prosperity through farming—but off-farm enterprises would support them. Pa worked as a carpenter and legal clerk. Almanzo found work hauling loads in Mansfield. Laura worked as the administrator of a government farm-loan program and, several years after arriving in the state, began her writing career as a columnist for *The Missouri Ruralist.*

Over their long lives, Laura and Rose seemed most comfortable somewhat removed from larger society. It wasn't that they didn't care about others. They strove to put down roots, but maybe because they had moved so much, they never quite got those roots in place. They worked to better their lives and, as hard-working, self-made people can be, both seemed impatient when others did not improve themselves and advance. They never expressed this overtly. But when I visited Mansfield fifty years after Laura's death, a local commented offhandedly that Laura and Almanzo Wilder had had trouble fitting in because they considered themselves better than the natives, even though they ultimately lived there for six decades. In Mansfield, Laura and Almanzo worked side by side, both on the farm and in town. They enjoyed some social life but felt that the local dialects and customs, particularly religious revival meetings, revealed a lack of restraint. Laura and Almanzo attended but never joined the Methodist church, and they made friends—one old photo shows them relaxing on a neighboring couple's porch during a visit—but didn't always feel close to them.

This is not to say they were completely removed from society. In 1897 Laura was involved with the organization of a new chapter of the Order of the Eastern Star, the ancient service group for relatives of Masonic Lodge members. For years, Laura's Pa, Charles Ingalls, had been a Mason. Laura had belonged to a chapter in De Smet, and by her third meeting in Mansfield, the new chapter had accepted her as a member. Soon Almanzo joined the Masonic Lodge, and a few years later he joined Laura in the Eastern Star. By the early 1900s, Laura was in leadership roles in the Eastern Star, and, as Masonic researcher Teresa Lynn writes, "It appears that Laura was a bit pedantic about the rituals and works of the Order." She would instruct members on protocol, for example, and, "When she became Worthy Matron for the third time in 1909, she immediately began having reviews of the degrees and work of the Order in meetings, even calling special meetings to practice . . . since she felt the Chapter needed more practice to perform them correctly."

In short, it seems the Wilders kept themselves at something of an arm's length from many people in Mansfield. And they occasionally laughed about the local dialect, customs, attitudes, or those who weren't educated. Once, in a letter to Rose, Laura made fun of conversations and meal preparation at Sunday suppers in Ozark country. Rose responded: write it down verbatim and work it into a short story.

For Rose, who did most of her growing up in Missouri, this experience of isolation colored her early life. As a child, she felt left out because they were poor. The farm barely yielded enough cash for seeds. She cringed at her simple clothes. Rose commuted to school in Mansfield in bare feet, riding a donkey called Spookendyke. She chafed against the apparently inadequate town school and made only a few friends. Years later, Rose called herself a "mal-nutrition child." She considered herself an expert in the disadvantages of farming life.

"No one can tell me anything about the reasons young people leave farms," Rose wrote in 1925, in an article for *Country Gentleman*. "I know them all—the drudgery of farm tasks; the slavery to cows and pigs and hens; the helplesslness under whims of weather that can destroy in a day the payment for a year's toil; the restlessness of ambition, with its sense of missing, on a farm, all the adventures and rewards that one dimly feels are elsewhere."

When Rose was fifteen, Almanzo's sister Eliza Jane Wilder Thayer (on whom Laura would base the character Eliza Jane Wilder in two of her books) visited Mansfield with her young son, Wilder. Eliza's husband had died, and she invited

Rose to return to Crowley, Louisiana, with her and her son to live in their house and attend school. Laura's dislike of her sister-in-law's bossiness—which dated back to when Eliza taught the frontier school and could not control the class—had not diminished with time, and it's easy to imagine her reluctance to send Rose off to Louisiana. But Rose went nevertheless, and probably eagerly, because she hated the Mansfield school. She spent a year in Crowley and appears to have graduated from what they called high school, which might have been the equivalent of ninth grade, and ended her schooling. Rose's journal entries and magazine articles from this time reveal Eliza as at once a busybody, a lenient aunt, and an indifferent guardian. After school, as Rose reminisced in a journal, she would go out with a much older man who picked her up in his buggy. Then she'd stay up all night doing her homework. What would Laura have thought?

After that year in Louisiana, Rose returned briefly to Mansfield, learning telegraphy at the Mansfield railroad station. Next she moved to Kansas City and worked as telegrapher. She wrote little about this time, except in a story she committed to paper but did not publish, "Faces at the Window." (It was published posthumously in 1988 in William Anderson's collection *A Little House Sampler*, with essays about Laura and Rose.) It's a perfect little horror story told through the eyes of a character based on one of Rose's telegrapher friends at her night job. Rose punched out messages at the Midland Hotel, while, across the lobby, Gladys (as Rose called her friend in the story) did the same for a competing company. On their breaks, Gladys told Rose the ghost story. Gladys had been adopted for a time by a family who settled in a haunted house in Mayfield, Kentucky, where apparitions would stare in at the windows at night, and there were reports of buried bones on the grounds outside. Rose insists in the story that Gladys, her narrator, was a reliable observer. Supernatural elements aside, "Faces at the Window" offers us a glimpse into Rose's early years as an adult, when she was "at the top of the world."

Rose's biographer William Holtz has suggested that Rose met her future husband, Claire Gillette Lane, when he traveled through one of the hotels. A surviving postcard from a friend mentions "Mr. Lane" and says, "It's your move now." Whether this postcard influenced her or not, soon after it was written Rose moved to San Francisco, where she continued working as a telegrapher and where Gillette (as people called him) worked for newspapers, probably as an ad salesman.

Rose and Gillette married in 1909; Laura and Almanzo did not attend the wedding. Rose tried being a housewife for a few months, but the couple often were on the road selling business schemes or subscriptions. They worked mainly in the Midwest that year. Rose was pregnant soon after the wedding. It seems reasonable to assume that she would have spent some time resting in Mansfield as her pregnancy advanced, with Gillette on the road. But her pregnancy did not go well. On November 23, 1909, she gave birth three months early to a stillborn baby boy in Salt Lake City, Utah. Why the couple were there, we don't know for sure. Rose never talked about it afterward. A photo believed taken the next spring shows Rose, in a white high-waisted dress, standing with Laura in the ravine at Rocky Ridge. She probably recuperated at the farm.

Only two letters survive in which she mentioned her son. When he would have been eleven years old, Rose revealed in a letter to her journalist friend Dorothy Thompson that she'd had a child but never talked about it with anyone. Thompson was expecting a baby; Rose advised her against visiting Rocky Ridge Farm in her condition, firmly stating that no good doctor could be found within 250 miles. This is hugely important, I think, because Holtz believes that, after losing the baby, Rose had surgery in Kansas City—which is within 250 miles of Mansfield. Almost certainly she was left unable to have more children, and the sting of this episode is suggested by her unwillingness to send another expectant mother to Missouri. Several years later, when Rose was living in Mansfield again, she clipped a newspaper article about a young woman who was challenging doctors' apparent view that women were supposed to suffer in childbirth. The idea that a woman's biology need not cause pain or difficulty was then revolutionary—and it got Rose's notice. Obviously, the loss of her child was a painful experience that had left lasting sadness.

Rose and Gillette lived together next in Kansas City, where Rose worked as a reporter for two newspapers. Back at Rocky Ridge, the farm was starting to yield. Laura tended a chicken flock and garden while Almanzo grew apples and raised cows, and in 1911 Laura started writing for her state's agricultural paper, the *Missouri Ruralist*, about the goodness of small-farm life. In her first article, "Favors the Small Farm Home," Laura advocated couples working together, piping water into houses, running machinery with gas engines, and bringing cultural activities like book clubs into the country. "In conclusion, I must say if there are any country women who are wasting their time envying their sisters in the city—don't do it," Laura wrote.

By 1911, Rose and Gillette were back in California, where Rose took a job for a hardware company but began writing freelance articles.

Soon both of them were selling real estate outside both San Jose and Sacramento. They weren't getting along for many reasons, partly because Gillette could not keep a job for long and also because Rose was very unhappy. A decade and a half later, Rose wrote a confessional article for *Cosmopolitan* harkening back to this period of her life. It was called, "I, Rose Wilder Lane, Am the Only Truly Happy Person I Know, and I Discovered the Secret of Happiness on the Day I Tried to Kill Myself." According to the story, Rose dampened a cloth with chloroform and lay down in her apartment to die, but she awoke some time later with a severe headache.

A new friend, the journalist Bessie Beatty, hired Rose as an editorial assistant on the women's page of the San Francisco *Bulletin*. Chillingly, the page was titled, "On the Margin of Life" and bore the subhead: "Truth is seldom on the written page. We must search the margins and read between the lines." Rose quickly moved from writing light features on the women's page to longer serials. Her serials and features blended fiction and fact. She often built her profiles of people around the challenges of their childhoods, usually on farms. Her subjects included daredevil pilot Art Smith, a prisoner named Jack Black, Charlie Chaplin, and automobile inventor Henry Ford. Her serial about Ford was published in 1915 as a book, *Henry Ford's own story; how a farmer boy rose to the power that goes with many millions, yet never lost touch with humanity, as told to Rose Wilder Lane.* She wrote that Ford was always tinkering in a shed with the goal of inventing something. No one believed the automobile would come to anything, but within a dozen years he was a millionaire. "We must have him as a symbol of something greater than ourselves, to keep alive in us that faith in life which is threatened by our own experience of living," she wrote.

That year, Rose sent rail fare home and Laura traveled to San Francisco for a visit with her and Gillette. Laura stayed three months. By then, the couple was near divorce but pretended they were happy. Laura spent much time in the newsroom with Rose, and it was there that she wrote her first children's copy—poems that appeared in the paper's children's column, the "Tuck 'Em In Corner." Laura wrote Almanzo that she didn't understand how Rose could stand the pressures of writing to deadline. Laura preferred to raise chickens, she said. While Laura was there, Rose paid her for lost egg income, although Laura and Almanzo had lent her and Gillette $250 that the young couple had yet to repay. They took Laura to the San Francisco Exposition, and Laura stayed long enough to cover the exposition for the *Ruralist*, an assignment Rose had urged her to request from the paper's editor.

We know nothing of how Laura felt about the Lanes' divorce, which was finalized in 1918. My guess is that she reserved this topic for private conversations with her husband. By then, Rose had become a nationally known writer for *Sunset* magazine. She believed that Laura should be a national magazine writer, too, and she got her mother an assignment for *McCall's*: an essay in which Laura was to persuade readers that marrying a farmer offered a better life than living in town. Rose edited the piece heavily, and evidently the editors at *McCall's* did, too. "Whom Will You Marry?" opens with a scene in the kitchen, where Laura kneads dough as she talks to a young woman trying to make up her mind about whether to marry a farmer.

In 1919, *Sunset* editor Charles K. Field recommended Rose to a publisher planning a new biography of Herbert Hoover, who was running for president. Field knew the Hoover family, and Rose gained access to Hoover's relatives. Rose's would be the second biography of Hoover published. Her version read like a novel. She used dialogue gleaned from Hoover's brother Theodore, whom she visited in January 1919, taking copious notes. She deliberately exaggerated events and, in her preface, defended this approach. She said that the facts were indisputable, but that she had interpreted them. Her preface for the Hoover biography could have served as a preface for the Little House books, too, for she explained the importance of using facts in a new way, as a route to someone's essence:

> The method used in handling this biographical material is so unusual that a word of explanation is necessary. The facts on which the story is based I do not believe to be open to dispute. Every detail of them has been collected with meticulous care from sources of unquestionable authority. The interpretation of them is my own. I have endeavored to present as a living human being the man whose life has been made by these facts, to show the influences of heredity and environment that went toward the making of his character as I believe it to be.

She began the biography with a history of the Hoover family. A grandmother had died before she could secure land for her sons to farm. That fact, Rose writes, is why Hoover's father became a blacksmith and later a salesman of farm machinery instead of a farmer himself. In the late 1860s, the first threshing machine to appear in eastern Iowa arrived in West Branch, and as Rose told it, Hoover's father, Jesse, was the only one who knew how to put it together. This happened four years before Herbert was born, but Rose felt this fact explained his character.

It was a marvel to the farmers who had never seen anything like it. . . . There was a significance in the incident of the threshing-machine; it marked the passing of a period in American history. The frontier had gone; agriculture was established; the era of the machine had come. . . . Four years later, in a small brown cottage near Jesse Hoover's blacksmith shop, Herbert Clark Hoover was born. His life began at the end of one pioneer age and the beginning of another.

Rose's embellishment of a childhood story in the book's opening models her technique of building drama in ordinary family scenes, an approach she would use when she revised the Little House books. In Hoover's biography, as with the early years of her pioneer parents, only a few facts or memories were available to her, and she used her imagination to embellish and elaborate on them. For example, she wrote that "Bertie" admired his mother's beautiful voice and painted an impressionistic scene of the kitchen: "This stillness, the sunshine on the green leaves, and the low humming of the tea-kettle on the kitchen stove, seemed part of the Presence to which his mother spoke." The young Hoover's blacksmith father made him a sled, and within a few minutes (Rose wrote) he cleverly turned a business deal with a boy who had made fun of it. Bertie told the critic that the sled was one-of-a-kind, and within minutes he had traded it for the kid's store-made one with steel runners.

The Hoover biography was published first in serial form and helped launch Rose to fame as a writer of serials. She'd laid a foundation for a career telling the stories of ordinary Americans displaying extraordinary courage as they rose to success. She published in *Country Gentleman*, the *Saturday Evening Post*, *Cosmopolitan*, *McCall's*, and other periodicals. Her first novel, *Diverging Roads*, was also published in 1919 and told the story of Rose and Gillette's marriage and breakup. Rose's writing career gained further traction as she began a period of wandering. Chasing subjects and sources, she was also seeking the perfect house and the ideal landscape.

She crisscrossed the country—traveling to Washington, DC, working for the Red Cross for a month, then to New York where, she later wrote, she attended an early meeting of communists led by Jack Reed. The idea of a progressive society using innovation to care for its people intrigued her, but she felt unsure enough at the time that she took no concrete steps toward joining the party.

After the New York stint, Rose visited California with a stop at Rocky Ridge, and finally, in May 1920, she left on a ship to Europe. Abroad, Rose gained enough distance from her roots that she rethought the value of her parents' hard life. Between spring 1920 and fall 1928, Rose lived more in Europe than in the United States, except for one long visit to Missouri lasting about a year.

PART II
THE FAMILY BUSINESS

3

THE ALBANIAN INSPIRATION

> This life is almost intolerable. I do not
> know how we shall endure it until I can
> get away. This is the sort of hell that
> taught me endurance, but now I am old
> and have so little time left in which to live
> peacefully.
> —*Rose, diary entry while visiting Laura,*
> *January 10, 1924*

After Rose's divorce, she wandered in Europe
for a few years, and by 1921, she ended up in
beautiful, mountainous Albania. She fell in love
with it. Albania is where she also fell back in
love with America.

Rose did not write much about the reasons she
went overseas, but probably she first went on a
lark. She worked briefly for the American Red
Cross in Washington, DC, and then soon after
took a job as publicist. In war-ravaged Europe,
the Red Cross's workers were scouting areas for
new schools. Someone who'd had the job told
Rose that all she had to do was write occasionally
for a newspaper or magazine, mentioning the Red
Cross. She visited Geneva, Vienna, Prague, and

Warsaw. Rose wrote a series for her old paper in San Francisco called "Come with Me to Europe."

On the train to Warsaw, Rose stumbled into her compartment and found it already occupied by a thin, brown-haired, laughing young woman. First she was angry and sputtered that there must be a mistake, but she quickly befriended Helen Boylston, a nurse from Massachusetts who was known as "Troubles" for the scrapes she supposedly got herself into. They spent the next two days talking nonstop. Rose very soon was calling her new friend by the nickname "Troub." Troub told her she'd just visited Albania, the tiny Balkan country newly separated from the Ottoman Empire that lay on the Adriatic Sea just north of Greece. She said Rose *must* see it.

Within months, because the Red Cross had wanted her to go also, Rose did visit Albania. When she traveled to a small Catholic school near the Yugoslavia border, she was astonished to find that students in groups as large as ninety-seven would stand in a cold room watching the teacher write words on a painted wall. Rose also rode a pony through native tribal lands of Albania's northern mountains with a group that included her Red Cross colleagues Frances Hardy and Margaret Alexander. The following year she returned and repeated the trip with American photographer Peggy Marquis (a friend from San Francisco), who documented their travels with photos of the locals, the Albanian state's new interior secretary, and a few young Albanian guides who led the ponies on their mountain trek.

Note that Rose was by no means the first daring Western woman here. Twenty years earlier, the British artist and writer Edith Durham had herself "discovered" Albania. The year before Rose visited the mountains, Durham's book *Twenty Years of Balkan Tangle* was published. Rose must have known about this book and probably drew inspiration for her travels from it, for she explored territory that Durham had visited a decade earlier. Still, the natives would have found Rose to be a most unusual sight. These trips through tribal Albania had to be her most adventurous ones to date.

Rose was fascinated by the people who lived far from the influences of the dominant culture. She wrote a book—some say it was her best because of its spare, engaging prose—about her mountain trips called *Peaks of Shala*. "We were in the sky; there is no other way to say it, and no way in which to describe that sensation of infinite airiness," reported Rose, who'd lived in low-lying areas most of her life. "Forty miles behind and below us Lake Scutari lay flat, like a pool of mercury on a gray-brown floor. At each side of our little gay-colored cavalcade a gray cliff rose perhaps two hundred feet, too sheer to hold the snow that thickly crusted its top. These cliffs were the posts of a gateway through which we looked into the country of the hidden tribes."

Rose admired the Albanians, who remained isolated from the outside world while keenly aware of their own particular dangers. The country's political situation was wobbly because of poverty and its recent independence, just as its steep, uneven terrain made travelers teeter. When the donkeys slid on narrow alpine paths across talus, the guides would grab the animals' tails and tighten the chains around their necks, Rose remembered. She wrote that these men had routed the group straight through dangerous tribal territory because they knew that natives would not shoot at a party with women in it.

On the trek, Rose became sick with what turned out to be malaria. Only one guide, a fifteen-year-old named Rexh Meta, realized that she needed a doctor. Rose would retell this part of the story to her agent and friends. She was delirious, but the other guides were ignoring her, just enjoying the freedom of going through hostile areas knowing they would not get shot. Rexh asserted himself, rerouted the trip, and got Rose to a hospital. Rose became attached to her rescuer, who she learned had witnessed his family's murder at the age of nine. Since then he had fended for himself and become a sort of caretaker of other homeless children. She eventually appointed herself Rexh's adoptive mother and would support him for years, paying his way to Cambridge University and providing the money he needed to win a bride.

It was in 1921, while in Europe, that Rose wrote the short story "Innocence" that I discussed earlier, where she examined her own early childhood trauma while her family homesteaded in the Florida Panhandle when she was three years old. She sold the story to *Harper's* and received a nice check. A few months later, an additional check for $250 arrived in Paris. Rose thought it was a mistake, but it was prize money. "Innocence" had won second place in the O. Henry Prize competition for 1922.

Reviewer Harry T. Baker wrote in the *Baltimore Sun* that Rose's story was better than winner Irvin S. Cobb's. "The second prize tale, 'Innocence,' by Rose Wilder Lane, is far above Mr. Cobb's and is the only truly notable story in the volume. . . . Its brevity, restraint, terror and pathos go straight to the heart. Anyone who wishes to see the difference between art and a bourgeois imitation should compare this story with almost any other in the book." I. Kaufman praised it in the *Brooklyn Eagle*: "It lacks the traditional O. Henry trick ending, which may be why it was rated by the Society of Arts and Science below Irvin S. Cobb's 'Snake Doctor.' It is, however, permeated from beginning to end with a psychological point of view, with a wealth of genuine emotion and restraint, which place it close to high art."

The expat life in Europe agreed with Rose. She spent many months traveling around, sometimes with Guy Moyston, a newspaper reporter with whom she began a several years' romance. After visiting the Mat River region in Albania in 1922, she headed back to the United States, not sure where she'd end up. Rose's adventures and perhaps her romance fueled unrest. "Eighteen months gone," she wrote in a diary. "The Albanian book sold in England and America. . . . I am on my way to San Francisco." She had a hundred dollars and felt some regret. "I must make a habit of thinking out carefully on paper the details of any project before I embark on it. The Mati trip is a failure because I did not do that." Rose looked for writing material in her adventures, and now she seemed uninspired for writing and therefore disappointed. "I must not be misled by my romanticism," Rose scolded herself in the diary entry. "I must take care of my dress and personal appearance. I must get myself, somewhere, a house."

For the time being, Rose's house would be the wood and stone farmhouse on Rocky Ridge Farm. Laura had written, asking her to visit, and Rose returned home with Troub. They stayed through most of 1924 and 1925, with Rose intending to return to Albania after two years.

She was now in a serious romance with Moyston, who was still working abroad but would come visit for many weeks. Yet she turned down his marriage proposal, arguing passionately in a letter, "I DON'T WANT TO BE CLUTCHED."

But she was clutched—by Laura. While Rose and Troub visited New York City, Laura sent a telegram asking for them to come to Mansfield. An illness or emergency must have arisen. "Mama Bess [Laura] said 'come' and Rose went," Troub said many years later, in an interview with William Anderson. "She was very much her mama's slave."

Laura and Almanzo were in transition. Laura's Ma had just died in far-off South Dakota, and Laura had stopped writing for the *Missouri Ruralist*. She was in her late fifties now and Almanzo a decade older. "Papa and Mama quarreling as usual about the farm," Rose noted one morning in her diary. On that trip, Rose made a payment of $500 to her parents. At some point before this, she had announced she would send them yearly subsidies. She didn't always pay it all or on time, but this decision to support Laura and Almanzo marked a reversal in her relationship with them. She was no longer the daughter who'd left home as fast as she could, shedding her Ozarks heritage. She was the responsible adult caring for her aging family. On this visit Rose named herself the head of household for income tax filings. Rose believed that her parents needed this help. Certainly, they did not earn much from their farming.

Rose made a lot of money—thousands of dollars for one short story in *Country Gentleman*, for example—but she spent it, too. She worried obsessively about the next check and made lists of stories written and money expected. Although Rose was one of the highest-paid writers at that time, she often overspent and had to borrow money—usually from friends, sometimes from Laura and Almanzo, the ostensible beneficiaries of her outsized income.

On May 4, 1924, Rose wrote in her diary, "I am on Rocky Ridge, where Guy is visiting. One Chekov story, 'Autumn,' written and sold to Harpers." On the next line, she wrote: "In bank, $500. Owing F.A. [Frank America, a friend who had lent her money in Europe], $1080. Mama Bess [Laura], $900. Finances incredibly and horribly growing worse, and Albania further away than ever." Some months later, Rose rationalized her cash-flow problems from this time in a rant about Laura's cautiousness to Guy, who seems to have lent her money for a car:

> I told her many years ago that I would give her five hundred a year, and though I have always given it to her—and often

84

much more—she has no comfortableness whatever about any probability that there will be another five hundred next year. . . . Mama Bess still occasionally says in the morning that the night before she dreamed that she woke up, and that there wasn't any car, that she had only dreamed there was a car. And the impression is sometimes so strong that she goes out to the garage and looks to see that it is there, after she gets up in the morning.

Around this time, Rose started an investment account with a stockbroker named George Q. Palmer. He was Troub's former employer, and Troub had invested an inheritance with him. Rose believed that if she, Laura, and Almanzo also invested with Palmer, they could earn nice returns and create financial stability.

Friends and family in Mansfield would probably not have guessed that Rose actually felt somewhat dropped back into her hometown, felt out of place there, and missed Albania. She also worried incessantly about money—when she'd be paid, how she'd keep up with bills and paying a cook and other helpers. Her letters to friends brimmed with cheer. Magazine articles she wrote during her visit home made her sound confident in her rural heritage. But privately Rose seethed. "This life is almost intolerable. I do not know how we shall endure it until I can get away," she wrote in 1924. "This is the sort of hell that taught me endurance, but now I am old and have so little time left in which to live peacefully."

Rose, Laura, Troub, and any friends who visited stepped out regularly into the small-town social life, attending occasional dinners, picnics, and club meetings. Laura belonged to two women's clubs, the Athenians and the Justamere Club. They gathered at each other's houses, sharing refreshments and listening to someone's program about whatever.

There were the fox hunts. Locals today in Mansfield still tell family stories handed down from almost a century ago of Rose's enthusiasm for the Missouri-style fox hunt, which involved setting up a campfire on which a pot of coffee boiled into sludge while the hunters smoked cigarettes and watched the dogs run around.

In 1925, Rose tutored Laura in the production of two more national magazine articles, "My Farm Kitchen" and "My Farm Dining Room" for the *Country Gentleman*. It had been six years since her first, "Whom Will You Marry?" had appeared in *McCall's*. When Laura complained to Rose about the editing, Rose scoffed that her work on the stories had been "an ordinary rewrite job." No more national magazine articles by Laura Ingalls Wilder would appear. This may have been because they got distracted by a very different project.

Together, they drafted a letter from Laura to Laura's aunt, Martha Carpenter, possibly the most important letter of their careers. The draft that I examined is a carbon copy of a transcription. (Historian and writer William Anderson typed it many years ago from a copy that a Carpenter descendent, visiting De Smet, South Dakota, lent to him.) The letter asked Martha to describe the early years of the Ingalls family in Wisconsin: "The *Ladies Home Journal* is wanting me to write an article for them on our grandmother's cooking brought down to date," the letter read, "and I am thinking that you could give me some old recipes for dishes that your mother or yourself used to cook." But then Laura asked for much more than this:

> There was something I wanted the girls to do for me, but they never got around to it and Mother herself was not able. I wanted all the stories she could remember of the early days in Wisconsin when you were all children and young people. Now it is too late to ever get them from her, but I think as I thought then that it would be wonderful for the family to have such a record. I want them principally for that, but I think too that Rose could make some

stories from such a record, for publication, and that would be fine, too. . . . Just tell it in your own words as you would tell about those times if only you could talk to me.

She offered to pay for a stenographer, "and I want lots of it, pages and pages of things you remember. . . . We have thought about going up to see you and talk about these things but I am not able to make such a trip and the *(fact that?)* we cannot very well leave home." (I have added the italics to show Anderson's insertion of what Laura probably meant.)

It's unfortunate that the original of this letter is not available for research. Anderson has confirmed that Laura typed it. We know that she briefly owned and used a typewriter that Rose had suggested she buy, but she didn't use it much and handwrote her book drafts.

In any case, it is certain that Laura did appeal to her aunt on her and Rose's behalf and that Aunt Martha did receive a letter. For she wrote back, warmly, a few months later in a long letter describing events that would eventually make their way into the Little House books: Indians walking into the house and taking whatever they wanted, maple sugaring parties, encounters with wild animals. "The wolves would howl first at the North then the East the South and at last to the West we would think they catch father before he got home and the panthers they was around with their noise to frighten us but I never saw one."

Martha's contribution was a gold mine. Her memories reminded Laura of events that would provide numerous details and scenes that ultimately found their way into Laura's early books, *Little House in the Big Woods* and *Little House on the Prairie*.

Rose continued writing for magazines, using the Missouri countryside as inspiration. Her serial stories were published as a book, *Hill Billy*, in 1926. She also wrote a series of "Green Valley" pieces about Ozark people for *Country Gentleman*. As she translated the world around her into stories for national consumption, in letters to Moyston she confided that she felt smothered by the chains of obligation to Laura and Almanzo, who Rose was sure found to be reckless this daughter "who roams around the world, borrowing money here and being shot at there, learning strange languages and reading incomprehensible books even in her own language."

She soon bid Laura and Almanzo good-bye, and left for Albania again.

Rose and Troub sailed from New York for Paris in March 1926. There they spent several weeks studying four languages—French, Italian, German, and Russian (teachers weren't available for Albanian, Greek, or Serbian). Foreigners were visiting the city in huge numbers that year. The franc had so little value that middle-class tourists from America could live cheaply, and there were so many of them that the Parisians demonstrated against the onslaught.

Rose didn't like Paris, and it's no wonder. American writers like Ezra Pound, Ernest Hemingway, and Gertrude Stein had adopted France as their vantage point in the postwar period. All of Europe after World War I offered something of a playground for visiting Americans. For Rose, it could have represented an escape from her Midwestern past, which she still felt ambivalent about. In a very real way, settling abroad was a conventional act in that time. But she did not write about it like her compatriots, although she was of the same generation, more or less.

While studying at the Berlitz school, Rose and Troub met a displaced Russian architect who promised to design them a new house in Albania. They bought a car they named Zenobia (after the third-century queen who conquered Asia Minor) and drove on back roads to southern Europe and onto a ferry to Tirana, Albania's capital city. In Tirana, they rented a capacious house recently inhabited by diplomats. It had a beautiful, walled garden. They hired servants and settled in to live there as partners in 1927 and 1928.

American relief efforts had changed Albania. The American Red Cross's Albanian Vocational School taught vocational skills in English, ran a government printing press, installed Albania's first electricity and running water, and encouraged its students to resist Italian domination. Rexh Meta, who'd saved her life in the mountains, had gone to this school. This strong American presence in Tirana provided Rose and Troub with a safe setting and probably many friends and acquaintances.

With no chores to do, Rose had only to write. She established a workstation in the house by sitting down in the same place every day for a few hours, even if it was just to write letters. She used this routine to block out all of the distractions (curtains, wall colors, objects in the room). "I try to be at the typewriter, in its established place, at a certain time every day," Rose wrote Guy on February 10, 1927. "All these little things help. Or perhaps not so much *help,* as remove hindrances. They're a help only negatively, by cutting off distractions."

At other times, she distracted herself by watching her servants, including a cook and gardener for an acre and a half of land, who cooked and cleaned or cared for walnut, cherry, fig, and hazelnut trees and a flower garden. "Old

Ibraim, the gardener, putters around all day in this garden, lovingly adding little trim of pebbles to the beds, digging a weed here and there, or sitting in rapt contemplation of a little wild daisy that's just blooming; now and then he pats it very gently," she wrote to Thompson. At the bottom of the letter's seventh page, Rose broke her reverie. "As to how we live; I am working as always, darn it! Just at the moment, doing an Ozark serial—or anyway, I ought to be. Troub writes a little, reads a little, spends a lot of time in the garden, goes riding. There's always tea from four o'clock on—usually in five languages. People drop in."

Just beyond the walls of her magical rented house, Albania's government wobbled on the shoulders of one man, President Ahmet Bey Zogu, whom she'd known since 1922, when she interviewed him in Tirana. Albania, once part of the Ottoman Empire, had gained independence after World War I with the support of the United States. Ahmet, who later became known as King Zog, impressed Rose because he seemed so sure of himself as he held together the shaky new government and dealt with ongoing threats from Yugoslavia, Italy, and Greece. Rose had fallen in with Zogu's own paranoia; she thought he would be killed if he left his house because of hundreds of blood feuds against him. Yet even this spurred her to idealize Albania, when she added, "Golly,

I love the Balkans! There is no other place on earth like it. Rather ten years of the Balkans than a cycle of New York. Only, I'd like to have enough of an income to live on, and—as our second-hand furniture man in the Village used to say—'just enjoy.' "

Unlike Troub, who had an income from her investments, Rose had to write to pay her bills even as she struggled with her dislike of the hardworking middle-class life she'd left behind. She claimed now to hate her home country. "I don't like The States because I don't like The States," she wrote Guy on February 16, 1927. "I don't like the American spirit; I don't like its energy, its deification of work, its insularity, its standardization, its terrific stress on possessions and comfort, its complacency, its ignorance, its idealism, and (mental sum-total of these) its unconscious hypocrisy."

Rose seemed to be arguing with herself, perhaps irritated with her own disingenuous approach to writing. While overlooking her Albanian garden, she wrote a romantic serial story, *Cindy*, inhabited by uneducated American backwoods people. The installments appeared in *Country Gentleman*, which paid Rose $10,000. They later were published as a novel. Rose seemed to squirm at her own stories' shallowness. Readers liked them; that wasn't the problem. Rose knew she was capable of something deeper

93

in her writing, yet so far she had rarely used her rural, hardworking upbringing as the source material to make deeper points. Most often the characters and tales she knew from the Midwest fed emotional, sentimental short stories.

But before the long sessions on *Cindy*, she'd written and sold a truly literary story, "Yarbwoman," about a snakebite, a tale from her father's days in Dakota Territory. Her agent said that the big magazines were too disgusted by the snakes, apparently, to print it, but *Harper's* bought it, and the story met with acclaim from the public—and from Guy, who told Rose the story was very good.

Rose quibbled with Guy over that assessment. She insisted she wasn't really trying to be a literary writer and that stories were just how she paid the bills. In July 1927, she wrote: "If I can't—*and I can't*—be Shakespeare or Goethe, I'd rather raise good cabbages. And that is why I would not write at all, except that there is more money in writing than cabbages, not only more money, but more freedom, more of the kind of life I like." Then Edward J. O'Brien wrote for permission to reprint "Yarbwoman" in *The Best Short Stories of 1927*. Rose wrote Guy, "So you see, your critical judgment is again confirmed. I must be blind as a bat about my own stuff. I wrote the darn thing for a *Country Gentleman* check, and my only genuine feeling about it was an agonized wail when C.G. turned it down and I had to take half the money from *Harper's*."

In an article, "How I wrote 'Yarbwoman,'" which appeared the following spring in *The Writer*, Rose admitted that she'd done it for the money. "Real stories come out of the subconscious, eventually, and write themselves. Nevertheless, the rent must be paid, and if only a story will pay it, and no story is ready to write itself, one must be written by main strength and awkwardness." Rose's preoccupation with money and the tension within her between being an artist and a self-sufficient breadwinner are obvious here.

Rose wrote friends that she envied Troub's freedom not to work, but she herself was restless. She took some of the money she was making in summer 1927 and traveled with Troub and one of their servants, Teko, to Vienna planning to buy a purebred Great Dane. They ended up instead with a Maltese terrier called Mr. Bunting.

Going to Albania might have been a mistake, Rose wrote to Clarence Day, the eccentric semi-invalid who wrote for *The New Yorker* and would later write *Life with Father*. He was one of her regular correspondents. Rose was changing. She was turning to simple truths. She sketched in one of her idea notebooks, on the page opposite one dated Feb. 6, 1928, the beginnings of a list:

Idea

A series of pioneer stories, featuring the woman.

    1. The Surveyors House.
    2. The Lotus Eaters.

(The list included numbers 3 through 10, but the entries were blank.) This is a remarkable relic. It is the earliest proof of Rose's eventual collaboration with Laura in the pioneer series. Both of these references point to Laura's life—stories Laura probably had told Rose growing up. She set this out before Laura wrote down her own life story. A decade later, "The Surveyor's House" would title a chapter in Laura's fifth book, *By the Shores of Silver Lake.* "The Lotus Eaters," a poem by Tennyson, would make an appearance in *Little Town on the Prairie*, Laura's seventh book, as verse Laura had read and puzzled over.

For now, though, Rose did nothing further with the pioneer idea, but the seed was planted.

Around this time, the dream life in Albania began to pull apart. It did so for a few reasons that, one by one, seem small in retrospect. Because the government seemed so tentative, she and Troub probably feared for their long-term safety. Years later, Troub remarked in an interview that the main reason they left was that there were too many fleas. These insects thrived so well that they had placed the bed legs inside cans of kerosene. This suggests that two American women used to a certain level of city comfort missed home. The greatest impetus to get back to America probably was this: Rose couldn't focus on her work in Albania, because she felt rootless there. She now felt she belonged on American soil.

Then came an excuse in the form of a cable from Laura, making the decision to leave much simpler. No letter or telegram survives explaining what was up, but Rose and Troub left the Balkans, bound, ultimately, for Missouri.

4

THE WRITERS' COLONY AND THE CRASH

> There was a long, scared sound off in the
> night and Pa said it was a wolf howling.
> —*Laura, writing about her early
> childhood in her memoir "Pioneer Girl"*

Ending eight years of restlessness and intermittent wandering, on February 6, 1928, Rose boarded the Italian ship *Saturnia* off the coast of Spain for the journey back to the United States. She told herself she had done the right thing, leaving Albania, and she promised herself she would spend the next two years saving and investing $50,000. She would write "one serial and a few short stories" each year. She calculated that she'd earn $6,000 but net $10,000 after investing with her broker George Q. Palmer.

In her notebook, Rose sketched a plan for three years in America, mostly on Rocky Ridge. She and Troub would need a car. "It involves delicate personal adjustments with the family and Troub. If only I can make it a fresh, sunny open-air life—without all this smothered smoldering." She would stay busy and study languages. She would try living in the present, removing the "weight of tomorrow."

Laura and Almanzo met her at the train station in Mansfield. Rose moved back into the upstairs and set out her Underwood typewriter. Soon she was typing stories and letters to friends. She worked, it seemed, during most waking hours, and she suffered insomnia. Laura took Rose to a meeting of one of her social groups, the Justamere Club. Troub, meanwhile, visited her father in New Hampshire but by June arrived with her father, who stayed a few weeks.

In July, Troub set up a platform tent in the field to serve as an office. She bought a horse from Almanzo soon after, which endeared her to him, for he'd raised horses his whole life.

For many weeks that summer, three writers joined Rose and Troub on Rocky Ridge: Catherine Brody, who had just sold the novel *Nobody Starves*, about the tribulations of working in Detroit's auto industry; Genevieve Parkhurst, who wrote for *Harper's*; and Missouri journalist Mary Margaret McBride, who soon would become a national radio personality. Rose had thus created an informal Midwestern writers' colony on the farm. (Brody would come and go for months at a time over the next five years.) Life there now resembled something more like a college or hotel. Laura and Almanzo used a bedroom downstairs. Rose and the others slept up the L-shaped staircase in low, windowed rooms under the eaves that Rose called the "sleeping porch." Rose soon would hire a cook and housekeeper, but it's hard to imagine that Laura ceded control of her low-countered kitchen in these first months of togetherness. Rose also sent out the sheets and clothing to town for laundering.

Gone were the days of cooking feed for chickens in the kitchen, with mud tracked onto the floor. Gone were the days of gathering cream, making butter, getting in the harvest for sale to the city, and doing their own laundry. Troub regularly disappeared all day on horseback rides with sandwiches in her basket and her dog running alongside. One can only imagine what Laura and Almanzo thought of sharing the farm with this group of literary women who saw the acreage as an opportunity to have fun. They had wished so much that Rose would come home—now their place had been transformed into something like an unending romp.

Rose herself remained the farmer's daughter with an earnest work ethic. She wrote most days, and she and Laura forged a relationship the best way they knew how. Laura would climb upstairs often, but always on the pretense of business. Saturdays and Sundays were like any other days; they seemed to hold no special purpose for either. I see little evidence that they were going to church. On Easter Sunday, April 8, 1928, while Rose sat typing a letter to one of her favorite correspondents, Clarence Day, Laura climbed the stairs to Rose's room so she could share a letter from a local woman farmer. The farmer had written to Laura thinking she still acted as secretary of the Farm Loan Association for the area. Laura read aloud: "Here is my wants is to borrou [sic] one thousand dollars on my property. And pay off to close the morages [sic] finish up my schooling." The two women shared a laugh.

Rose described all this to Day in her letter, adding, "There's a cruelty, in forcing ambition upon this poor creature, who, without ambition, as a servant born and bred, accepting the inevitability of being a servant, would be a busy, contented, and doubtless most excellent servant all her days." Rose's tone sounds downright mean, and the moment she and Laura laugh at a woman trying to better herself seems so much worse than simple meanness because both of them had suffered through poverty and lack of opportunity in that very town. Rose sounds dismissive, almost as if she has judged that this woman, unlike some self-made character in a Horatio Alger novel, lacked the ability to work hard and elevate herself, and, by extension, her failure proved that the Wilder family was superior for their courage and strength.

The companionability didn't last long. Over the

rest of the spring, Rose found herself wanting her own space. That summer, she hired an architect in Springfield, sixty miles away, who said he could design an English-style rock cottage on their land. Rose had seen a picture of a Sears Roebuck kit house known as "the Mitchell" and asked the architect to duplicate the basic layout.

For thirty years, Laura and Almanzo had bought land whenever they could and cleared large hillside fields. In 1928, the year that Rose moved back, the farm totaled almost 200 acres, including remote acreage the family called the "Newell forty" after the family who had sold it. Rose, who had once hoped to build her own house in Albania, now threw herself into planning a brand-new house for her parents on the Newell forty. The house would be an English-style cottage with a fieldstone exterior, with electricity and new plumbing and all new furniture.

Rose probably felt responsible for the newly crowded conditions in and around the farmhouse. Why didn't she instead build a house for herself? Many people have interpreted Rose's decision as her attempt to control her parents sugar-coated in an extravagant present, a modern house where two people who loved to work must stop doing so. Her whole life, Rose was a generous, emotional, warm person with her friends. But her relationship with her parents was more complicated. With them, her warmth came out more in letters and presents, which she sent often, but in person she seemed to balk. It was as if Rose's own expectations stifled her, and she felt vulnerable to criticisms, especially from Laura. Perhaps in building a house for them, she could show them how much she cared—while also keeping them at a distance.

She ignored one problem: her parents had not asked for a new house.

The house project began in August. The architect said he was surprised at how much Rose knew about construction. She fussed over details and, with equal fervor, worried about the cost. "August 1, 1928, the day after saying I will build a $4,000 house on the Newell forty for Papa and Mama Bess," Rose wrote in her diary, referring to her parents by their nicknames, "I have about $19,000 in P[almer] and Co. In local bank, $200. One story out—doubtful—and a blank mind."

Four and a half months later, the total cost had come to $11,000.

Sometime around Christmas 1928, Laura and Almanzo saw their new house, supposedly for the first time although Almanzo had hung around the construction site. Rose had furnished it in Mission style. The leaded glass windows, electric lights, wood floors and tile sparkled. Laura would have taken stock of the modern, open layout. Expectations must have been high—and perhaps created a kind of burden, because when Laura and Almanzo walked in, they weren't that happy. What they said we don't know.

Rose hinted at wounded feelings or some sort of conflict in a letter to her old newspaper boss, Fremont Older: "Certainly I should have thrilled all over when my mother walked into the new house. I expected to, and would have done, but for a strange unexpected turn of events, which I might tell you about, but won't write. The longer I live, the more I am amazed and fascinated by the endless variety of living."

It's likely that Laura considered the house too fancy and that Rose bristled at the apparent lack of appreciation for the grand gesture of building it. All three followed through on the plan, though. Laura and Almanzo moved in, and Rose wrote the architect that Laura liked the house. A few days later the architect wrote back: "I look forward with eagerness to the starting of your new Lodge on Rocky Ridge." (Plans for a "lodge" apparently never went beyond a simple sketch.)

The Wilder/Lane family expanded into two houses during a brief period of easy wealth. Income from Rose's and Laura's separate stock market investment accounts had relieved the near-poverty of the Wilders' farming life. A photo from around that time shows Laura and Almanzo in front of the Rock House with their dog, Nero. Laura's hair is cut in a neat bob, and she wears a dropped-waist dress and white stockings. Almanzo wears a suit and has combed his hair. They look citified—and uncomfortable. One might think material ease would have been wonderful and welcome. The life that unfolded with their move into this house intensified their leisure time. They had even more time for the trappings of middle-class contentment they'd been involved with for some years— club meetings, dinners with friends, visits with Rose and her companions. The free time likely unsettled them. Laura did keep house in the new cottage, but she and Almanzo no longer ran a farm. Nor was she writing regularly. The loss of daily chores created a void.

Rose had not lived on Rocky Ridge much growing up—the family had been in town earning money for the time when they could build their house. So in her diary she confessed feeling trapped in Wright County, Missouri. "Mon. Feb. 11, 1929," Rose noted in her diary. "Took a little drive with both dogs in the afternoon to Cedar Gap and back. No tongue can tell how *I want to get away from here!*"

The townspeople had never seen such a life: groups of un-attached women coming into town on the train and spending weeks at a time at the Wilder farmhouse. The laundry service Rose had hired was run by Corinne and Jack Murray. Corinne became a friend very quickly—and she had lots of work. Rose sent the sheets out to the laundry every other day.

"April 8, 1929," she wrote in her diary. "Monday. Joyous day, of discovering via Corinne what Mrs. Young thinks of our using so many sheets."

The metamorphosis in Rose that had begun in Albania continued. The farmer's daughter and writer in her had merged, creating yet another Rose, the agrarian philosopher. In the last year and a half, she had gone from hating the "American spirit," which she had railed against in letters to Guy, to feeling the pull of her home soil. Over the summer, around the time the Rock House project started, Rose wrote her friend Floyd Dell, the playwright, that she was feeling a new, deeper impulse to her writing: "I find that I have a conscience, and that it is concerned with my writing," her letter said. "Yes, money has nothing to do with it. . . . I don't know why the job of writing has suddenly taken on a new aspect, a moral aspect, to me."

Her bank accounts held thousands, but Rose still felt mounting anxiety over money. She wrote to Fremont Older—whom she often confided in—that she feared she was not writing well. Her agent was peddling three stories, but no one had yet bought them. The "bank account's draining rapidly away to nothing." She contemplated running away, she said, but then wondered where she'd vanish to.

On Wednesday, October 23, the day before the stock market crashed, Rose drove to Springfield and bought a blue velvet dress. Five years later she would reflect in her diary (apparently missing the date by one day) about Black Thursday: "This was the day of the Great Crash—the evening I said to T[roub], knowing it but not believing it, 'This is the end.' " Five days after the first crash, on the day that became know as Black Tuesday, most stocks had lost all their value, and the Great Depression had begun. The reality took months to set in, however, as the stock market rallied and dipped. The Wilders were used to money problems, of course, beginning with the Panic of 1893, which had contributed to their having to leave Dakota Territory.

In the winter of 1930, a few months after the crash, Laura worked on her life story, sitting at a small desk in the Rock House, penciling stories on "Fifty-Fifty" pads from the Springfield Grocer Co. The earliest draft that survives from this time starts on a tablet she labeled "Pioneer Girl No. 3." In it, she revisited her earliest memories in a guileless, moment-by-moment account. Laura had a gift for description, and a scene in the covered wagon just flowed out of her as if she were talking to her family:

Once upon a time, years and years ago, Pa stopped the horses and the wagon they were hauling away out on the prairie in Indian Territory.

"Well, Caroline," he said, "here's the place we've been looking for. Might as well camp."

So Pa and Ma got down from the wagon. Pa unhitched the horses and picketed them, tied them to long ropes fastened to wooden pegs driven in the ground, so they could eat the grass. Then he made the campfire out of bits of willow twigs from the creek nearby. . . .

I lay and looked through the opening in the wagon cover at the campfire and Pa and Ma sitting there. It was lonesome and so still with the stars shining down on the great, flat land where no one lived.

There was a long, scared sound off in the night and Pa said it was a wolf howling.

It frightened me a little, but we were safe in the wagon with its nice tight cover to keep out the wind and the rain. The wagon was home, we had lived in it so long and Pa's rifle was hanging at the side where he could get it quickly to shoot the wolf. He wouldn't let wolves or anything hurt us and Jack the brindle bulldog was lying under the wagon guarding us too, and so we fell asleep.

Through the spring, in the tablets, Laura told stories from the childhood she'd lived itinerantly, in covered wagons and shanties. For some years, she had wanted to write about her childhood but had managed only short vignettes in her farm-paper column. Embarking on the project now, she didn't think about plot or theme. Instead she revisited the practical facts of living on open prairie, traveling in wagons, surviving among wolves and panthers and bears, and cooking on woodstoves.

The stories she wrote down seem to have come easily to her. She set them down in strict chronology, starting with her family's brief stay on the prairies near the current Kansas-Oklahoma border. Months after Pa Ingalls finished a new log house on the prairie, they were already leaving. "We took everything out of the house and put it in the wagon," she wrote. "Then we all got in the wagon and with Jack running under it we drove away leaving our little house standing empty and lonely on the prairie. The soldiers were taking all the white people off the Indians' land."

The stories filled almost two hundred pages. Laura wrote in earnest, yet it's very likely that she embarked on this project not because she was struck with inspiration and pluck, but rather because Rose asked her to: On May 7, 1930, Laura delivered a few tablets to her daughter. In a brief journal entry, Rose noted the manuscript's arrival. It seems she'd been waiting for it. From what happened next, we know that the women's plan was for a magazine article or serial. They hoped to make some money during a dry period in Rose's income.

We know from Rose's meticulous diary-keeping in those years that she spent six of the next ten days typing up Laura's pages. The diaries that disclose so much about these events comprise a few, small line-a-day notebooks; without them, this story might have remained lost to us. Consider how hard diary-keeping is for most people, yet Rose devoted tremendous effort to filling the pages of almost every day, especially between the years 1930 and 1935. The very fact of these meticulously kept diaries reveals more than the details recorded in them, for they show how much Rose needed discipline on the farm. She hung onto her daily record as proof that, amid the smell of manure and stressful encounters with Laura, she made a full life. We who have gone back searching for the true story of the Little House books benefit from this.

Rose sent several early pages of Laura's memoir to her literary agent, Carl Brandt, in New York, and waited. Brandt said to send more, and so Rose sent the entire manuscript. On June 4,

Rose complained in her diary that she had only $150 left from a short-story check and "no word from Carl about my mother's story, which I think has been badly handled."

Brandt returned the pages Rose had sent, with no prospects for a sale, a few weeks later.

Rose was getting panicky about debts. Meanwhile, her friends on the farm played. On many days, Troub and Corinne rode horseback and romped with their pet dogs while Rose worried about how she could make the pioneer story sell. Laura and Almanzo had planned a trip to see family and old friends in South Dakota, but Laura stopped in at the farmhouse on July 29 and told Rose they wouldn't go because they couldn't afford it. Rose must have promised them she'd fund the trip; she hadn't delivered the money. "I am a failure and a fool," Rose wrote. "Why was I such a fool as ever to get into this mess?" She dreamed about debts that night. The solution would be to work more on Laura's story. Two days later, "at typewriter till 4 pm rewriting my mother's story. She says she wants prestige rather than money." This dry comment revealing that Laura had great hopes the public would respect her book made me wish again that, like Rose, she had kept her own diary.

Rather than prestige, Rose wanted money. She wrote to Brandt a few days later, asking if they could enter the story in contests. The next day Corinne played chess with Rose, but Rose couldn't concentrate. "Bad night, smothering and very much depressed about money, failure, old age, death, etc.," she scrawled in the diary. Rose and Laura were so different. Laura lived with a sense of satisfaction about her choices, while Rose was still searching. Between them, they shared a watchful fear that the money would not be enough.

Meanwhile came the first of four record-breaking droughts that would eventually lead to the Dust Bowl. Rocky Ridge's garden dried up. One night, Rose went out at midnight and left the hose running on the lilacs. She also noted in her diary that the stock market report looked grim. Rose had continued to rely on dividends from her brokerage account with George Palmer, who also administered the account she'd convinced Laura to open. Despite the crash, her account with Palmer had apparently held on. The next day, August 6, Brandt wired Rose that her story "Grandmother's Silver" had sold to *Good Housekeeping* for $1,200. Rose called Laura and told her she'd pay for the trip to Dakota as a wedding anniversary present. But a week later, during an afternoon visit from Rose at the Rock House, the ever-frugal Laura broke the news to her daughter: she and Almanzo would take the money, but rather than travel, they'd use the cash toward ponds and a meadow on Rocky Ridge.

Laura could not accept money without feeling that it ought to be saved or put to careful use improving the farm for the future. It was her nature.

"God! I need money," Rose wrote that night in her diary. She realized that the Palmer account probably would fail and that the expenses of the farm were more than she could handle. She confessed to herself that her own writing was stuck; she couldn't think of new ideas. The next day, she was back at work on her mother's memoir.

Over the next several days, Rose took Laura's manuscript and decided to try part of it out as fiction for children. She excerpted pages about the years living in a cabin in the Wisconsin woods, where Laura had been born, and where they had farmed, hunted, and preserved their food. Laura didn't know what Rose was up to. Rose called this draft "When Grandma Was a Little Girl."

By August 17, Rose was wrapping up work on "my mother's 'juvenile,'" as she was calling it in her diary. The next day, she made a few final edits and mailed the manuscript off to her children's book writer and artist friends Berta and Elmer Hader, who lived in a stone house they'd built themselves in the Hudson River village of Nyack, New York. The Haders were pioneers in the children's literature world. The draft of "When Grandma Was a Little Girl" survived in Laura's papers, with its opening page stamped with the Haders' name and address, and beneath it PLEASE RETURN TO. (In 1933, Laura would use the back of that opening page to work on an early draft of *Little House on the Prairie*.) This is one way we know that the Haders were the first to see this manuscript that would become the first Little House book.

Rose was not done with working on Laura's memories. A couple of days later she turned back to the full "Pioneer Girl" manuscript to rewrite it—"stupidly," she wrote, second-guessing herself, "for will it come to anything?"

The idyllic writers' colony on Rocky Ridge was fracturing a bit. Catherine Brody left for the time being at the end of August. Troub was still there, but her father had written from Connecticut that he needed money. She might soon have to start working. Rose finished revising "Pioneer Girl." In September and early October she drafted two new short stories, calling them "Dangerous Curve" (eventually published as "Winding Road" in *Ladies Home Journal*) and "Paid in Full." She got on a train bound east, carrying "Pioneer Girl" and the stories, and arrived in New York on October 15. That day she learned from her agent's secretary that *Country Gentleman* had bought "Paid in Full." Two days later, though, Brandt advised her not to try to sell Laura's story. Whether he meant the "juvenile" story or the longer memoir "Pioneer Girl" she did not say in her diary. Perhaps for this reason, and because she was generally unhappy with Brandt's marketing of her own work, Rose began looking for another agent.

Rose spent the next few weeks in New York, visiting the Haders and other friends like Betty Beatty, her former boss in San Francisco. Brandt held a meeting at his office with *Saturday Evening Post* editor Graeme Lorimer. Rose "gave him a sales talk on 'Pioneer Girl' after which he came up to the apartment and got the manuscript." But during this trip, Rose switched to agent George Bye, a former Kansas City newspaper reporter known for his soft spot for former newspaper reporters. Bye had become the literary agent of Eleanor Roosevelt as well as novice writers with unusual stories, so-called "stunt books."

On November 12, 1930, Rose wrote to Laura that *Ladies Home Journal* had turned the "Pioneer Girl" manuscript down. Lorimer had telephoned her saying he found the writing to be "most intelligent" but that they had another story that was similar enough to Laura's to make hers redundant. "I'm awfully sorry," Rose wrote Laura. "They said if the same material were used as a basis for a fiction serial they'd take it like a shot. But I know you don't want to work it over into fiction. I haven't any doubt at all that it will go in a book, but what I want to do is to exhaust serial possibilities before offering it for book publication."

In a note to herself on her diary's "Memoranda" page at the end of January 1931, Rose wrote: "I think I must stay in America and write American stuff. Sometimes I can almost *feel* this."

Her intuition would pay off well, for the Haders had come through. Rose noted in her diary that she'd visited with the editor of children's books at Alfred A. Knopf, Marion Fiery, at the Haders' house and that Fiery had told Rose she was taking the "juvenile."

On February 12, 1931, while Rose was still in New York, Fiery wrote to Laura about "When Grandma Was a Little Girl." "I have read it with the greatest interest. I like the material you have used: It covers a period in American history about which very little has been written, and almost nothing for boys and girls." She asked if Laura would be willing to revise the story, making it long enough to be a chapter book for children between ages eight and twelve. She recommended it be lengthened to twenty-five thousand words from its length of between six to seven thousand words. "The more details you can include about the everyday life of the pioneers, such as the making of the bullets, what they eat and wear, etc., the more vivid an appeal it will make to children's imaginations."

Rose wrote to Laura from Westport, Connecticut, on February 16, with instructions. Westport was Rose's base of operations that winter. She was living in the house of Sinclair Lewis and his wife, Dorothy Thompson, taking care of their eight-month-old baby while they were abroad attending the Nobel Prize ceremony. "Dearest Mama Bess, Marian Fiery (if that is the way she spells it?)"—in fact her name was spelled Marion—"said she had written to you. Knopf's will take the juvenile in book, if you can make it twice as long."

Rose wrote that she was sure Laura could easily do that. She then set to telling Laura where in the farmhouse to find her notes. She directed her to a file cabinet upstairs at Rocky Ridge, in the room Rose called the sleeping porch. She warned Laura that the drawer included many scraps and pages from drafts Rose had been working on out of "Pioneer Girl."

Rose next came out with the fact of just which manuscript Fiery was asking Laura to expand. "It is your father's stories," she wrote, "taken out of the long PIONEER GIRL manuscript and strung together, as you will see."

Clearly, this was the first Laura learned of what Rose had done with the "Pioneer Girl" pages after Brandt had rejected the manuscript. Rose not only told Laura where to find the children's book pages. Elaborating on Fiery's requests, she also suggested that Laura just sit down and start writing "any and all details about the way of living, what you played, what you ate, wore, everything like that." On the letter, Laura made a note: "cleaning and oiling gun." She was gathering details in her mind.

Rose also suggested giving the longer book a structure by following the seasons. The early draft of the "juvenile" was set in the winter. Rose suggested adding back some episodes she had removed in plotting the children's story: the anecdote of a cousin, Charley, who taunted the adults with fake problems and then actually stepped on a hornets' nest but no one believed him; and the story of the family dance at Laura's grandparents' house. These scenes would become memorable sections of Laura's first book.

As she put her letter of instruction into the mail, could Rose have feared Laura would be angry? She had no choice, of course, because Fiery had sent off a letter directly to Laura. She probably hoped Laura would be so thrilled at a publisher's interest that she would do what Rose said.

She wrote that the book would be lovely and would probably cost two dollars, and that the copy would have to be submitted by October, eight months hence. "Marian Fiery is crazy about your writing; indeed, everyone is who has seen it. She says you make such perfect pictures of everything, and that the characters are all absolutely *real*. If you find it easier to write in the first person, write that way. I will change it into the third person. later. [sic] For juveniles you can not use the first person, because the 'I' books do not sell well. But probably you will write it more easily that way. However, do as you please about that."

Rose sounds breathless, if it's possible to sound that way in a letter. Her instructions bounce between orders and encouragement. She next told Laura that her main character would be "Laura," not "I." Laura didn't know at this point that Rose had changed the narrator to "Grandma" speaking as if the elder were addressing little children. In this one letter, Laura was finding out that Rose had typed and edited a small part of "Pioneer Girl" and shopped it to Knopf as a very short story of happy evenings in a log cabin listening to Pa tell stories. There was no time to apologize.

I wish you would just get another tablet, and put down in it somehow the other fifteen thousand words that Marian wants. When I come home I will go through the whole thing and we will send it off to her and get the contracts signed up, and all. . . .

Of course, I have said nothing about having run the manuscript through my own typewriter, because the changes I made, as you will see, are so slight that they could not even properly be called editing. It is really your own work, practically word for word.

And so, on the back of Fiery's letter, Laura drafted a response in longhand. "In reply to your letter of the 12th, I have many more memories of the days of my story and am sure I can make it the length you wish. I feel sure agree [sic] on any changes for the good of the story and I would be especially glad to have Knopf publish those stories of my father's. They impressed me very much as a child and I still have a great deal of affection for them."

On March 3, Fiery sent the short "Grandma" manuscript back to Laura so she could start revising. "Our interest in having this book is very definite, and if the complete book is as well done as the part you have submitted, there is no reason in the world why we will not accept it."

Rose carried on a secret writing project separate from her mother's at the same time the first Little House book was beginning to take shape. We know this because she wrote about it to her dependent, Rexh Meta, who was in Cambridge,

England, studying at the university. On March 1, 1931, Rose had been up until midnight "working like mad to finish a book," one of a series she would ghostwrite for Lowell Thomas, the travel writer and broadcaster known for having made Lawrence of Arabia famous. Thomas was paying her $1,000 per book. She told Rexh that "this kind of work is called 'ghosting' and no writer of my reputation does it."

Laura and Rose spent May 21 together, "roughing out" fifteen thousand words for Laura's expanded book, as Rose noted in her diary. Laura had made additions to her "Grandma" draft, but the new episodes were rough. Over the next five days, from Friday to Tuesday, Rose typed a new draft of the book, according to her notes. Laura read the partial manuscript on Saturday night, when she and Almanzo came to dinner. On May 27, Rose wrote to Marion Fiery, pretending that Laura had done all of the work. (The available version of the letter is a rough draft; it's not clear how similar the final letter might have been or even if Fiery received it.) "My mother is just sending you the revised manuscript of those tales of her childhood in the Big Woods," she wrote, adding that she hoped the editor would like it because Laura was so attached to the stories. "I don't know just where or how I come into this, do you?" she went on. "But somehow I do, because my mother naturally consults me about everything concerning her writing." Rose wrote that the agent George Bye represented Laura, too, but that Fiery should go through Rose for changes to the manuscript.

On a separate sheet, Rose typed at the top, "Laura Ingalls Wilder, Mansfield, Missouri" and, beneath it, a list of "suggested titles: Trundle-bed Tales. Little Pioneer Girl." She x'ed out the next seven lines. "Long Ago Yesterday" she let stand as an idea. The next line she x'ed out. But "Little Girl in the Big Woods" survived the brainstorm.

In this way, Rose directed the production of Laura Ingalls Wilder's first book. Having selected Wisconsin stories, turned these into a manuscript, sent the manuscript off to Berta and Elmer Hader, traveled east and peddled it, visited in person with the Haders and Fiery—having, in effect, found the manuscript a publisher—Rose was now determined that Laura would see the thing through.

Rose returned from the East to Missouri. The summer of 1931 bore down, hot and oppressive. At the end of July, Rose wrote in a notebook, "Everything still and parching. The locusts are loud and near, then suddenly faraway. The vibrant stillness swells and wanes, now slowly, now abruptly, + is never still. The sky a soft gray blue, to deeper v blue at the zenith, all scattered over with gray-white clouds. The walnut trees' green glitters with bright-yellow, dead leaves. The elm's topmost leaves turn up their little pale, curled bellies."

In the late summer, Rose turned to her own fiction—she sold "Dog Wolf" to *Good Housekeeping* for $1,200, and began drafting chapters of a pioneer story based on Laura's parents, Charles and Caroline Ingalls, calling it, for now, "Courage." Both of them were working on stories out of Laura's "Pioneer Girl" pages, and the future looked as if it would be filled with pioneer stories.

Suddenly, in early November, came disappointing news. Knopf abruptly closed its children's department. Fiery sent a handwritten letter to Laura, strongly advising her not to accept the three-book contract they had offered, because "heaven knows" what would happen to the publisher over the next few years.

Rose acted quickly. She airmailed the manuscript to her friend Ernestine Evans, who was working as a literary agent and was a sometime recruiter of children's books for publishers. Ernestine was one of Rose's old gang in New York. She had gone there from Chicago around the time Rose migrated east from San Francisco in 1919. They had congregated together in Greenwich Village during Rose's brief flirtation with communist ideas and Rose had socialized with her just before she went abroad in 1920.

But, apparently, Ernestine's help was not necessary. Fiery had asked Virginia Kirkus at Harper and Brothers to take a look at the book. Kirkus would write about her "discovery" years later in an issue of the *Horn Book* honoring Laura Ingalls Wilder. Sitting on the train, she pored over the manuscript (the expanded version Laura and Rose had done for Fiery). The narrative so drew her in that she rode past her train stop. "The real magic was in the telling. One felt that one was listening, not reading," she wrote. "All of us were hoping for that miracle book that no Depression could stop."

5

THE BIG AMERICAN NOVEL

If ever I write my beautiful great novel and no one cares, I will be so hurt—and as always, coward that I am, I shrink from risking.

—Rose Wilder Lane in her journal,
June 25, 1933

The epic droughts that coincided with the Depression parched Rocky Ridge Farm, even though it lay fully five hundred miles east of the Dust Bowl states. Rain was scarce in 1930. Fields dried up in 1931. In 1933, the spring ran dry and Almanzo hauled water to the farm. More extreme dry conditions came in 1934, 1936, 1940, and 1941. Farming was a disaster, and the Wilder-Lane family felt relieved, for sure, that their living came now from stories.

But their finances remained precarious. On December 10, 1931—the same week Virginia Kirkus at Harper and Brothers had bought Laura's book—Rose finally broke the news that she'd concealed from Laura for several days. Their Palmer and Co. stock market investment accounts had no value. "She took it very well, considering," Rose wrote in her diary. Rose's anxiety was high; she realized that even after giving Troub their jointly owned car she would still owe her $2,495. A few weeks later, Troub— whose income also had evaporated—tore out of there, as she put it years later, driving the car back East to find a nursing job.

Laura visited Rose "to get me to answer Harper's Letter" on December 11. The day after that, Laura received her official letter from the receivers for the Palmer account. There was hardly time to feel stunned about that loss. Eight days later, the Junior Literary Guild announced it had chosen Laura's *Little House in the Big Woods* for its "April list": it would print and distribute copies of the book to all of its members—an enormous boon for a new author.

Rose turned back to Laura's wealth of stories in "Pioneer Girl" for herself and resumed writing her own pioneer novel, "Courage." She noted: "am doubtful about it." And on January 10, after reading the latest *Saturday Evening Post*, she wrote, "My own stuff is no good."

In "Courage," Rose sketched Laura's parents as newlyweds several years later than they actually were married. In her portrayal, they lived in a railroad camp and then a dugout in Dakota Territory in the 1870s. In real life, the Ingalls family didn't follow the railroad builders until much later, 1879, and years before that they lived near Plum Creek, close to Walnut Grove, Minnesota. (Laura would write about the Plum Creek period four years later.) Rose created a narrative compressing events from Laura's actual childhood into a few quick years.

Rose's novel was taken fairly purely from her mother's family experiences sketched in "Pioneer Girl." (At this point, Laura had no immediate plans for writing books on these events, but of course she did write about them later.)

One day, Laura ended a conversation with a comment, "Oh well, *let the hurricane roar.*" Rose, intrigued, asked where she'd gotten that line. It was from an old song, Laura said. Rose asked if they could get the words to the song, and Laura, who couldn't remember all the words, went to her old friends the Pooles, asking if they knew. They didn't. Laura wrote to her sister, Carrie, who sent the words—written by Irish hymn writer William Hunter—in a letter.

> Then let the hurricane roar,
> It will the sooner be o'er;
> We will weather the blast and will land
>   at last,
> Safe on the evergreen shore.

Rose loved this. She decided she'd rename her book *Let the Hurricane Roar.* "We'll weather the blast" would, much later, inspire a chapter title in the sixth Little House book, *The Long Winter.* The song search showed the two women at their collaborative best. Rose realized, through this song, just how deep her roots went in her family's experience. Her own hard childhood obviously inspired her now.

With some interruptions for summer socializing, chastising herself all the way, Rose worked on *Hurricane* until the second week of August, when she sent it to her agent.

Meanwhile, buoyed by the success of *Little House in the Big Woods*, Laura spent the summer of 1932 working on a book about her husband's childhood on his family's small, prosperous farm in Malone, New York, in the 1860s. The story of Almanzo Wilder's early years would be called *Farmer Boy.* In August, she gave the penciled pages to Rose. Over the space of a few weeks Rose revised the story into a book draft. Preoccupied with *Hurricane*, Rose sent off the manuscript to Bye. She told herself she had little faith in either manuscript. But Bye, jubilant, telegraphed that *Let the Hurricane Roar* was a classic. "I am so upset by hope that I can't work," Rose noted. A few weeks later, Bye told her that the *Saturday Evening Post* would pay $3,000 and run it as a two-part serial. Longmans, Green and Co. would publish it as a book in 1933.

Laura fared worse this time. In late September,

the editors at Harper and Brothers returned "Farmer Boy," asking for a complete rewrite. It appears that Laura set to work alone at first, while Rose and Corinne, by now Rose's close friend, visited Malone during a loop journey through the East. Rose sent home postcards of upstate New York, writing that she'd walked through the old house and that it hadn't changed from Almanzo's time. The trip gave Rose a feel for the landscape that she obviously believed she needed. Laura kept working on the revision until mid-January 1933, when Rose noted that Harper editor Ida Louise Raymond was asking after it. A week later, Laura took her pages to Rose. Rose put aside her own work and began revising Laura's.

The challenge was finding a theme for Almanzo's story. Rose built the narrative around the Wilder farm's stability and the economics and freedom of farming. Young Almanzo's father teaches him again and again that farming offers independence. Rose also drew on a reminiscence of Almanzo's about bullying and a story of Laura's about a teacher in Burr Oak, Iowa, who had whipped unruly boys who then escaped out a window. The two made a dramatic episode in which town bullies try to beat up the soft-spoken teacher, who beats them with a blacksnake whip and watches them scramble out the back window, crying.

Full of turmoil, Rose revised "Farmer Boy" for two months. "There's a curious half-angry reluctance in my writing for other people," she wrote in her journal on January 25, 1933. "I say to myself that whatever earnings there may be are all in the family. And I seize upon this task as an excuse to postpone my own work. But there can be no genuine pleasure in generosity to my mother who resents it and does not trouble to conceal resentment."

She might have predicted the cold blast that unleashed on her later that week. This is the story as Rose tells it:

At the farmhouse, Laura had joined Rose, Corinne and Jack Murray, and the writer Catherine Brody, who'd been staying there with Rose. They were celebrating an ad for *Let the Hurricane Roar*, which Rose had received from her editor, Maxwell Aley.

The ad, Rose wrote in her diary, had been "splendidly done and I was very happy over it." While the tear sheet doesn't survive, another ad from that time reminds readers that the pioneers had overcome difficult trials, just as readers were now facing, with skill and strength through tough times. It quotes President Franklin D. Roosevelt's inaugural address: "A recognition of the old American spirit of the pioneer . . . is the way to recovering . . . the immediate way." It described Rose's novel as "the story of a young pioneer couple who faced Dakota cyclones, blizzards and grasshoppers with faith and magnificent courage—the kind of courage we need today."

Brody held the ad up to the group, but Laura said she didn't have her glasses and wouldn't look. Some time later, after retrieving her glasses, she picked it up and did look, and interrupted the gaiety. Rose recorded the exchange in her journal:

"Why do they place it in the Dakotas?" Laura asked.

"I don't know," Rose replied.

"The names aren't right," Laura said.

"What names?" Rose asked.

"Caroline and Charles. They don't belong in that place at that time. I don't know—it's all wrong. They've got it all wrong, somehow."

In her journal, Rose lamented that the conversation "effectively destroy[ed] the simple perfection of my pleasure."

Laura must have felt blindsided, betrayed. While she was used to her daughter writing short fiction using family stories, she had never made characters right from the family; she'd never narrated the family's homesteading attempts. Probably Laura never read *Hurricane*—she seldom read anything of Rose's—but she didn't need to. The ad said it all.

Laura got quiet. And Rose's evening was ruined.

Their spat shows how trust eroded when two writers mined the life of one of them; only Rose knew who was using what. Yet, awkward though their competition was, they continued at top speed. Rose finished her work on Laura's "Farmer Boy," which *Harper's* accepted in March 1933 for September publication. This time it offered a lower royalty, blaming the Depression. And Rose's *Hurricane* presented itself as a leader in a new genre. The book's flyleaf proclaimed, "This novel places Rose Wilder Lane among the few American writers who have drawn from the deep roots of our national life to create fiction of lasting value."

The same month in which Rose was revising *Farmer Boy* and celebrating the publication of *Let the Hurricane Roar*, she drafted notes for a multivolume novel about America, sketching outlines across thirty-three pages of a notebook. She would link dozens of character types in a "swirl" of events across "an enormous canvas, covering horizontally a continent, vertically all classes." Rose, whose schooling had ended with the equivalent of perhaps ninth or tenth grade, had gained a broad historical knowledge through her own voracious reading. She now considered the vitality of ordinary working-class people. She had become interested in how leaders take power over ordinary citizens and how those citizens react to it. "Power really lies *between,* not in the hands of any person or class, but in the issue of their reactions to each other, outcome of conflict of their desires. Power an imponderable thing."

Rose listed potential characters—farmer, industrial worker, communist, office worker, small business man, financier, politician, and more. Under this she wrote: "One family may comprise all these, and incidentally show complete destruction of the Family as a social unit, a social concept. But since the Family no longer exists in America, it is not proper framework for an American novel—What is a framework for chaos?" From this we might infer that Rose did not believe—yet—that a family provided a suitable framework to tell a uniquely American story. She viewed American life as chaotic. But perhaps the passage implies something else: that, to Rose, family life in early 1930s America lacked structure, integrity, the ability to nurture future generations. If that was what she meant, the belief contradicts what she and Laura were beginning to express with the Little House books, portraying a wholesome pioneer family life. Yet perhaps that is the point. Pioneer novels gave tributes to what had been lost.

Rose's Big American Novel would cover every region of the United States. Characters would illustrate the growth of America. Two systems that influenced Americans were movements like Protestantism (after the Reformation, shown in the Puritans from England, for example) and Feudalism (shown in Southern states that relied on slavery). She thought the Civil War had ended traces of Feudalism and that the struggles in 1933 were between farmers and industry. All this sketching showed she wanted an encyclopedic history.

The most surprising part of the Big American Novel outline—when we consider the emerging Little House project—was Rose's page-and-a-half sketch of the American pioneer. The character she drew here is an outright contradiction of the pioneer as hero as portrayed by Laura and Rose in their pioneer writing:

> Anti-Aristocratic, and increasing irresponsibility. Because he was typically the poor man, of obscure or debased birth, without ability to rise from the mass, and his westward movement was largely escape. . . . He evaded difficulties and responsibilities (such as debts) by running away from them. He had some physical courage and he was forced to physical endurance (or killed by frontier conditions) but he had little moral stamina.

Her Big American Novel would probe current American society rather than evoke nostalgia. What she was setting out to do was a tall order. In subsequent months, Rose retreated upstairs to her writing and sleeping porch. "All these days and weeks I am trying to work out my novel," she wrote on June 25. "The complications are terrific. They overwhelm me. I am not even sure where the choices are, and if I found them, have I the character, the courage, to make them clear? I want to make a big, popular success." She fretted that she'd work hard, produce, and then no one would care. "Courage is what I most lack," she wrote.

Before long Rose's efforts collapsed under the sweeping canvas of the novel she'd dreamed up. She confided in her diary that she couldn't see how to get it going. On June 26, she wrote, "Yesterday I worked out the basic plan of the novel—ten books, and suddenly I was overwhelmed with despair. I knew I haven't the power to do such a thing, and saw myself as the absurd and piteous ambition that attempts and fails to do more than it can."

She had told no one of her plan and soon abandoned it. "It is a cheap vanity in me, never to attempt big work, so that I can always say I didn't (try and) fail."

Her fears about the Big American Novel seem a bit odd, given the wild success she'd just seen.

Rose's *Let the Hurricane Roar* was short—152 pages—but she did not fail in that. The public loved it. Reviews showed that the pioneer experience spoke profoundly to Americans in the bleakest years of the Depression. On February 26, 1933, the *Minneapolis Tribune* wrote: "Perhaps Mrs. Lane wants us to take a lesson in courage from the early settlers." Margaret Wallace wrote in the *New York Times Book Review*, " 'Let the Hurricane Roar' is the story of a courageous struggle, told with such simplicity and sweeping directness that the reader is fairly caught up in it. Mrs. Lane, who knows her frontier Americans thoroughly"—Wallace understood Rose's background—"has captured a good deal of the reality, and some of the romance as well, of the stirring early days of our national existence." The public was eating this up. The reviewers couldn't have known whether Rose was an expert, but the authenticity of her family story did come through.

In April, the *Boston Evening Transcript* added its admiration, connecting hardships with heroism. "In Miss Lane's attempt to portray the hot winds, snow blizzards, prairie fires and the scores of other obstacles which confronted Charles and Caroline in their heroic effort to pioneer, there is conveyed a sense of realism. Time and again you get the feeling of utter futility which gripped the early settlers. Also you get the spirit of gigantic achievement."

Rose's readers seemed to feel that early settlers had forged westward in order to carry out some larger national purpose, that of testing themselves against difficulties and nurturing generations of courageous people. It could be that Rose read or at least had heard of Frederick Jackson Turner, whose frontier thesis had gained popularity during her early years in newspaper writing. Turner contended that the movement west, building on wild lands on the frontier, defined American character. *Let the Hurricane Roar* describes two brave people who survive a difficult year on a new homestead. To many readers who have compared it closely to the Little House books, it rings hollow. Charles and Caroline, the main characters, work hard and love each other, but they say very little. The man's jubilant vernacular, such as when he calls their baby "the little shaver," seems forced. The narrator takes readers inside Caroline's mind but fails to describe her feelings as deeply as Rose's editing later would bring out Laura's feelings in the Little House books. Something about the overall tone of Rose's first pioneer book betrays the fact that Rose, the writer, had never lived through the weather and conditions she was describing. The landscape and weather were only "fresh mornings," or "the prairie was lost in heat." The locust plague, which Rose based on Laura's description from "Pioneer Girl," fails to horrify in the way it would in Laura's later book *On the Banks of Plum Creek*, because Rose described how it made them feel rather than merely describe it outwardly: "The descent of the grasshoppers was, mercifully, a nightmare. It was a horror, but it was unbelievable." As we will see in Chapter 6, Rose later pulled much more out of Laura in a very similar scene: the family heard the insects chewing, watched their jaws make willow tops fall to the ground, and heard the quality of Pa's voice, which the fires he's burning in the wheat field have made raspy.

Rose wasn't the kind to bask in the joy of her *Hurricane* readers. She always worried that the money would stop. So she continued her practice of drafting new short stories for magazines. Two she worked on around this time showed her ability to weave plot and melodrama in whatever direction she thought the major magazines might want. The homey "Pie Supper" told of a church auction where men bid for desserts made by their imagined sweethearts. This was published in *American* magazine. "Vengeance," which she called "A Spool of Thread" during its composition, constructed a grim love triangle involving a newly released prisoner and his former fiancée. It ends with a murder by pitchfork—which drops from the thread by which it is hung above the barn door—and the sick revelation that the ex-convict has killed the wrong rival. "Vengeance" showed Rose at her most contrived. It was published the next year in *Liberty*, whose editors informed their readers: "Reading time: 20 minutes 20 seconds."

Writing for the big markets was a game Rose played because she thought she must. Her book *The Peaks of Shala*, story "Innocence," and even her long letters to friends and her early newspaper writing all showed she could write sparely and beautifully. Rose noted around this time in her journal of books read that writers in the early 1930s could not expect their readers to dive into a story thinking, "It's only a story." Instead, Rose noted, "We must now convince them that our tale is more real than 'real life.' "

Rose's writing routine in early 1933 included long journal entries about her day-to-day life on Rocky Ridge, in addition to the three-lines-a-day diary entries that she had been making almost daily for a decade. The longer journal notes provide a more complete picture of farm and garden, interactions with Laura and her friends, and money anxieties. She didn't write in it at all during February, when her other diary reports she was revising Laura's *Farmer Boy*. On February 7 came Laura's sixty-sixth birthday. Rose noted only that she had "sent candy" over to the Rock House—probably through a delivery man from town.

One morning three days later, Rose let her little dog, Bunting, out, as usual. Her diary tells what happened next: "At 11, Catherine saw him crawling up the highway. Badly hurt, stood in pool of blood till I picked him up. Called Dr. Fuson to sew him up." Bunting later died on the floor of the living room while Rose and Corinne kept vigil during a game of chess. The next day, they buried Bunting "on the hill."

The following day, she visited Laura, and the day after that, February 13, 1933, Rose started crying. Over the next seven months, until late September, Rose descended into a physical and mental collapse. She noted regularly in her diary, "Crying." Her head pounded, she was exhausted, and she wrote that she didn't care about anything. "He's gone just as I will go," she mourned in her journal, "everything lovely in us wasted, uncared for, lost and forgotten. I *know* all the time now that I am dying and that it makes no difference at all to anybody."

Rose's misery, recorded in her journals, is moving, but is it out of proportion to reality? Consider the success that her and Laura's writing enterprises were achieving. *Let the Hurricane Roar* went into a second printing that very month, February 1933. *Little House in the Big Woods* was still selling well. Other stories were bringing in thousands of dollars.

Unarticulated emotions—neediness, guilt, resentment—seemed to lurk beneath the surface of many of the interactions Rose recorded. It's tempting to psychologize and wonder whether Rose returned to Missouri for reasons having nothing to do with caring for her parents, but in fact as a way of settling a score with her mother, so as to forge a good relationship with her in adulthood. See, for example, Rose's reaction to what might have been a perfectly businesslike discussion. On March 28, Laura showed up at the farmhouse while Rose was eating breakfast. She told Rose that someone had offered to buy the Rock House. Should she and Almanzo pursue this sale?

If the Rock House sold, Rose wrote later, Laura and Almanzo would move back into the farmhouse and Rose would leave. At times in the coming two years, Rose would revisit, in her notes and letters, this idea of leaving. The truth is that the Depression had cut way into the income that Rose had projected back in 1928, the year she'd built the new house for her parents. Now, five years later, Rose wrote that she'd be relieved if she could recoup some of the money she'd put into her parents' retirement house and get away. But she doubted the offer would come to anything. And at that point, it didn't.

A few weeks later, Laura stopped by the farmhouse again with money on her mind. She asked Rose for the electric company's contract.

"I must have known, without knowing, what was coming," Rose wrote in the journal, "for I *ran* upstairs, saying I'd bring it down, telling her—behind me—that she needn't come. Of course she came. She sat at my desk, I in my typewriter chair." As Rose told it, Laura slowly read the paper. "Then she began. Cheerful, almost playful, and brave. She has it all planned. Cut off the electric bill and she can manage indefinitely. Well, after all, she didn't have electricity before; I've given her six 'wonderfully easy years.' How she hates it that I'm her 'sole source of support.' Implicit in every syllable and tone, the fact that I've failed, fallen down on the job, been the broken seed." The relations that bound them to each other were interwoven with money fears. Rose seemed to feel like a wounded child when Laura talked about money, while Laura managed to imply that Rose was extravagant for keeping the electricity on during an economic collapse.

Rose's recollection was that this conversation went on for an hour, with Laura saying they should cut off the electricity and Rose responding they should not. Finally, Rose offered to pay the overdue February rent. She handed Laura the check. Laura said she'd take it only if Rose would tell her if she needed it back, and suddenly left. "The curious thing is, that she's sincerely reaching for some kind of companionship with me. . . . She wants genuine warmth, sympathy.

She had not the faintest notion what she's doing to me."

Yet Rose, even in her emotion and disappointment that she could not hold a frank conversation with Laura, acknowledged that both of them were misers.

> But underneath, there's not a trace of generosity in her. (Any more than there is, really, in me.) Only my refusal to give is on another basis, concerns other things. She doesn't intend to let me get away with owing her a penny, not any more than she'd give a tramp a crust of bread, or a neighbor a taste of first strawberries.

Rose still corresponded with her writer friends, but at this point only Catherine Brody remained on the farm. She and Rose didn't really get along, which suggests that the strains of the Depression and personal sadness, as over Bunting's death, clouded some of the earlier fun. One evening, Brody asked Rose to read a rough draft of her new novel; her editor in New York was asking for the manuscript, which was overdue. When Brody, frowning and anxious, later appeared in her nightgown at Rose's bedroom door, Rose (with the pages in her lap) managed only, "Catherine, it's grand!" before Brody snarled and accused her of not being honest. Rose offered her a cigarette.

She actually had some criticisms but didn't share them. She later wrote in the journal that although the book held promise and "could beat" Brody's earlier book *Nobody Starves*, it was rough and lacked structure. Rose also thought her friend was deliberately not doing her best work, perhaps was sabotaging herself. Apparently, Rose said none of this to her, though Brody continued to live with her for months more.

Rose's fearlessness confined itself to her typewriter and pen. In person she seemed to freeze, afraid to speak her true thoughts. Rose wrote of Laura, "She made me so miserable when I was a child that I've never got over it. I'm morbid. I'm all raw nerves. I know I should be more robust."

While these personal dramas played out, circumstances in America so alarmed Rose that she spent time commenting on them in her journal. It was as if the news gave her something to think about other than her pounding head, writing, and the bills. Everyone on Rocky Ridge Farm listened with a combination of alarm and horror to the radio reports emanating from the Franklin D. Roosevelt administration. Rose followed the US Senate's Pecora investigation into the practices of Wall Street banker J. P. Morgan and his partners. News accounts from that time reported that the public was dumbfounded that Morgan and his partners had found loopholes in the tax laws and paid no income taxes since the stock market crash of 1929, even though they were making more money than they had before the crash. Rose talked to herself about this for a page and a half in her journal. She didn't seem to harbor anger that Morgan might have acted unethically. She wrote, "Wild hullabaloo because the Morgan firm handled big stock flotations by selling blocks at cost to—o horrible crime!— the men who could pay cash for them: i.e., rich men. Morgan seems amused; I don't know how he could be otherwise. Also he is, naturally, quite safe within the law."

Awkward though rural Missouri life probably felt to Rose, she had over the past several years matured in how she approached her craft. She believed that she belonged on the soil where she'd grown up, and that American values and experience should drive her work. Although the Wilders had spent their lives striving to better their standing, Rose now seemed to value what poverty and moving around in covered wagons had given them. "There's room for a movement of American writers," she wrote in her journal on June 2, 1933, "loving the American scene. Many inarticulate common people do. Such feeling in our literature would express authentic feeling, and bring (if they could come) our writers home."

Rose set off on a road trip to Kansas in

July 1933. The *Saturday Evening Post* had commissioned her to write two articles about wheat farming, especially in the Dust Bowl states of Kansas, Oklahoma, and Texas (where winter wheat was a major commodity), and the effect the Depression and drought had on wheat trading. Rose was suffering from headaches, low energy, and despondency, but she pushed herself hard on this trip. "Wheat and the Great American Desert" came out in the *Post* in September. The editors gave Rose the byline "A Grain Trader." For her narrator, she created a fictional wife who couldn't sleep over the uncertainty of her husband's income, but the narrator understood that no external controls on markets could change the human urge to produce, trade, and negotiate fair prices based on actual conditions. Rose compared the Dust Bowl to the federal government: both, the "grain trader" wrote, acted to reduce the harvest. Nature, she wrote, was a better equalizer than government policy. She believed that in two years the land could recover and become productive again. "The dust storms, the dry, harsh winds, the sudden reversions to low temperatures, the alternate thawing and freezing had been doing on a large scale what the Government in Washington was trying to induce farmers to do by subsidy," she wrote. "The climate was accomplishing an acreage reduction on a scale that made the Government's offer of a subsidy to farmers not to grow wheat seem needless."

The supposed "trader" went on to say that he got out of the wheat market in July 1933 because he could not understand the policies of the New Deal for controlling the markets. "I understand the grain trade. I do not understand propaganda."

The rainy evening of September 26, 1933, brought an unexpected visitor, who would join her family circle. Rose was reading, or perhaps washing dishes, inside the farmhouse. She heard a rap on the screen door nearest the garage and gardens. The farm dogs ran to the knock, and Rose quickly followed and reached up to latch the door so the dogs wouldn't push it open. A bedraggled teenage boy was standing there, looking crestfallen because she'd locked the door. He asked if she had any food.

Rose started asking questions: Where was he from? Where were his parents? Where was he headed? He told her he was alone. He'd come from Tulsa. "On an impulse I put him to work," she wrote in her diary. "Weeded border in the rain and did good job. Parents died August 1932."

Rose gave him a room (perhaps the one Catherine Brody had vacated just a few days earlier) and ordered clothes for him from the Sears Roebuck catalog. The farmhouse was now home to at least three or four people— Corinne Murray (who probably left her husband behind at their home), Rose, and a new charge. He started at school in town.

Now that they were done with *Farmer Boy*, Laura began drafting her third book, covering her early childhood in "Indian territory." These were the memories with which "Pioneer Girl" opened, and Laura used those pages to start the draft of what she was then calling "High Prairie," after the high-elevation grasslands where the Ingallses had tried to settle in 1870.

She'd been so young at the time—she was only three in 1870—that she felt obliged to do some background research in order to understand the family stories Pa and Ma had told. She and Rose did the work together.

They began searching for information about the Indian tribes in the area where the family had lived, and they set out by car for Kansas and Oklahoma. From that road trip, Laura saved a highway map of Oklahoma that showed the town of Independence in southern Kansas. She circled the area roughly forty miles south of Independence that was immortalized in family lore. She didn't know at the time what US Census reports would reveal years later to dedicated amateur historians—that the Ingalls family home was not in the future Oklahoma but in the land that became Kansas, as I discussed in Chapter 1.

Rose corresponded with Grant Forman of

Muskogee, Oklahoma, who had written an article in the *American Historical Review*'s July 1932 issue on John Howard Payne and the Cherokee Indians. His letter to Rose, dated March 27, 1933, detailed defiant settlers who established farms on tribal lands in 1870 and whom the military removed. Forman told Rose that the area she and Laura were focusing on did include white settlers who had moved onto Indian lands without permission. He quoted Captain John N. Craig, an Army officer, who wrote in 1870 that the illegal settlers were "quite defiant and cannot be removed without a military force." Forman went on to say: "The period referred to in these reports does not quite agree with your mother's account—65 years ago; but the facts seem to fit the situation described by you." He believed that Laura could have encountered "wild Indians from various of these tribes, whose identity it would be difficult to determine. There were doubtless Cherokee and Osage Indians there of course."

Laura tried to recall the name of an Osage chief who had been kind to the white settlers. She remembered something about this from her parents. She wrote to R. B. Selvidge, also of Muskogee, Oklahoma, who wrote back on July 5, 1933: "In reply to your letter, I will say that the chief of the Osages at that time was named Le-Soldat-du-Chene. This Man was very friendly to the white people. Hoping that this information is satisfactory." Laura used this name in the book, as we know.

Laura and Rose knew from Aunt Martha Carpenter's letter in 1925 that, during that period, Indians would enter white people's houses and ask for food. Aunt Martha's letter probably inspired them to reconstruct similar stories about Indians in this manuscript. The book also continues the detailed description of pioneer skills that Laura had begun in the first book, showing Pa building a log house with Ma's help. After an account of meeting a family friend, Mr. Edwards, it ends with the government getting ready to tell them they have to leave and Pa's angry complaints. In real life they would return to Wisconsin, partly because they weren't supposed to be on that land but mostly because the buyer of their farm couldn't pay for it.

The research trip Laura and Rose took and the letters they sent prove that, thin though the manuscript evidence is, they were collaborating from day one on Laura's third book. They worked in concert, piecing together the story of the time and place as best they could. While they were off by a few dozen miles in the location of the house site, and consequently the history on which they based what became *Little House on the Prairie* wasn't strictly accurate, the important point is that they did the research together. The letter from Forman guided both of them in creating a story out of Laura's very hazy memories from when she was a toddler.

Laura wrote a rough draft of "High Prairie" in early 1934. Some of these tablets have survived, but most of the drafts the two women must have produced have been lost. A handwritten and incomplete draft of "High Prairie," with several starts and stops, was found in Mansfield at Laura's death. With it were a handful of working pages in Laura's handwriting from the chapters "Fire on the Hearth" and "Two Stout Doors," full of cross-outs.

The early part of the story matches the opening of "Pioneer Girl," which describes the Ingalls family's arrival to a prairie campsite, where they will build their house. The gulf between the handwritten tablets and the finished book *Little House on the Prairie* suggests that Rose accomplished a major rewrite, but it is difficult to compare the early handwritten pages, because the versions open to scholars are white-print-on-black microfilm with faint handwriting. Still, we can infer that Rose again guided Laura's factual memories into narrative and theme. For example, Laura wrote in her early pages the story of Pa Ingalls taking Laura and Mary on a walk through an abandoned Osage Indian camp while, back at their cabin, a neighbor was helping Ma deliver their little sister, Carrie Ingalls. During the revisions, probably it was Rose who decided to leave childbirth out of this children's story. Carrie appears as a character and the older girls visit the Indian camp for an outing.

We know from Rose's diaries that in the late spring she spent about five weeks revising "High Prairie." Susan Wittig Albert, who conducted extensive research of Laura's and Rose's work together for her novel *A Wilder Rose*, observes that Rose noted only five times in those five weeks that she had seen Laura. That means they weren't talking about the work as Rose revised this book. Rose's diaries during this time were filled: she recorded people she saw, places she traveled, books and articles she read, and writing projects she labored over. There's no evidence of any discussion with Laura about Rose's typed draft. All this is a reminder that, for this book more than the others, the two women had to use their imaginations for every event, since Laura was too young to remember more than the stories she'd heard from the family over the years.

6

THE BREAK-UP

It is none of my business but I would suggest that you give the key to the house over there to someone that takes care of their own things.

—*Almanzo Wilder to Rose, 1937*

In January 1935, Laura and Almanzo started their seventh year living in the Rock House. Laura wrote at a small desk in the living room. Almanzo kept a herd of goats and a few dogs. A hired man lived in an outbuilding. It all seemed calm and quiet. But a half-mile over the hill, the Rocky Ridge farmhouse resounded with the activities of Rose's assembled "family." Rose had charge of her "sons," John Turner and now his older brother Al, who had moved to the farm in November. She supervised Corinne Murray, who had become a close friend and who now lived at Rocky Ridge full-time as a combination housekeeper and den mother to the boys and their friends. Even the novelist Catherine Brody spent another few months on the farm that year, although she left at the end of the month, finally, making her way to California for a movie-writing job.

Rose would not have found much peace in the cramped farmhouse, even after Brody left and after she had a bunkhouse built for John and Al on the foundation of the burned-down garage. And so, craving solitude to write, she left Rocky Ridge, planning a temporary respite from the distractions. This was the first time she would live away from the farm since she'd babysat Sinclair Lewis and Dorothy Thompson's child for three months in 1930 in Connecticut. It's a common story for many women of privilege—especially mothers—who write: seeking peace and quiet, they secure household help and leave home to get some work done. It seems that despite years of experiments in living, Rose hadn't found her ideal working environment. The past five years had shown only that she could not live or work happily at Rocky Ridge. She could not have admitted this to Laura and Almanzo, let alone the Turner boys, Corinne, and the others. And she didn't. She just told them she was going away for a little while.

Rose first retreated to the Old English Inn on Lake Taneycomo, south of Mansfield. She spent a month there and then moved north, into Suite 916 in the modern skyscraper Tiger Hotel in Columbia, Missouri. It could have felt like a huge relief. But going to the inn also would entail sorrow: her attempt at constituting a surrogate family in adulthood was failing. Yet Laura and Rose's writing partnership was moving into a novel phase, and the new arrangements would give Rose more control over the Little House manuscripts after Laura sent them to her.

At the inn and the Tiger Hotel, Rose worked on an anthology of her magazine fiction first published in the *Saturday Evening Post* and *Ladies' Home Journal* between 1932 and 1935. The collection, titled *Old Home Town*, would join nine stories set in a small, fictional town similar to Mansfield. Rose wrote a preface to the book that revealed a new appreciation for what childhood in Mansfield had given her (notwithstanding how stifling she still found the town). She had spent much of her adult life working to undo the lingering feelings of shame over her family's money struggles when they had lived in town and on the farm, and she had become self-consciously gentrified. Now she celebrated the penury of her early years and found the attitudes that the adults in her life had held back then to be wise, moral, and necessary rather than oppressively strict and sober.

Laura, the strict mother of that old home town, had celebrated hard work as a core value in her *Missouri Ruralist* columns two decades earlier. Now Rose had evolved a firm opinion of what hard work in marginal circumstances should mean for the American experience. This change in her perspective is important, because she and Laura were midway through the Little House books and it would influence Rose's approach to the subsequent volumes.

The stories in *Old Home Town* are narrated by an adolescent named Ernestine. Ernestine struggles for love and freedom, maneuvering around her parents' rigid expectations to achieve her ends. The stories contain slick turns of plot. In her preface, Rose labored to connect them through certain unifying themes. William Holtz, Rose's biographer, writes, "As she attempted to draw these together in a single volume, she began to uncover ambiguities that had not been manifest in the stories individually."

Rose turned away from ideas inspired by her earlier personal experiences, such as the need of young people in small towns to wrench free of the rural chokehold. Using language much like today's "family values" political code, she advocated for the repression of individual expression, an adherence to tradition, and a strict work ethic. She argued in the preface that the exasperated parents in the "old home town" did not suppress individual freedoms but actually held the key to a meaningful life. Her growing identification with farm life as the foundation of American values was manifest when she wrote:

Now some of us seem to see, in our country's most recent experiences, an unexpected proof that our parents knew what they were talking about. We suspect that, after all, man's life in this hostile universe is not easy and cannot be made so; that facts are seldom pleasant and must be faced; that the only freedom is to be found within the slavery of self-discipline; that everything must be paid for and that putting off the day of reckoning only increases the inexorable bill. This may be an old-fashioned, middle-class, small-town point of view. All that can be said for it is that it created America.

She added, "It was a hard, narrow, relentless life. It was not comfortable. Nothing was made easy for us." Depriving oneself in order to pay off debts was better than procuring comforts while owing money. Honesty meant something: it meant avoiding the unpleasant outcomes of dishonesty.

These ideas show how strongly Rose believed that, left alone, individuals and the markets would settle scores, that hard work brings success. These are the same ideas *Farmer Boy* underscored: No valuable goods or services should come free in this life, and no one should delay their costs by borrowing. The consequences of that take a toll.

The perspective shift can be seen as personal, an argument Rose was having with herself. Laura and Almanzo were still—in a rather convoluted arrangement—Rose's landlords, and Rose still owed Laura thousands of dollars in overdue rent. Rose sometimes missed paying her parents the $500 yearly allowance she'd promised them many years before. Laura had invested some of her money in the Rock House, and Rose was paying her interest on that. Rose had lent her parents money for some of the costs of building and furnishing the Rock House, but Laura and Almanzo—demonstrating, once again, their ability to stay out of debt—had already paid this back.

Between the lines of her discourse in the preface appears a woman criticizing not only other Americans but herself. Rose the writer lauds stoicism, financial discipline, and repression of desire. Yet in her own life she ignored some of the key lessons that the stern adults had given her by remaining in debt and subcontracting the simple chores of daily living. Rose herself had misbehaved, and writing a preface that celebrated those modest values was perhaps a form of self-flagellation—a whipping like one the parents might have administered in the old home town.

When *Old Home Town* was published in 1935,

Rose wrote an autobiographical sketch that the publisher issued in pamphlet form. A typed draft of the sketch was filed with biographies collected for the Works Project Administration in 1940. When she was young, Rose wrote, the family had fled the parched prairies bereft of hope— "But everyone felt the courage of despair." She implied that hitting bottom had given them ground on which to stand, from which to view the situation with bravery, and act.

She characterized Rocky Ridge Farm in 1935 this way: "This submarginal farm, in a largely submarginal but comfortably prosperous county, helps support some seven hundred families on relief." At that time, the Wilders had not grown fruit, raised cattle, or tended hens for income since the late 1920s. So what did Rose mean by this? She might have been referring to a comment she'd heard from the town banker, that any taxpaying entity like Rocky Ridge was supporting, by paying taxes, all those struggling Wright County people who had to accept government relief. The population of Mansfield, Missouri, in 1935 was 922 people.

Rose drafted a sequel to her *Saturday Evening Post* article on wheat, but the magazine rejected it, and no manuscript survives. The same year, she wrote a long article that she referenced in her journal as a piece on individualism, which the *Post*'s Adelaide Neall had asked her to try. In

August 1935, Neall rejected all 11,500 words of it.

Robert M. McBride, a writer and publisher of travel books, commissioned Rose through her agent George Bye to write a book on Missouri. In the spring and summer, she read up on the state in the University of Missouri library. She started writing the book on October 11 while in exile in the Tiger Hotel. Over two weeks and one day she wrote a first draft of eighteen thousand words, weaving stories into her descriptions of Missouri's pre-settlement, farming, and modern landscapes. It would seem she had the project under control, but she hadn't yet figured out how the whole book would serve its purpose as a travel guide.

The manuscript that survives, stamped with her agent George Bye's address, opens with the story contemporary fans know well: the Wilder family rattling by wagon into Mansfield in 1894, having escaped drought-parched Dakota Territory, when Rose was seven.

> My mother was happy because there were trees. We had driven out of the wind and already I was growing accustomed to the silence in which every sound was clear. There was no longer the rushing of the air that could become a whistling, a wailing, shriek and a buffeting of the wagon.

Their first days in Mansfield Rose characterized this way:

> One day we had a farm again. Such good fortune was almost too good to be believed. My father saw it, then my mother saw it, and they bought it—40 acres of flinty hillside covered with trees and underbrush. But it could be cleared. And I could go to school. . . . The deed was signed and my mother put it in the pen till where there was now no money at all. Early in the morning we started from our last camp to our farm. ("Our really own farm?" I said. My mother replied, "As soon as we pay the mortgage.")

She went on to say, "I now felt some quality of magic. . . . I knew that under this low sky and in this strange softness of light and shadow and blue air, anything might happen."

Rose labored over this project, which had a working title of "The Name Is Mizzoury," and expanded its scope beyond that of a travel book. Instead of a simple text of state history, she composed a novelized depiction based loosely on actual events. Her story went deep into Missouri history, imagining the arrival of French and Spanish settlers on Sioux tribal lands, then continuing with farming and cities. It's clear that

Rose identified deeply as a Missourian, which was ironic, since she had just escaped Rocky Ridge.

But she hadn't moved to Columbia thinking she'd settle there. At the beginning, on some of the weekends she drove the 160-mile journey back to Rocky Ridge, where she mediated arguments and reestablished order among the Turner boys, Corinne, and Laura and Almanzo.

Rose's friendship with Corinne was intense, perhaps as intense as the one with Troub had been. Since fall 1929, Corinne had been spending late nights out at Rocky Ridge, playing chess with Rose. Her marriage appears to have been unhappy, judging from some of Rose's diary entries. "Corinne tired and Jack suddenly yelled at her at dinner, upsetting my stomach," Rose wrote on January 27, 1935. The two women corresponded intimately when Rose lived in Columbia. A few of Corinne's letters to Rose are available, but Rose's letters to Corinne during that time don't seem to have survived. One letter from Corinne in late October 1935 hints at the closeness of their rapport: "Gosh! Rose your [sic] such a sweet person. I just had to start this letter tonight after reading yours. Nothing you wrote but the feeling I had when I read your letter. . . . I believe you are the only person I ever knew who really is genuine. I can't begin to write what I think and feel. If I could that God d— New York crowd might think they had some grounds for their gossip. I'll just *bet* Ruth pumped Troub." (The identity of Ruth isn't known.) By then Troub, who also was close to Corinne after the years they had ridden horses together on Rocky Ridge, was back on the East Coast.

Corinne's letter also detailed tediously a party John and Al Turner had had on Rocky Ridge, underscoring the fact that Laura and Almanzo, living at the other end of the farm, were not involved with the Turner boys in Rose's absence. Corinne's account suggests she was a lenient guardian who didn't notice that the teenagers were taking advantage. When a group of girls didn't bring food for the party as they'd promised, Corinne made popcorn for all of them. Two of the Turners' female friends talked Corinne into lending them a car so they could pick up yet more friends, and Corinne soon realized that the girls had lied to their parents about where they were going. She also described love affairs that she was witnessing between the young people. It's easy to imagine that Laura was very uncomfortable about all this.

"Remember, dear," Corinne finished the letter, "we all love you a lot and hope you will get that damn book out of the way soon and be with us."

Rose, though, seemed dedicated to staying away and figuring out the next step in her life. On April 12, 1936, she wrote to former President Herbert Hoover, with whom she had not corresponded for at least fifteen years. She aired an old grievance: she'd heard for years that Hoover had not liked Rose's biography of him and had ordered the plates for the book destroyed. (This rumor was reported by Rose's journalist friend Garet Garrett in the *Saturday Evening Post*.)

When he answered Rose's letter, Hoover admitted that he'd complained about someone's manuscript but hinted it was some other writer's that had never published and denied it was Rose's. The notes between Hoover and his staff over this matter do leave open to question whether Hoover actually had criticized Rose, but Hoover denied strenuously that he'd found fault with her, and from then on, the two of them would stay in touch, sharing their opinions about conservative political thought.

Rose's solo career was faltering, but Laura needed her for their next Little House book. In 1936, while Rose remained in Columbia, she and Laura completed their work on the fourth volume in the series, about the Ingalls family's migration to the prairie on Plum Creek, near Walnut Grove, Minnesota. Rose had already mined some of the episodes of Laura's recollection in *Let the Hurricane Roar*, so Laura might have felt nervous about taking up this part of the family history and tentative in how to tell it. Almanzo told friends that he was angry Rose had used Laura's stories without asking her—this report circulated in Mansfield for years and was relayed to Rose's biographer in the late 1970s.

As Laura sketched the story, the Ingalls family first lives in a dugout right in the bank of a sometimes-raging creek. Pa promises he will grow a splendid wheat crop and builds a house out of lumber acquired on credit against the crop. But—in some of Laura's most vivid work, in an early draft—a giant cloud of grasshoppers visits the land and eats everything green. Pa leaves home for paying work, and Ma and the girls find the courage to go on. This was the Rocky Mountain locust plague that had already made its way from "Pioneer Girl" into *Let the Hurricane Roar.*

A look at how the two women wrote about the insect invasion underscores their mutual dependence. Rose obviously depended on Laura for inspiration and for reliable memory, in great detail, of incredible past events. Laura could remember not only what the land and the flora and fauna looked like but how they appeared to her as a child. For her part, Laura depended on Rose to give her material scope and a theme.

Here's how Laura rendered the arrival of the locusts in her original draft of "Pioneer Girl":

> We raised our faces and looked straight into the sun. It had been shining brightly but now there was a light colored, fleecy cloud over its face so it did not hurt our eyes.

And there we saw that the cloud was grasshoppers, their wings a shiny white making a screen between us and the sun. They were dropping to the ground like hail in a hailstorm faster and faster.

And here's how Rose wrote it in *Let the Hurricane Roar*:

A cloud was coming from the northwest, moving swiftly over the sun. It was a cloud like none that Caroline had ever seen. . . . This was a cloud ineffably beautiful, soft as moonbeams, iridescent as mother-of-pearl. It covered the sun, and the sun shone through it gently with kindness. . . .

Grasshoppers were coming out of the sky, out of that cloud. They were dropping by dozens, by hundreds. The air twinkled with their shining wings, coming down. The cloud was grasshoppers.

Finally, this is how Rose revised Laura's description in the "The Glittering Cloud" chapter of *On the Banks of Plum Creek*:

A cloud was over the sun. It was not like any cloud they had ever seen before. It was a cloud of something like snowflakes, but they were larger than snowflakes, and thin and glittering. Light shone through each flickering particle. . . .

Plunk! Something hit Laura's head and fell to the ground. She looked down and saw the largest grasshopper she had ever seen. . . . They came thudding down like hail.

The cloud was hailing grasshoppers. The cloud *was* grasshoppers.

In both Rose's and Laura's tellings, the grasshoppers ate the wheat despite frantic efforts to stop them with smoke. They ate every plant. And the crops died quickly the next spring, after the grasshopper eggs hatched. Rose knew Laura's line in "Pioneer Girl," that Pa had *had* it and "wouldn't stay in such a 'blasted country'!" But that would be too negative for "Plum Creek," she decided, and created instead a hopeful supper scene, full of dialogue: " 'Oh Charles, what will we do?' . . . 'I don't know. . . . but I do know this, Caroline! No pesky mess of grasshoppers can beat us!' "

Rose pressed Laura to define what the theme of the book was. Eventually, they settled on the hopes for the wheat crop. This left them with the difficulty of injecting hope after the grasshoppers came, but they—brilliantly—managed to bring it off by making a maturing Laura Ma's capable helper after Pa left, walking a few hundred miles east to become a farm hand.

"The Darkest Hour Is Just Before Dawn" is a powerful chapter, based on Laura's short anecdote in "Pioneer Girl." The character Laura is forced to give her beloved rag doll to the younger Norwegian neighbor, Anna, who takes it and then leaves it in a mud puddle. In Rose's revision, Laura not only finds the doll face down in the neighbors' yard—she rescues it and takes it to Ma for redemption. The chapter's title originated with seventeenth-century theologian Thomas Fuller, but in Laura and Rose's time the line appeared in *Little Orphan Annie*, Harold Gray's anti–New Deal comic strip that in 1930 was adapted for the radio.

Rose was a rigorous editor. For every incident in the book, she asked her mother to defend its place there. She eliminated Laura's true story of Ma's grave illness during the spring floods, but she left in Laura's brave trip into the creek. Laura crept, fascinated, onto the rickety footbridge during a raging freshet. The water knocked her off and under, and she had to claw her way back onto the narrow board. In Laura's early draft, as in real life, Laura had been going for a doctor, but in *On the Banks of Plum Creek* she's just exploring.

As Rose revised the draft of "Plum Creek" in Columbia, she would ask Laura for more details of daily life and about some of the events. "Look, Mama Bess," Rose wrote in a letter accompanying manuscript pages. "If the grasshoppers eat all the tops off the garden vegetables—potatoes, turnips, carrots, onions— and here it is hot July with no rain for weeks, how can Ma dig potatoes in the fall? Seems to me the thing to do is dig what potatoes there are right away." Laura wrote back that in Minnesota soil, even when the plant tops had died, the safest place for the root vegetables was underground. Laura knew farming better than Rose, and she knew the land where she'd lived. Rose didn't.

Rose was incredulous that, as Laura wrote in her draft, a giant crab lived in the creek. "Surely it would not be a crab. . . . Could it have been a crawdad?" Laura responded that it had been a crawdad, but that they had *called* it a crab back then—reminding her daughter that local parlance made the books authentic.

Although she didn't say so outright, Laura must have resented Corinne's residence in the farmhouse she and Almanzo had worked so hard to establish, while Rose lived in Columbia, seeing them only on weekends. By July 1936 the tension exploded. "This week all shot to hell by my mother's yowls," Rose scrawled in her three-line-a-day diary for July 15. "I have written Corinne to take everything on the farm and I will close the place. End 9 years of an utterly idiotic attempt." She did not elaborate, but we can infer from this—and from a few notes she made years later—that Laura asked Rose either to return or to leave for good but not run Rocky Ridge as an absentee head of the household. Rose noted in the same entry, "and have to finish my mother's goddamn juvenile which has me stopped flat."

This was a full-blown falling-out. Rose decided she wasn't going back to what had become a chaotic situation at the farm. Almanzo's and Laura's frustrations are obvious in the epigraph at the beginning of this chapter, which he wrote on the back of a letter: "It is none of my business but I would suggest that you give the key to the house over there to someone that takes care of their own things." Laura wanted to regain control of their property, but Rose had not cleared out the farmhouse of her invited guests and effects. Laura supposedly asked the hired man to kill Rose's dog (evidently a successor to Bunting); Rose recorded that woeful news four years later.

The diaries show little evidence that either Rose or Laura felt saddened by this turn of events. Perhaps their spat released the tension of trying to live and work together on the same property, and an atmosphere of calm followed the storm. John and Al Turner were getting ready to leave Missouri. (Rose was sending them on a trip to Europe.) Rose may have felt she'd run out of purpose on Rocky Ridge. Nonetheless, dismantling the household would take many months, for Corinne had moved too many of her belongings there to vacate quickly. When she was gone, Laura and Almanzo moved back into the farmhouse as soon as they could. The Rock House was closed and sat vacant.

In the midst of this discord with her family, Rose published an essay in the *Saturday Evening Post* celebrating the freedom she had learned from them. She wrote that Americans and especially pioneers often lived messy lives; freedom for them sometimes meant skipping town ahead of debts. Nowhere but in the United States, Rose argued, could people choose in a relatively unfettered way where and how to live. Rose titled the article "Credo." Most of it was a manifesto railing against the communist way of life, but she cited as heroes the generations of struggling pioneers in the Ingalls and Wilder families.

Rose's Missouri book was now in jeopardy. The editors at Robert M. McBride and Company wanted a modern guidebook, but Rose had thrown herself into a romantic history. McBride demanded the return of the $1,500 advance Rose had received on signature of their contract. She appealed—or perhaps her agent Bye wrote—to Maxwell Aley, her editor at Longmans, Green, to see if he could publish it instead. In late August,

Aley wrote Rose that he had yet to compare two versions he now held of her manuscript. Despite this, he offered some soft-pedaled criticisms, such as that it "has great possibilities for a long time sale"—meaning, he went on, that it was not a book for the general public but for schools. According to him, Rose had portrayed the French and Spanish settlers as "a bit grander than they were in some of your fictionalized passages." The other version he describes has not survived. And despite his criticisms, Aley added, "By God, Madam, you can write!"

While coping with the strain in family relations, Rose continued doggedly on the "Plum Creek" manuscript. By September 21, she wrote in a letter to Laura, "Dear Mama Bess. . . . I meant to send you at least a note, but I have been finishing Plum Creek and not even stopping to sleep." She then gave Laura line-by-line instructions on how to write to the agent and the editor at *Harper's* and mail off the final manuscript, which was on its way to Laura for her final review.

In her letter to her editor, Laura apparently did more than what Rose had directed her to. She asked the publisher to stress on the cover of *On the Banks of Plum Creek* that the stories were true. We know this because of the response from Ida Louise Raymond on December 22, 1936: "I think you are quite right in saying we have not sufficiently stressed the fact that these stories are true. We shall do so in the future. . . . what do you think of having a line on this jacket, in small type of course, saying, 'The True Story of an American Pioneer Family' or something of the sort?" In fact, the cover of the first edition of *Plum Creek* did announce that it was a true story. A poster the publisher distributed in 1937 (on display at the museum in Mansfield) promised: "More about Laura, Mary, baby Carrie and Jack the bulldog. Their further true adventures in the pioneer west." By requesting that her publisher emphasize the veracity of the account, Laura may have been asserting her hold on the stories of her life. Modern readers obsess over the differences between fiction and nonfiction. When twenty-first-century nonfiction writers make something up and the public learns of it, the scandal can end their careers, but in that age Laura might not have understood or considered important the difference between fiction based on facts and strict nonfiction. Rose, we know, played somewhat fast and loose with facts in her writing.

With the publication of *Plum Creek*, Laura affirmed her success as a standard-bearer for simple, wholesome values. And Rose seemed to be coming somewhat unglued. She still had some important fiction ahead of her, as we will see. But, in October 1936, Rose wrote an article for *Ladies' Home Journal* under the title "Woman's Place is in the Home" that, while ostensibly looking back on her own life, once again celebrated values that had nothing to do with how she had actually lived. The article honored homemaking and repudiated the kind of independence that Rose worked so hard to achieve. "Be deeply, fundamentally, wholly feminine. Be proud that you are the bearer of life, the giver of life values," she wrote. In the early 1900s, Rose and her friends had not sought to be like men, she wrote. They sought rewards from their skills and intelligence. They sought not to be "parasites."

In rambling prose, Rose rejected her varied accomplishments, such as becoming the first woman to sell real estate in California and traveling the world to write about her experiences. She disavowed her past by altering and omitting facts. She claimed that she owned "two homes," one in the Ozarks and one in Albania, while at this time, in 1936, she owned no house at all. She referred to having adopted sons—meaning Al and John Turner and, in Albania, Rexh Meta—but, though she did support them, in fact she hadn't legally adopted them.

In such lies and exaggerations, Rose painted herself as austere, without roots. She pointedly failed to mention the long marriage of her parents except by noting, "Some of our mothers had gone so far as to ask the minister to omit the word 'obey' from their marriage vows." The minister agreed, Rose went on, because back then "man and woman were indissolubly made one, and that in this unity woman was no more submissive than man was." But Rose's generation, she went on, missed the meaning of marriage vows because "the words we repeated had no meaning for us."

This is an amazing article, because Rose seems to be coming back to her family through a veiled announcement in a magazine. She admired her parents' marriage; that's clear. She claims that in her own choices she lost more than she gained in giving up femininity for accomplishment. When girls asked her whether they should become writers after their teachers had praised their writing, "what I see is the prodigal blithely leaving home to eat husks." In these lines Rose seems to mourn her choices. She ends by advising women to be creative at home—cooking, decorating, nursing, gardening, and understanding the arts. These are the words of a person with regrets—or, possibly, of a writer who'd say anything to make some money. Whatever she meant to say, Rose was changing, pulling away from old situations, and unsure where she'd be next.

In November, Aley wrote Rose again, asking how she was doing on her revision of the history book, by then titled, "Call It Mizzoury." He didn't mention he was about to resign from Longmans, Green, Rose's publisher. Aley's departure shortly thereafter killed the Missouri project. As the year 1937 began, Rose was in precarious financial shape. Wesley Winans Stout, the editor of the *Post*, wrote to their literary agent George Bye early in 1937: "If Rose needs money badly, I'll break all the rules of The Curtis Publishing Company and advance her enough for her needs. That's how strongly I believe in her."

Rose had kept in touch with John and Al Turner, visiting them many weekends back at Rocky Ridge. In June, Rose and John together left Columbia on a bus for New York. John would join his brother Al a few weeks later in Montreal where, with Rose's support, they lived for the summer. After a few weeks, Rose settled in the Grosvenor Hotel in New York. She was almost out of money when she arrived, but the pioneer stories came to the rescue, again.

In March, Rose had begun work on a novel based on her father Almanzo's trip from Minnesota to Dakota Territory in 1879, covering five years during which the character based on him struggles to "prove up" and own the land. The theme would be that "free land" had never been free. It was paid for, she wrote, with hardship and loss. Almanzo and his brother Royal, and sister Eliza Jane, had ridden west to Dakota together in a wagon pulled by Almanzo's team of horses, one of which died en route, a great loss at the time. (Almanzo revealed later that he had owned such valuable horses because "I earned them.") Characters in the book included a banker, a school teacher, a claim jumper, a "half-breed," a merchant, and an Easterner.

Perhaps because Laura and Almanzo had been so upset at finding their family stories published in *Let the Hurricane Roar*, this time Rose was transparent about it and asked them to help her get the details right. And they helped eagerly, it seemed. Both sent Rose in New York long, detailed letters about Almanzo's first homestead, before he married Laura. Laura quizzed Almanzo for more details and sent her own letter to Rose, explaining that homesteading had not been a successful venture for most. The fact that homesteaders failed conflicted with the central message of the Little House books, of course. "Farming there was like the chicken business. . . . we could get rich on paper—*If*— but the 'If' was too big."

Almanzo, not normally a letter writer, scrawled pages of descriptions and memories. Like Laura, he viewed his whole life as enduring hard luck. Rose typed questions for him, leaving space to answer. She sought details that would show pioneers' courage and strength. "Did folks generally feel that free land, homesteading, was *a new thing?* Dating only from 1861? A kind of triumph of the poor man in America?" she asked.

And her father responded, "I don't think they did."

Rose asked Almanzo to describe "*moments* of satisfaction" in homesteading. He replied that he couldn't remember any such moments except "when we threshed the first crop that was the best crop we ever had, but it was only a few acres because it was before we had much land broke up. My life has been mostly disappointments."

It's a telling line. Almanzo didn't have any investment in creating an uplifting message. Rose, who did, clearly knew that her father's assessment—"My life has been mostly disappointments"—was a pithy line, for she would include it in *Free Land*. She just wouldn't allow the hero, based on Almanzo, to say it. She gave the line to the grandfather, who said it early on, before anyone left for the West. The grandfather said it about his life in the East.

Rose's new pioneer book would be decidedly darker and more adult than any of the Little House books, and it would dig deeply into a growing attitude Rose and Laura shared, as shown in their 1937 correspondence, an attitude that would infuse the next four Little House books. They distrusted and even hated Franklin D. Roosevelt's response to the Depression. As Laura wrote to Rose, "People drive me wild. They as a whole are getting just what they deserve. 'What's the use,' they ask. 'It won't do any good,' they say. I simply can't read it in the papers anymore. It makes me sick, actually." People who couldn't survive and thrive were "getting just what they deserve." They should figure it out, she seemed to say.

Rocky Ridge farmhouse, the home they had worked for over half their lives, now stood empty; Corinne had moved out. Laura and Almanzo wanted very much to move back in, but they didn't want the government to detect that Rose was no longer the head of the household. By now, Laura had an income of several hundred dollars a year from royalty sales. Rose was earning thousands a year, and she relied on the tax deduction stemming from the fiction that Laura and Almanzo relied on her for support. Laura figured that they could get around this problem by continuing to lie on the tax form. "Even if we move to the other place, you can still be head of the household and we can keep it up for you," Laura wrote.

Laura by now was famous if not yet prosperous, more famous than Rose, and she was apparently more confident as a writer because of it. That September she wrote a letter to Berta Hader (the artist and author who'd helped Laura get her start in 1931) and proposed a collaboration: Would Berta illustrate a set of poems? "Some time ago Rose sent you some of my children's verses and some of hers which were to be signed with my name if used," Laura wrote. "Has anything been done with this book of children's verse?" She added that her books were selling well and that she thought her name would guarantee a good sale of the book, as she thought Berta's name would, too. Apparently, this came to nothing.

Laura generally stayed at home and had never made an author's appearance. Her editors had never met her. Finally, she ventured out to her public that year. In the fall of 1937, the J. L. Hudson Department Store in Detroit invited her to speak during "Book Week," to be held in October. Amazingly, because she had never done anything like this, Laura accepted. Rose, from New York, fussed over many details of Laura's trip, and they probably had phone calls about it. Possibly at Rose's insistence, Laura and Almanzo hired their friend Silas Seal to drive them from Missouri to Detroit. Seal had worked for a Ford plant in Detroit, and so he knew the area. Rose sent a letter ahead to her mother at the Statler Hotel, where the three would stay. She began, "Welcome to Detroit! Remain calm, darling. . . . Pause, be quiet, and look around for the person whose business it is to do for you whatever you want done." Rose gave advice on what Laura should wear and how she should let her editor know via a note that she'd arrived. She reminded Laura, "Every one who sees or meets you will buy all your books."

And Rose warned her mother that with fame

comes jealousy, quoting Sura 99 from the *Koran*: " 'I flee for refuge to the Lord of the Daybreak, that he may protect me from the mischief of the things which he hath created; from the mischief of the night when it cometh on; from the mischief of women blowing on knots; from the mischief of the envious when he envieth.' Especially the last, because a lot of people are envying you."

Rose, who'd been a household name during most of the 1920s for her widely circulated magazine stories, would know about fame. Was she now learning about envy?

Nevertheless, in the jaunty tone that she used at the outset of Laura's career, Rose encouraged her: "You will make a grand talk and be a lovely lion."

Laura had with her a seventeen-page hand-written speech. It's almost certain that she'd discussed with Rose by telephone what she should cover in this speech, since she had never appeared at an event larger than club meetings in Mansfield.

The whole experience must have felt over-whelming. Hudson's was a grand institution: the tallest department store in the country, made of pink granite and brick, with thirty-two floors and fifty-one elevators. Laura stood up before an audience of librarians, book buyers, and editors in (probably) either the book department or one of the store's dining rooms. Holding her pages before her, looking down under her hat brim, she began. She and her sister, she said, had listened to her father's stories many years back, in the "little house in the Big Woods." Her mother was a refined woman, descended from the Scotch. Her father's people had come to America on the *Mayflower*, and he'd been born in New York state. He was "inclined to be reckless" and loved music and poetry. Her childhood, she said, was busy and happy and, she realized, unlike any life a modern child could live. She said she'd put off writing down Pa's stories until she was past age sixty.

Laura was a tiny woman, standing less than five feet tall, and attractive, her mostly white hair now cut short. Her voice was colorful, with a very slight twang, as she expressed humility over her fame. "When to my surprise the book made such a success and children from all over the U.S. wrote to me begging for more stories, I began to think what a wonderful childhood I had had," she said, certainly reading straight off the pages. "How I had seen the whole frontier, the woods, the Indian country of the great plains, the frontier towns, the building of railroads in wild unsettled country, homesteading and farmers coming in to take possession. I realized that I had seen and lived it all—all the successive phases of the frontier, first the frontiersman then the pioneer, then the farmers and the towns."

She told the crowd that her purpose in writing the Little House books was to help children "understand more about the beginning of things[,] to know what is behind the things they see—what it is that makes America as they know it." She said she had come up with the idea to write the story of her life in seven books. Since the series actually had not unfolded out of such a deliberate plan on Laura's part, it seems a prudent guess that Laura and Rose had talked out how Laura should present the concept. Laura went on: "When I told my daughter . . . about it, she said it would be unique, that a seven-volume novel for children had never been written." (In 1937, with the fourth book *On the Banks of Plum Creek* just coming out of revisions through Rose's typewriter, Laura thought the series would include seven books; it ended up with eight.) She had kept going after the first few, she said, because children kept on writing, asking what happened next. "Someone has to do a thing first. I would be the first to write a seven-volume novel for children." Note that Laura did mention Rose, but only once and as a confidante, not as an editor or cowriter.

Laura also emphasized that the books were about her real life. "Every story in this novel," she said of the forthcoming *Plum Creek* book, "all the circumstances, each incident are true. All I have told is true but it is not the whole truth. There were some stories I wanted to tell but would not be responsible for putting in a book for children, even though I knew them as a child." She then recounted a few stories from her life that she had kept *out* of the books—like the story of the Bender family, which, she told her audience, chronologically would have been in *Little House on the Prairie*. The Benders ran an inn, which the Ingalls family had always passed by. Guests there disappeared. The Benders' garden was often plowed but never planted. A missing-person investigation found dead bodies in the basement and garden and showed that the Benders had been killing guests with ax blows to their heads while they dined, burying them out back or dumping them in the basement, and taking their money. Laura surely included this tale because it would give the speech some zing. The Bender story was family lore. It had taken place when Laura was three or four at the oldest. She'd heard it from her father and retold to Rose and friends for years. Laura told her Detroit audience that she'd always felt shielded from the terror of the story somehow.

But apart from adding zing, why did Laura tell them this? Rose probably suggested it. Rose was the one who'd actually written it into one of the later drafts of "Pioneer Girl," as Pamela Smith Hill has documented carefully in the annotated edition of *Pioneer Girl* published in 2014. Laura herself didn't write down the Bender story; Rose did.

Laura ended her speech with stronger truths from her childhood: "The spirit of the frontier was one of humor and cheerfulness no matter what happened and whether the joke was on oneself or the other fellow." It was a grand day for Laura Ingalls Wilder, the "lovely lion."

Yet Laura the writer of home truths was feeling unsettled over Rose's extensive revisions to *On the Banks of Plum Creek*. She must have written or called her to say so, for a few days after returning home from Michigan Laura received a letter from Rose facing head-on the awkwardness or perhaps competitiveness between the two of them: "As to similarity in our writing, of course. You often write lines and whole paragraphs that I feel are what I could have written or anyway wish I had. What you haven't developed is structure, a kind of under-rhythm in the whole body of the writing, and a 'pointing up' here and there. And you often fail to put in detail." Next, Rose made a very strange suggestion. She told Laura to take one of the published Little House books and copy it over by hand, to give herself the attitude and mood she needed to keep the "under-rhythm" in the whole body. "Copying gives you the attitude of the writer, not the reader," Rose wrote. "You will find many things you want to change, and when you do, just change them, write them your way."

Laura seemed to have sought some encouragement, because she had started a new manuscript, "Silver Lake" (which would become *By the Shores of Silver Lake*). In one of the letters giving Rose details for *Free Land*, Laura admitted that she was having trouble drafting the next Little House book. This book would cover the same time period as Rose's *Free Land* but from Laura's point of view. Laura was an adolescent in the year covered in both books. Almanzo (ten years older than Laura in real life, but not as old in the book) had already started homesteading. The Ingalls family had gone back to Plum Creek, and there was the problem of whether to talk about that. She apparently decided very early on not to mention the year spent in Burr Oak, Iowa, in this book.

The advancing railroad had provided an excuse for Pa to get out the wagon again and leave for Dakota. His sister, Docia, and her husband, Hi, offered him a job as the paymaster for the Silver Lake Camp. Laura struggled to write an opening for this story, using pages from "Pioneer Girl" that Rose sent her. "Thanks for the pages from Pioneer Girl," she wrote Rose. "All that time is rather dull to me now for some reason. Not nearly so vivid as when I wrote P.G." The pages Rose sent Laura came from the revised "Pioneer Girl" that magazines had rejected in 1930. Laura still had her original handwritten version at Rocky Ridge. Rose's fleshed-out version might have helped her get in the right frame of mind to begin the next book.

In their letters in mid-1937 and 1938, Rose and Laura debated major plot points. Rose did not want Mary to go blind in the novel, as she had in real life. Laura insisted that this remain. Rose rewrote the entire opening of the book, beginning it on Plum Creek. She added a made-up scene of Jack the bulldog dying of old age (which Laura had said must happen—they had to get rid of Jack, who, in reality, the family had traded with their horses in the period covered two books ago) and they settled on the theme of the book: homesteading. Everything the family went through would be worth it because they were working toward their own land. This was a much more optimistic take than Laura's original approach. "There were no jobs lying around to go begging while the government hired men as now," Laura wrote on March 23, 1937. "A man once in debt could stand small chance of getting out." She told Rose that "Pa" Ingalls had worked for a butcher, had lost an investment in a hotel in Iowa. "Pa was no business man. He was a hunter and trapper, a musician and poet."

Rose already knew well the move to Dakota from her simultaneous work on *Free Land*. This had to help in her redrafting of "Silver Lake" and inspire Laura's trust in her, but it also created competition. In one letter fulfilling Rose's latest request for details, Laura noted, "I am using a mob scene at the land office when Pa files the next spring [for the homestead in Dakota], so please don't use that."

In the same letter, Laura told Rose about the death of Almanzo's horse. She gave it an economic theme. "Imagine the loss of such a valuable horse to a poor man making a start in the west and the courage and resourcefulness needed to go on and make a success in spite of 'hell and high water.' There was no whining in those days, no yelling for help. A man did what he could with what he had."

This correspondence buried the tensions and conflict that had ended Rose's years on Rocky Ridge. It seems clear that they were bonding over Laura's pioneer past, together creating a new narrative of American bravery. The warmth probably resulted from their constant communication over Laura's writing and Rose's new pioneer novel.

Wesley Winans Stout, the *Post* editor, didn't have to advance money to help Rose after all. In late 1937 she sold *Free Land* to the *Post* as a serial. It was soon published as a book under that title and became a bestseller. The *Post* paid her almost $25,000. The fivefold increase in her income appeared on the carbon she kept of her 1937 income tax return: "Total income: $24,976. Earned income credit: $1,400. Personal exemption: $2,500." And even though she was not living in Missouri by then: "Credit for dependents: $966.67. Dependents: Mother ($400), Father ($400), Adopted son ($166.67, because he turned 18 partway through the year)."

The sale of *Free Land* ought to have settled Rose's finances and left her, Laura, and Almanzo with no worries. That was a fantastic sum for mid-Depression. Rose began to think about buying a house in the East and settling there.

But Rose spent the income, and she began to conclude that no amount of money would get her out of debt unless she changed how she lived. She opened an account in New York, depositing $8,050 on August 3. Six months later, she explained the situation she was in as 1937 came to a close in a letter to her friend, journalist Mary Paxton Keeley:

> Like a fool, I paid up all my debts. With my agent's advances (to live on while I was writing the thing) and commission deducted, and then all those debts, interest and everything, I was all clear with around $4,000 left and I felt fine till I suddenly realized, it is not enough to pay the income taxes and live on (and

support everybody on) till I can write something else. Well, I am going to write short stories, very cautiously—not too many—and hope somehow to back out of this. . . . if I earn enough in 1938 to pay the two or three thousand dollar 1937 income tax (pay back the money I borrow to pay it, I mean), then that amount on top of what I must make to live on, brings up my 1938 income again, and increases the *rate* of taxation. And at that high rate, I have to pay tax on (the money I borrow to pay) 1937's tax. Because nothing is allowed for what you pay on debts, as you know. So unless I am careful, I will have to borrow again next year to pay this year's tax, and so on, forever and ever.

Rose remained on the East Coast. She and Laura (and Almanzo) were physically separated by a gulf of miles that guaranteed they would no longer share a social life. Rose would not look west again for many years. But the writing of *By the Shores of Silver Lake* marked the strongest period in their collaboration on the Little House books, and it might have been the closest they could become to each other, or would ever be. The next three books would unfold without much apparent discussion between them. It was as if Laura was ready to cede more control to Rose.

PART III
THE ESTRANGEMENT

THE HARD WINTER

"We knew we could expect no help from outside. We must depend on ourselves."
—*Laura recollecting the Hard Winter of 1880–81 in De Smet, South Dakota, in her memoir, "Pioneer Girl"*

Rose shopped for a house in Connecticut during the winter of 1938, but she didn't find anything and in mid-February told herself she'd decided not to buy a house. She sent Laura $500 then, noting that she was making the yearly payment she'd been trying to keep up with for the last decade. Laura wrote back, "Your check was one big surprise. I suppose it is meant for [the] expense of running the house, on your 'head of the household' exemptions. I can't think what else." Laura added she feared her income that year would mean having to pay income taxes.

By letter, perhaps the same one that included the $500 check—the women were writing back and forth often that winter—Rose apparently assured Laura that she was a talented writer and should not worry that her drafts required restructuring and rewriting. This letter has been lost, but Laura's grateful response on February 19, 1938, survived. "You don't know how much good your letter did me and I can't tell you," she wrote. "You see I know the music but I can't think of the words. I didn't suppose any one else ever felt such a failure as I did. It surely was a sick stomach I had. Anyway your letter picked me up and gave me courage. It is sweet of you to say the nice things you did about my writing and I will try to deserve them more."

By this time, Laura was working on the next book, "The Hard Winter." Rose, though, hadn't finished with the previous one. She held onto Laura's "Silver Lake" manuscript for months longer before finally finishing with it. She was distracted. She decided after all that she would buy a house. Her friend Isaac Don Levine, a Russian-born journalist she'd met in Berlin in 1922, lived in Norwalk, Connecticut. He had urged her not to squander all the money from *Free Land*, and Rose had managed to set some aside after paying off an old loan from Troub. By early spring, she had made a down payment. On April 1 she moved to a small farmhouse on three acres off King Street, a few miles outside of Danbury, Connecticut. At that time, Danbury— almost seventy miles northeast of New York City—was an outlying country location, but the trains ran regularly. The day she moved in, she had one ton of nut coal delivered for $13. "For the first time a normal happy feeling of coming home," Rose wrote in her diary on April 14. "Rooted here already more than ever on Rocky Ridge."

Rose's new house was small, uninsulated, and in need of renovation. With her hard-coal stove (Laura and Almanzo had advised her to get one) and basic provisions, Rose camped out there off and on the first year. The rest of the time, she lived in a rented (for $12 a month) cold-water-only walkup apartment in New York's Gas House District, at the edge of what today is Stuyvesant Town. Her neighbors there were journalist Norma Lee Browning and her husband, the photographer Russell Ogg. Rose and Browning had first met when the younger woman was a student at the University of Missouri in Columbia. They'd met up again in New York in 1937. The apartments were apparently quite wonderful, and both women wrote articles about fixing them up. Rose was a mentor to Browning, and the Browning-Oggs spent the spring and summer of 1939 at Rose's house in Danbury.

In the ten months that Laura waited for Rose to finish the "Silver Lake" manuscript, Laura ran interference with *Harper's*. No one at the publisher seemed aware that Rose had, all along, been revising Laura's work. Ida Louise Raymond, Laura's editor, wrote Laura repeatedly through 1938 asking for the manuscript. Laura kept stalling. In late January 1939, almost a year after Laura had finished her part of the work on it and started on her next book, Raymond wrote, "As you may have guessed, I am again asking you if you have any idea when we can get the finished manuscript of SILVER LAKE."

Laura forwarded this letter to Rose, writing on the back, "I have used up all my excuses etc. and think I will just not answer this letter. She can think I have gone to Timbuctoo or am sick or mad or just to [sic] lazy to write."

The next day, Laura sent another letter, four pages long, praising Rose for taking care of her and Almanzo so well. "Without your help I would not have the royalties from my books in the bank to draw on." Laura listed the dining room curtains, table and chairs, Simmons beds, and down comforters, all presents from her daughter. "When I go to count up our comfortablenesses, and the luck of the world we have it all leads back to you." In a chatty P.S., Laura described curtains she was working on and tea sandwich recipes but confided that she did not feel comfortable with her clubwomen friends. "I can't fit in with the crowd someway," she wrote. "Never could very well and now I am tired of them more than ever." This effusive tone contrasts with Laura's personal style—she was not a demonstrative mother, by Rose's accounts. With this acknowledgement of her debt, was Laura cajoling Rose to finish the draft?

Rose sent Valentine candy the next month, but if she sent letters, too, they haven't survived. Perhaps she and Laura spoke on the phone about how they'd make the "Silver Lake" deadline. For now, Laura's letters remained full of friendly chatter. On February 20, she alluded to her and Rose's emerging political views while writing more prosaically about her and Almanzo's decision not to put in a bathroom upstairs at Rocky Ridge farmhouse. "And we are living within our income in spite of your advice," she added. "I wish Mrs. Roosevelt would have to scrub her own floors and do her own work."

Mother and daughter agreed, of course, on the topics of Roosevelt, the rise of Adolf Hitler, and communism. "Hitler's word is about as good as Roosevelt's, isn't it," Laura wrote. "I am worried though, for between dictatorship and communism what chance has a simple republic. If the dictators are stopped the communists will get 'em."

On April 2, Laura wrote that they'd missed the deadline for the fall release of "Silver Lake." But she had come up with another stalling tactic; evidently she wrote to Raymond that she'd been sick. Laura sent Raymond's sympathetic response on to Rose, noting on the back of the letter, "You will see by this that we have a little more time on Silver Lake."

• • •

During the time Laura was waiting nervously back in Mansfield and beginning the book on the Hard Winter, Rose had become engrossed in a campaign against the United States entering World War II. In early 1939, she was writing several magazine articles about the Ludlow amendment. This proposed constitutional amendment—introduced several times between 1935 and 1939 by Democratic representative Louis Ludlow of Indiana—would have required a national referendum before Congress could declare war, except in the case of attack by a foreign entity. Rose told her friends she didn't think it would pass, but she wrote articles in its favor for *Good Housekeeping* (March), *Liberty* ("Why I Am for the People's Vote on War," April 1), and twice in *Woman's Day* (April and December). In her April 2 letter, Laura praised Rose's *Liberty* article, calling it "plain and fair and true."

On May 10, 1939, Rose testified before a subcommittee of the Senate Judiciary Committee in Washington. One of only two witnesses that day (the other was a lawyer also in favor), Rose wore a dark suit with white pinstripes, a black straw hat with a feather, and a white corsage. The *New York Times* reported that Rose told the subcommittee she appeared not as a pacifist but as a revolutionist. Despite her quick explanation that she referred to the American Revolution and that she advocated the proposed amendment as a means of preserving American democracy, Senator [William Edgar] Borah took alarm. He tried to get the witness to say that she "meant 'Americanism,' but she stuck to her own terminology."

The same week, Rose's long friendship with the journalist Dorothy Thompson nearly cracked under the strain of their divergent attitudes about communism and Stalin. It started when Rose's friend Isaac Don Levine, the journalist and Russian émigré, ghost-wrote articles for a former Russian intelligence officer named Joseph Krivitsky. The articles said that Stalin supported Hitler. Thompson, in a speech to writers at the International PEN Congress at the New York World's Fair, used the Krivitsky story as an example of the muddled atmosphere journalists faced as they tried to cover the war in Europe and the public's response. Rose seemed to believe that Thompson had attacked the credibility of an eyewitness to communism. She wrote to Thompson that their friendship was over. The two patched things up somewhat in the next few months, but they were never close again. Rose was willing to sacrifice a friendship for political principles.

Laura's fifth book must have been far from Rose's mind in those first months of 1939.

However, after Rose returned from Washington, she seems to have turned immediately back to the "Silver Lake" manuscript, because, on May 23, Laura wrote again: "I might have known you would fix things!" Rose had finished and sent the manuscript to *Harper's*, probably via the typist or agent. Laura and Almanzo were preparing to leave on another trip to De Smet, South Dakota, for Old Settlers' Day. "May I send you 'The Hard Winter' now?" Laura asked. "I would rather you had it so if anything should happen on our trip, you could finish it."

Laura and Almanzo would drive themselves and would take the journey slow. "You see, if we are by ourselves, we will be independent," Laura wrote. The ideal of independence was dear to both of them, of course, and would resonate with Rose. Laura encouraged Rose not to lose the Hard Winter manuscript—it was the only copy, after all. "I expect you will find lots of fult [sic] in it, but we can argue it out later. If the [manuscript] is with you, it will be where you can work on it when you please and get it over with when you like."

At the beginning of June, Laura sent another letter informing Rose they would leave for De Smet on June 6. This letter contains an important clue to how Laura would begin her final two books, which at that point she thought would be one. She told Rose where to find notes to this last volume in her writing desk at Rocky Ridge, with the understanding that Rose should finish the series in case Laura didn't survive the trip. "You could write the last book from them and finish the series if you had to do so," she wrote.

I imagine Rose glowering at such cheerful exhortations from Laura, not only because Laura was enjoying her authorial fame and prosperity—a status that relied on Rose's secret work—but because Rose's own writing career was suffering. That same summer, Rose drafted a story she called "Forgotten Man." It traced the tribulations of coal miners who chafe under government regulations and taxes. The heroes of the story migrate to Jackson, Wyoming, where the main character "steadily lifts himself by the bootstraps," as Rose explained in a note to the editor, adding, "His struggle is against governmental interference with individual initiative."

"I hope," she went on, "that it won't smell like a tract, or a political pamphlet." Apparently it did smell like a tract. In September, the *Saturday Evening Post* rejected it. Rose wrote in her diary, "SEP turns down serial because it is propaganda." Rose's current work was emerging as a body of ideas shaped by her politics. "Long May Our Land Be Bright," for example, in *Cosmopolitan*'s August 1939 issue, stated: "Freedom is self-government, for a human being is free only so far as no one else governs him."

But from being Laura's editor and writing

coach, Rose had developed her role in another direction, slipping firmly into that of trusted collaborator. Sorting out the structural and plot problems of "Silver Lake" (which finally would be published that fall under the title *By the Shores of Silver Lake*) had worn Laura out, it seems. She sent "The Hard Winter" to Rose with no stated expectation of revising it herself; she wanted to leave enough time for Rose to do the job. This marked a turning point; Laura had realized that she no longer wanted to be as actively involved in the revisions. Two manuscripts—"The Hard Winter" and "Prairie Girl"—remained to wrestle with. They would eventually become the last three books of the Little House series: *The Long Winter*, *Little Town on the Prairie*, and *These Happy Golden Years*. Laura would rely on Rose to make her rough drafts into coherent books. In future work on the series, freed from her mother's input and possessing more creative control, Rose would work on the drafts more quickly and add more scenes that reflected her personal and political ideals.

"Nov. 12, 1939 – Sunday," Rose wrote in her diary, sitting in her apartment at 550 East 16th Street. "Halgar says this is my unluckiest day. Feels like it. Began typing from tablets Hard Winter." (Halgar was a newspaper astrologist. Rose frequently mentioned his columns in her diary.)

The story of the winter of 1880–81 in Dakota Territory should have almost told itself; it was so self-contained—lasting one winter—and so awful. But narrating it presented a problem, Laura had explained to Rose in a letter, because it had no clear plot. Would a few hundred people's struggle to survive be enough? The Ingalls family took refuge for almost seven months in the back of Pa's store building. The townspeople relied on trains from the East for their food because they had only just busted through the sod and slough grass the previous summer and had raised almost no grain or other food. Blizzards started in October, and the trains stopped before Christmas. Ice and rock-hard snowdrifts covered the tracks until May. Most families were on the verge of starvation.

The arrival of the "Hard Winter" draft hit Rose hard. It took her back seven years, to 1932, when she had failed in writing the story of that blizzard season under her own byline. By the time she started working on the draft, Rose was probably furious. But she had no choice. She was locked in and had to rewrite this book. Rose's New York City neighbors, Norma Lee and Russell, spent a summer living with her; Browning later reported she'd seen the manuscript arrive and knew from Rose's deflated reaction that Rose felt only obligation; her heart wasn't in it. "They were collaborators in that they were Laura's stories and Mrs. Lane did the professional job of putting them in publishable form," Browning told a reporter many years later. "Rose did not want her name on the books. It wouldn't have done Rose's literary reputation any good."

Seven years earlier, back in 1932, Graeme Lorimer, the editor at the *Saturday Evening Post*, had suggested the idea of writing about that blizzard season to her, based on her vivid storytelling during a visit to his office. She misunderstood his initial enthusiasm, thinking that he had mixed her up with her mother, whose "Pioneer Girl" he had earlier rejected. "Graeme Lorimer's note confuses me rather," she wrote to her agent that April 23, "because I cannot do a first-person pioneer story myself. My gray hair makes me seem more ancient to him than I am. Pioneer life ended with the Oklahoma rush of '89, when I was a year old. Would they take third-person fact-story of the HARD WINTER of '73, about my father and my mother?" (Rose had her dates and events mixed up at that point. In 1873, when Laura was just a toddler, the Ingalls family had just settled on Plum Creek, where a bad blizzard did immobilize the family for a while. Rose wrote about that blizzard in *Let the Hurricane Roar*.)

Rose told Bye that the De Smet settlers survived the Hard Winter because they never expected life to be easy. The article would be, Rose promised Bye, "just a simple record of De Smet, Dakota Territory, during the winter known as the Hard Winter in pioneer history. There was plenty of friendliness, but not a trace even of 'community spirit.' " In that last remark, Rose was presumably dropping in a little social criticism of what she must have felt was a modern idiom.

She recounted for her editor: "The famous 'October Blizzard' stopped the trains. No train got through till the next May. (Railroad company made herculean efforts; most dramatic.)" Rose went on to list many details she could have gotten only from family stories and from Laura's "Pioneer Girl": the people quickly ran out of meat, flour, sugar, coal, and kerosene. They could not hunt. Their shanties and store buildings had such thin walls that only snowdrifts insulated them, until the winds tore the snow away in the next blizzard. They huddled around stoves kept going because they twisted hay into sticks.

Next she listed other elements in the story that would later appear in Laura's Hard Winter book: Almanzo Wilder and Cap Garland made a risky journey between blizzards and bought seed wheat from a homesteader who'd been overwintering in a shanty a dozen miles from town; Pa Ingalls shot a starving antelope and butchered it for the women and children; the women ground up seed wheat in a coffee mill and baked it into bread.

"Really, they took the whole experience as a matter of course; a hard winter, but they didn't expect winters to be easy. 'The Hard Winter,' they called it, almost wholly in reference to the extraordinary weather."

In fact, Lorimer loved the idea, although he asked her to shorten the story to a single article of seven or eight thousand words. But Rose didn't ever write it. Perhaps she couldn't start on it because she still felt stung from Laura's hurt feelings about her using "Pioneer Girl" stories in *Let the Hurricane Roar*. Rose didn't let go of the Hard Winter idea, though. Almost two years later, in June 1934, she corresponded with another editor at the *Post,* Adelaide Neall, about it. She said the story had struck "a snag. It is now off again and speeding toward the next rapids ahead. I truly think it will be a good story." A month later, she wrote Neall that drought and 110-degree temperatures meant she could work between three and six in the morning. "But the long, hard haul of HARD WINTER is beyond my present strength."

The Hard Winter stories clearly had a grip on her. But as Laura established herself as a pioneer author, Rose realized that she had to be careful which stories she used. Maybe she and Laura talked about the Hard Winter and Laura asked Rose to hold off. Whatever the reason, Rose gave up writing her own version.

• • •

In the fall of 1939 and winter of 1940, while Rose revised the draft of Laura's "The Hard Winter," she lived through a hard winter herself. It wasn't snow that piled up against the windows; it was unpaid bills. A few entries in her now mostly neglected diary tell the story: On the spaces for March 7–10, 1940, she wrote the words "Hard Winter." On March 9 she wrote, "Check for $500 received from mother. Working on Hard Winter."

So the tables were reversed, and Laura had sent Rose the same amount that Rose had formerly sent home. Nonetheless, the family continued the charade of Rose's taking care of Laura and Almanzo. Rose claimed on her tax return for 1940 a personal exemption of $800, again for being the head of the Rocky Ridge household. She also claimed $949 as an exemption for the Turner brothers, despite the fact that they were both living on their own now. Rose wasn't even sure where John was; Laura passed on a rumor that he intended to join the Army.

As a writer, Rose was undergoing a metamorphosis. She confided to her diary that her successful novel *Free Land* had exhausted her. It would be her last work of fiction. She blamed her money troubles on the fact that she'd had to pay taxes on her earnings.

Simultaneous with the Hard Winter rewrite, Rose wrote a proposal for a nonfiction book with the working title "Underground," apparently based on her recently published story, "For Humanity." She'd chronicle the life of an underground worker in the Comintern, the association of international communist parties established by Lenin in 1919. "The book," she wrote, "is the first candid exposition of the Underground, a stratum of today's life that is unknown and important," Rose wrote in her proposal. "It will be a startling revelation even to well-informed Americans."

In the rejection letter of February 15, 1940, Angus Cameron of Little, Brown seemed to assume Rose would be ghostwriting this for the Comintern member; the editor pointed to the difference between writing fiction and writing nonfiction, and his reasoning might have caused Rose to rethink the sorts of stories she wanted to write from here on out. "If this material were to be handled by you in the form of a novel, that would be another thing, of course; but this being a non-fiction book, we felt perhaps that enough of the facts aren't known to us. On the other hand, I realize that you had very good reasons for preserving the author's anonymity and for divulging no more about the project than you did."

And so, putting aside her interest in the growing communist movement, Rose must have leafed through the nineteen pages of "Pioneer

Girl" that covered the Hard Winter period. She had not looked at these pages since revising them in 1932, but she must force herself into the story again. This time she had no alternative but to do what she'd said she could not: write it as a novel, told from her mother's perspective. She had to either prod her mother for more details or invent them. The novel must satisfy the insatiable young Little House fans and their parents and grandparents. Because Laura spent that fall on the road with Almanzo, it seems likely that Rose rewrote what would be published as Laura's book *The Long Winter* almost entirely without discussing it with Laura.

The Long Winter could be the greatest book of all the Little House volumes, because of the powerful way it conveys the stress and drama of near-starvation in blizzard upon blizzard. Literary scholar Janet Spaeth has observed that *The Long Winter* is a "conventional novel, with rising and falling action based around one major climactic point." Laura had been uncertain how to handle that problem when she'd started her draft, as we saw. "I can't seem to find a plot, or pattern as you call it," she wrote Rose at the outset. "There seems to be nothing to it only the struggle to live, through the winter, until spring comes again." From this narrative puzzle—if Rose responded to Laura's perplexity directly, the letter hasn't survived—to the finished book represents a long journey that we can only sketch because of the incomplete documentary evidence.

All the evidence we do have suggests that Laura's draft of this sixth book was the sketchiest she'd sent to Rose so far. We know that she started with the seventeen-page section on the Hard Winter in "Pioneer Girl." She also probably referred to a longer section, nineteen typed pages, that Rose produced in revising the memoir. The first draft that Laura sent to Rose is missing. Some pages of intermediate drafts were found at Rose's house in Danbury after she died. Laura worked with those intermediate drafts, certainly, to produce the handwritten near-final draft she laid out in yellow tablets that she would eventually donate, along with a later typed draft, to the Detroit Library.

But even that late typed draft now in the Detroit Library wasn't final. I believe that after Laura saw this draft, she excised scenes Rose had added to the manuscript. This is just a guess, but it seems the only answer to the following mystery: Historian William Anderson has identified several pages in this typed manuscript Laura donated to the library that are missing from the published edition of *The Long Winter*. They include a section in Volga with the character Mr. Edwards, a bachelor who'd shown up in earlier books but who apparently was based on no real person. It seems likely that another, more final, draft of the manuscript went through Rose's typewriter before publication.

The final important revision was, of course, editor Ursula Nordstrom's decision to change the title from "The Hard Winter" to "The Long Winter." Laura and Rose both objected to this change, and Rose wrote to George Bye, who quoted her letter to Nordstrom on July 3, 1940. "I would suggest to Harpers, as a selling scheme, honesty." Nordstrom obviously was unmoved. This is certainly one exception to the statement the editor made later that she had never had to edit the Little House manuscripts because they arrived in perfect shape. *The Long Winter*, with its cheery title and dramatic events, was published late in 1940.

The struggle to survive the seven months of blizzards in De Smet, as told in *The Long Winter*, created a new contest in the telling. I believe that Rose jumped into her mother's manuscript with a great deal of energy and fascination with that terrible winter. It was the story both of them had longed to tell. It represents the best that both of them had to offer.

Laura Ingalls, looking determined, stands (at right) with two of her sisters, Carrie (left) and Mary (who was blind), in 1881. *Courtesy of Laura Ingalls Wilder Home Association, Mansfield, Missouri.*

In 1889, at age two, Rose posed for a photographer in Spring Valley, Minnesota. She later wrote that she had switched her hands despite the photographer's preference because she wanted her ring to show. *Courtesy of Laura Ingalls Wilder Home Association, Mansfield, Missouri.*

Rose's graduation photo, taken in 1904 in Crowley, Louisiana, where she finished secondary school and lived with her aunt. *Herbert Hoover Presidential Library.*

Laura, left, stands in the ravine with (almost certainly) Rose, in 1910. Rose had lost her baby a half-year earlier and is believed to have recuperated at Rocky Ridge Farm. *Herbert Hoover Presidential Library.*

Rose in the early 1920s in Paris. *Herbert Hoover Presidential Library.*

A portrait studio in Mansfield, Missouri, photographed Laura in 1917 or 1918, when she was fifty or fifty-one. *Herbert Hoover Presidential Library.*

Laura, seated on the porch, and Almanzo, at left on the steps, visited with neighbors in Mansfield. The likely date of this photo is 1919, judging by Laura's hair color.

In 1916, Rose reported a series of articles for the *San Francisco Bulletin* on the damming of Hetch Hetchy Valley for San Francisco's water supply. *Herbert Hoover Presidential Library.*

Rose visited an outdoor market on one of her trips to Albania, where she lived for two years. *Herbert Hoover Presidential Library.*

The kitchen at Rocky Ridge Farm had a pass-through window and low counters to accommodate Laura's small stature. This photo was taken to illustrate Laura's 1925 article, "My Ozark Kitchen" in *Country Gentleman*, January 17, 1925. *Herbert Hoover Presidential Library.*

The living room in the Rocky Ridge farmhouse as it looked in the late 1920s. *Herbert Hoover Presidential Library.*

Laura, Almanzo, and their dog, Nero, at the Rock House, which Rose had built for them in 1928. They lived there in semi-retirement only eight years before returning to the house they preferred at the other end of Rocky Ridge Farm. *Courtesy of Laura Ingalls Wilder Home Association, Mansfield, Missouri.*

Rose with her beloved Maltese terrier Mr. Bunting, right (the black dog is probably Helen Boylston's), Rocky Ridge Farm, 1929. *Herbert Hoover Presidential Library.*

Helen "Troub" Boylston lived with Rose in Paris, Albania, and Mansfield, Missouri. Rose suffered a mental and physical collapse after Troub's departure from Mansfield in 1931. *Herbert Hoover Presidential Library.*

Editor, writer, and literary agent Ernestine Evans (1889–1967) wondered in the early 1930s whether Rose was involved with the Little House books. *Author's collection.*

In 1929, Rose called herself a revolutionary as she testified to a US Senate committee in favor of the Ludlow Amendment, which would have required a national referendum in order to declare war. *Library of Congress.*

Journalist Norma Lee Browning, shown here reporting a travel story for the *Chicago Tribune*, witnessed the arrival of Laura's manuscripts while living with Rose in Danbury, Connecticut, in the early 1940s. *Author's collection.*

Laura signed copies of her books for schoolchildren at Brown's Bookstore in 1952. Standing at left is her companion, Irene Lichty, who would become the curator of Laura's effects five years later. *Photo by Betty Love.*

Rose's close friend and heir, Roger Lea MacBride, ran for president as the Libertarian Party's nominee in 1976. He took his daughter Abigail on the campaign trail. *University of Virginia Library.*

8

LIBERTARIANS IN CONNECTICUT

"I owe Rose, for helping me, at first, in selling my books and for the publicity she gave them."

—Laura, in a letter to literary agent George Bye in 1949

During the spring of 1940, Rose lived frugally in Danbury. She survived on garden produce and food shared with her neighbors. It was the sort of simple life that she'd known as a child and portrayed as desirable in the Little House books. But Rose was in distress. She wrote in her diary on May 9, 1940: "Something must be done to enable me to write fiction. I have no ideas whatever, no spark, I see no stories, I do not desire to write. I am living on borrowed money. . . . Have just looked through the notebooks of twenty years ago; that 'I' no longer exists. What interests me now? I kept those notes because I was interested. Perhaps, in gear, the wheels may turn the engine. But truly I would prefer to die."

She was fifty-three. Rose had been depressed before, but now she and Laura had reversed roles. Rose was a struggling homesteader, relying on help from her mother, while Laura was a bourgeois author, basking in her admirers' praise, collecting armfuls of fan letters, banking more money than she had ever thought she would earn. And Rose was obligated to keep this going.

Two years earlier, Laura advised Rose to cut income and avoid taxes. "Couldn't you work less and pay less and get by just as well?" Laura had suggested. "I mean—You say you can live in your Connecticut place for $500. Suppose then you write enough to earn $1,000. That would cut out the tax and be as much for you as though you earned twice as much and gave 1/2 to Roosevelt. The figures are not right of course but there's the idea. As you say 'Dam' 'em."

Rose appeared to follow that course, earning only a little money writing short articles on women and needlework for a new magazine, *Woman's Day*. The magazine offered much lower rates than she'd been used to. And when the editor's assistant wrote to her asking for a biographical sketch, Rose squirmed and complained to her diary that this had to be the lowest she'd sunk.

Rose's articles for *Woman's Day* suggest she yearned for something settled and traditional that she had never sought nor obtained as an adult. In "All Men Are Liars," which appeared alongside a piece by J. P. McEvoy that claimed women never told the truth, Rose painted the picture of a trusting wife: "Of course (for she has no fear of the truth) his wife sees him as he is—an ordinary man, a human being who has had the nerve and endurance and courage to live fifty years or so, to marry, raise a family, pay the bills, build a house and carry the mortgage, to keep on living valiantly through triumph and disaster, and to hold the respect of honorable men and the steadfast affection of his wife, who is herself an ordinary woman."

Rose's subject here had nothing to do with any life she herself had led or even observed. One wonders what was going on—whether she wrote this simply sketching out some new idea she was developing of an ideal and happy woman, or whether it was purely because she needed money.

Laura began sketching out the last book, which would become two books, *Little Town on the Prairie* and *These Happy Golden Years*. A clue to how she and Rose worked on them comes in the letter from Laura, cited in the last chapter, in which she listed events in the three years before Laura's marriage to Almanzo in 1885. The notes for "Prairie Girl" filled only a few pages; they constituted a rough list of incidents Laura thought the next book should cover: "Platform boards for seats. Reading of Declaration.

Speeches. Singing—" "When you hear the first whippoorwill" began this list.

No one knows exactly how Laura's early drafts read, or whether there were early drafts. No handwritten early version of the last two books exists. It seems that their working method now was that Laura trusted Rose to create rough drafts from "Pioneer Girl." Before long, Rose, or both of them, realized that the intended single final volume would have to be two. The seventh book, eventually titled *Little Town on the Prairie*, would cover the time until Laura began teaching school. The last, *These Happy Golden Years*, would tell the story of her teaching and of Almanzo's courtship.

If Laura sent letters to Rose during the work on *Little Town on the Prairie* and *These Happy Golden Years*, Rose did not save them. Nor does Rose seem to have written to Laura. They must have talked on the telephone about the manuscripts instead. They'd been speaking via phone, after all, since the mid-1930s, when they'd lived just a hayfield apart in Missouri.

The dearth of early notes and letters around the production of these books matches the mystery around *The Long Winter*. Rose almost certainly threw away drafts, leaving us playing a detective game to piece together the collaborative work. Only letters to George Bye, a few late typed drafts with notations here and there, and two neatly recopied later drafts in Laura's handwriting have survived. Sparse though the material is, it's enough to hint at two possible scenarios. In the first, perhaps Laura actually drafted very little of the manuscript, but instead sent a list of scenes to Rose and instructed her to create or greatly expand a draft from sections of "Pioneer Girl." Under this scenario, Rose would have mailed Laura drafts of each book for her to revise. (There's no evidence of such intermediate drafts for either book, but Laura must have edited and revised the respective manuscripts.) In the second scenario, Laura did more of the early writing herself, using "Pioneer Girl" as a source and reference, and then expected Rose to take the draft apart and structure it thematically as she had done for the previous books.

We know that, at their deaths, Laura had the full handwritten version of "Pioneer Girl" in Missouri and Rose had the typed versions in Connecticut, although it is also true that they sometimes sent pages from various versions they held of "Pioneer Girl" to each other. It is possible, under the second scenario, that Laura mailed Rose her drafts and those drafts didn't require much work before being sent on to the publisher. Even so, Rose did clearly add scenes, as I will discuss shortly. In either scenario, Rose or Laura produced the first draft as a progression of stories about town life and Laura and Almanzo's courtship and did not concern themselves with tying the stories together with a theme. Both books show little evidence of thorough review and revision. Unlike the previous titles, they lack purposeful structure and narrative drive. The stories, charming though they are, seem aimed at satisfying readers who yearned to know what happened next in Laura's life. By now the family has stopped moving and building houses. Laura has become a most sympathetic character; she is growing up, teaching school, sharing her earnings with the family, guiding her blind sister Mary when Mary is home, and falling in love.

Still, Rose found a way to add stories of independence, courage, and free market beliefs, again changing the tone from Laura's recollection of the family as taciturn homesteaders who made do to something else. She rearranged the stories and created new scenes that depicted the Ingallses as principled and optimistic heroes who forged individual destinies. Among many examples, this recasting shows clearly in the evolving portrayals of the Fourth of July celebration that Laura attended in 1881. Laura herself wrote little about that afternoon in "Pioneer Girl," except to say that it included "speeches and singing and reading of the Declaration of Independence in the morning and after noon horse and foot races." She even called the proceedings "tiresome."

A later draft, in Laura's handwriting and

donated to the Pomona Library, contains just a bit more, but still expands only slightly on the bare details: "Then another speaker talked about 'our glorious country' and how our ancestors fought, bled and died that we might be free as the Declaration said we should be."

In contrast, the Fourth of July story in the published version of *Little Town on the Prairie* goes on for five dramatic pages. Fourteen-year-old Laura listens to a man's passionate speech and then stands, resolute, realizing that she herself must strive for maturity and accomplishment. She must use her freedom well.

The final portrayal of the Fourth of July reflects Rose's evolving attitudes about individual freedom as being uniquely available in the United States. By the early 1940s, she hardly wrote a magazine article without discussing freedom. In a draft article that she never managed to sell entitled "Don't Marry for Love," Rose spends the entire first page going on about American government: "We revolt against the murderous insanity of war, and send a million men to war to stop it, as one would stop fire by deluging it with kerosene. . . . Nevertheless, our country actually is the finest, happiest, and most powerful country on earth, the ultimate hope of humane civilization." She then goes on to say that one failure of American civilization is romantic love. She argues couples should view union as a business deal.

• • •

Through the late spring and summer of 1940, as Hitler advanced across Europe, Rose assiduously recorded military updates in a small notebook. She wrote with a thick fountain pen, documenting events on the European stage. She also recorded events closer to home—particularly the blossoming of her friendships with anticommunist thinkers. She cultivated few friends locally except her journalist friend Don Levine and his wife, Ruth, and the writer and anticommunist activist Isabel Paterson. It was Don Levine who'd persuaded Rose to buy her Danbury house, warning her not to spend all of the money she'd earned from her last novel without having something to show for it. Rose was now visiting the Levines frequently at their house in Norwalk and later in Danbury.

The Levines spoke fervently and often of the trouble overseas. Sometimes the conversations with Rose turned sour, when Rose and her friends argued about America's response to the conflict. "Don and Ruth *want* this country in the war *now*," Rose wrote in her diary. "Don says, this means we go in. Japan will attack Dutch East Indies. Hitler will seize Brazil. F.D.R. will *certainly* be reelected. They both (Ruth and Don) turned against me. Three times I said, There are valuable things, the most valuable to me, our friendship. Don replied merely that he is sick, physically sick: he will take a rifle and fight. He will die before he will submit to Hitler. Ruth answered once by explaining that Don and she are pro-Ally. The second time by saying, This is hard on 'those of our faith.' I said passionately, 'Ruth, you are no more Jew than I am English: we are *Americans.*' She was polite."

The three had planned to go together that evening to see Isabel Paterson's shadbush (serviceberry) in bloom, but Rose ended up taking a taxi there by herself.

That same night, sitting by the radio, Rose made detailed notes of a speech by FDR, recording diligently, almost as if devising a novel: " 'I am a pacifist: you, my fellow citizens of 21 American republics, are pacifists. But I believe we will act together, with all our strength, by *every* means, to protect, to defend, our science, our culture, our American freedom, and our civilization.' Star spangled banner, great applause." Next on the radio, Rose wryly noted, came "popular music, 'Last night you kissed him, aren't you ashamed? You couldn't resist him, aren't you ashamed?' "

The Levines' alarm at Hitler's treatment of Jews drove a wedge between them and Rose, for they wanted the United States to enter the war and Rose did not. Perhaps ignorant of what it means to be a mistreated minority, she asked herself in her diary why she did not understand "the Jew," believing instead that religious differences did not matter. By the end of the spring, the friendship with the Levines seems to have cooled. Despite this, on June 4, the couple drove Rose to New York City where she had tea at the Algonquin Hotel with her *Woman's Day* editor Eileen Tighe and a few others. That night at home, Rose continued taking notes from radio reports. The French cabinet had resigned. Rose grimly recorded numbers of casualties: 420,000 Dutch; 580,000 Belgians; 460,000 French and British; 144,000 Germans.

On the next page, she sketched an idea for a novel. It would explore the "problem of good and evil." It would be about a "woman hated all her life because she assumes that others behave according to their common standards. Compare with: Evil exists because men trying to be good."

That was the extent of that project. It went no further.

All the while, Rose's growing horror of the war and interest in the cause of freedom remained foremost in her mind. Hitler's forces entered Paris and Rose, while still against going to war, followed the action in Europe closely and became a fan of Winston Churchill because he championed people's rights to make their own destinies. "Churchill speaks 'in solemn hour for life of our Empire, of our allies—above all, the cause of *Freedom!*' " she exclaimed on the page.

"A marvelous speech—a historic document."

Rose had become quite close to Isabel Paterson, whose views of unrest abroad seemed to fuel the running narrative in her diary. As she tried to grasp the political situation, Rose appeared unsure of herself. Paterson, whom Rose called I.M.P., made sweeping statements that suggest she thought Europe was inherently socialist. Rose noted: "I.M.P. says the Allies have not fought. As Europe did not fight Napoleon. Being rotten with collectivism, false by the Marxian lie, which Germany revolted against and went to despotism." Paterson said this, too, was a lie. And Rose noted to herself that "despotism has a kind of authenticity, (on wrong basis) coherence, a truth of a sort."

As the news from Europe grew more awful by the day and the United States grew ever closer to joining the war, Rose recorded the movements of Hitler's armies as if intending to write her own war book. She documented the news as diligently as she'd recorded the budding of flowers and bushes in Mansfield a decade and a half earlier. The king of England remained on the British island, yes, Rose noted. But he'd sent Princesses Elizabeth and Margaret away on a ship to Halifax. In Belgium a bomb had overturned Hitler's car. She carefully wrote notes from Wythe Williams' radio broadcast: "Hitler, uninjured, took refuge in a ditch. End. At least he is not safe in Berlin headquarters while he spends a million lives. W.W. says Allies will win this war."

Rose leavened her journal with notes on the natural world outside her window. Early on May 23, she wrote: "no fog; clear-cloudy, almost white, sky. Rain stopped. Lilacs opening, redbud still gorgeous. Forsythia passed and daffodils gone. Bridal wreath full." At eight that same morning she returned to her European war narrative, sourced by her radio. The Allies were evacuating the port of Boulogne. The stock market had dropped in New York; steel stocks were down. At midday, she wrote, "I ask myself, May it be possible that the whole effort of human freedom was a mistake? That the effort is too great for the results, which perhaps after all are too largely material?"

Rose was angry that America seemed poised to go to war for its economy, and as she began thinking more deeply about the political forces that lead to war, she seemed horrified to the point of not expressing herself well. The war seemed to remove poetry from her personal writing. In an extraordinary understatement, she wrote on May 24, "It is a misfortune to be aware of what is occurring. The happy man is he who knows no history."

Rose's engagement in her mothers' series waned to obligation only. Rose's own writing would now focus entirely on individual liberties. She recorded in her journal that Congress signed a $1.5 billion "defense" bill—the quotation marks are hers.

We know that Rose and Laura must have been working on the manuscript for *Little Town on the Prairie* during these months. The final manuscript went to the agent and then the publisher in the summer of 1941. Bye wrote Laura that he had enjoyed it and had repeated some of the stories to his friends. Laura wrote an affectionate, jaunty letter back to him, saying, "Ask Rose to tell you the one I told at Detroit Book Fair [in 1937] about the Easterner who saw his first Dakota mirage and took a short walk before Breakfast to the lake he saw from the hotel. Like all my stories, it is true." In a postscript, Laura wrote, "The days of Little Town were great days and at times I have a strong feeling of nostalgia for them." Readers shared her nostalgia on the book's publication later in 1941.

The last book, *These Happy Golden Years*, probably emerged from Laura and Rose's collaboration in sections, judging by the way Rose communicated with their agent the following year. "Dear George," Rose wrote to Bye in September 1942, "here is the second installment of my mother's copy. There is a third which should come through soon."

"Should come through" must mean that Rose was waiting for Laura to make some additions or to send the end of the manuscript back to her. Laura and Rose continued to perpetuate the fiction that Laura wrote the drafts and Rose's role was simply to have them typed.

Ironically, Rose's revision of the characters based on her parents discussing getting married in *These Happy Golden Years* transformed taciturn, practical settlers into principled romantics. Laura, in the rough list of incidents she sent to Rose, had sketched the scene thus: Almanzo got up his nerve and asked Laura if she'd like an engagement ring. Laura answered that it would depend on who gave it to her. He said he would. Laura said, "Then it would depend on the ring." In an aside on the bottom of the page, Laura noted to Rose: "Fact! . . . It was what you might call laconic and illustrates once more the something about us at that time and place I have tried to express."

We know Rose agreed that marriage was a practical matter. But perhaps she knew a laconic interchange over a ring would not make great reading. So Rose again worked around that "something" Laura had tried to express and infused the scene with emotion, particularly joy. Laura's original, impudent response remains in the final version, but only after Almanzo has picked up Laura's hand, closed his over it, and—the two of them bathed in beautiful moonlight—put the ring on her finger.

Laura says, "It is a beautiful ring. I think . . . I would like to have it." And then they kiss.

Perhaps the most dramatic revision in the series' last two texts shows up in *These Happy Golden Years*: Rose rewrote a story that Laura's uncle Tom Quiner told the family in 1882. The story was missing from Laura's first draft of "Pioneer Girl," but versions appeared in a later draft that Rose sent to George Bye in 1930, and, finally, in the last of the Little House books. In the book, Laura comes home from school in De Smet, Dakota Territory, finding Ma's brother, Uncle Tom Quiner, sitting in the front room on a surprise visit. He tells them that eight years earlier he had traveled west of there "with the first white men that ever laid eyes on the Black Hills," with a party looking for gold. Ma and Pa are surprised and ask him to elaborate.

Uncle Tom tells of traveling in the fall of 1874 with a group of twenty-six men, one woman, and one boy, from Sioux City to the Black Hills. They built cabins inside a log stockade meant to protect them from the Lakota Sioux Indians. They nearly starved that winter, but in the spring, they heard a bugle and knew that American soldiers had arrived. They rushed out to see the soldiers, expecting to be greeted warmly and offered help, but the soldiers arrested the group for trespassing on tribal lands, marched them out on foot, took their belongings, and burned their stockade.

Here, in the book, Pa Ingalls jumps out of his chair and paced the room in exasperation, saying, "I'd be durned if I could have taken it!"—meaning, having to surrender to the government after enduring a difficult winter in the hope of prospecting for gold.

Laura did not include the Tom Quiner story in her first drafts of "Pioneer Girl," when they were aiming for a magazine sale to adult readers. It's likely Rose had heard the story from Laura over the years and thought it was a good one to add. However, Rose had gotten her facts wrong: Thomas L. Quiner did indeed go to the Black Hills that winter with the John Gordon party (Pamela Smith Hill documents this in her annotated *Pioneer Girl*), but Civil War hero George Armstrong Custer had made a more famous expedition to the Black Hills just ahead of John Gordon's expedition. Meanwhile, President Ulysses Grant, who'd been trying to make peace with the Lakota Sioux, "belatedly recognized what was obvious to everyone else from the first: that the Black Hills expedition was simply incompatible with the successful operation of the Peace Policy," writes Richard Slotkin in *The Fatal Environment: The Myth of the Frontier in the Age of Industrialization*. Hill writes that no evidence of the soldiers burning their stockade survives; it appears the government gave the men time to collect their belongings and promised they could return to the area when the federal government officially opened it for settlement. It appears that Tom Quiner did not go back.

Why, then, did Laura and Rose include this story? It's an odd intrusion in Laura's coming-of-age narrative in *These Happy Golden Years*. Unlike most of the Little House scenes, it's told as a story within a story from the point of view of a different character, previously unknown. So it isn't like Pa's anecdotes about encountering bears and panthers, which are presented in indented passages in *Little House in the Big Woods*; for that reason, it feels dropped in. The character Laura, who is supposed to be fifteen years old at the time, listens and reacts ("Then one morning they heard, far off, a bugle! . . . Laura remembered the sound, long ago, echoing back from the Big Woods when Uncle George blew his army bugle. She cried out, 'Soldiers?' "), but she draws no conclusions. On the other hand, Pa thinks the federal soldiers acted recklessly, destroying the efforts of well-meaning prospectors. The character Uncle Tom replies, "We couldn't fight the whole United States Army," while Ma agrees: "To this day I think of the house we had to leave in Indian Territory. Just when Charles had got glass windows into it."

It is Pa who might reveal the underlying

purpose of Uncle Tom Quiner's anecdote: When Pa reacts to it, Laura, on the verge of adulthood, listens to him attentively and absorbs what he says, turning over in her mind her uncle's actions when the government moved him out. The whole thing seems unfair to her, and readers are invited to share that feeling. Yet the anger and emotion that the character Laura evinces contrasts with the stoic courage that the elder Laura tried to explain to her daughter about those times. That discrepancy suggests that Rose was the one who inserted this emotional reaction in the scene.

Rose sent along the last section of "Golden Years" to Bye only a few months before the presses were supposed to roll. There would not be time for Laura to review what she had done before typesetting, though Rose knew that Laura would want to see the changes. "One requirement is that my mother *must* have a set of proofs by air mail as soon as possible," Rose wrote. "Harper's can NOT put this book through without my mother's OK on the proofs. This is absolutely imperative." *These Happy Golden Years* was published in March 1943. Within six weeks, readers bought five thousand copies. "The book is certainly being well received," Laura wrote Nordstrom. "Already letters are coming to me from children and teachers who have read it." Readers apparently bemoaned the announcement at the end of the book that it was the last of the series, and Laura spent hours every day responding to dozens of letters that landed in the mailbox at the end of her curving driveway. The book won the Spring Book Festival Award from the New York *Herald Tribune.*

One of the letter writers asked about Rose. Replying that Rose was her daughter, Laura explained that Rose had written *Let the Hurricane Roar* before the Little House series had been conceived. "She had of course learned of those things from us," Laura wrote. "Her use of family names and characters came naturally." Laura suggested that the writer of the letter read some of Rose's books.

Laura responded to another reader who had asked about Rose: "She is a better writer than I am, though our style of writing is very similar."

9

FREEDOM

Rose had never waded into matters of race in her journalism, and some of her 1920s fictional stories portrayed blacks as simpletons, so it is surprising that in late 1942 she began writing a column for the activist black newspaper the *Pittsburgh Courier*. An African American woman Rose had hired as a domestic in Danbury had brought a copy of the paper with her to work. (That Rose was hiring a domestic worker indicates that she was not as poor as her diaries suggested in those years.) Reading it, Rose was impressed. The *Pittsburgh Courier* had a circulation of about a quarter million readers who opposed the New Deal, according to historians David and Linda Royster Beito. As they tell it, "She liked what she saw and wrote a fan letter to Joel A. Rogers, one of the columnists. . . . Rogers, a self-taught leading popularizer of black history, apparently was instrumental in getting her hired."

While writing for a black newspaper was new territory for a white Midwestern farm daughter, Rose and the *Courier*'s leadership held core beliefs in common. Both denounced Roosevelt's policies and communism. George S. Schuyler was "the paper's star attraction," according to the Beitos—an "unrelenting anti-Communist, always ready to denounce the party's infiltration and manipulation of black organizations and causes." Rose loved the *Courier*. "Here, at least, is a place where I belong," she wrote in her October 31, 1942 column. "Here are Americans who know the meaning of equality and freedom."

Writing in plain language about her favorite topics, including the value of hard work, ordinary citizens' power, laissez-faire government, and the evils of communism, Rose seemed much more at home on the *Courier*'s pages. Here's a sampling of her opinion nuggets:

On August 21, 1943, she wrote, "Tyrants will always reappear until workers learn the meaning of words and stop being in awe of writers and talkers."

"The effort to create a free economy is very new; it has hardly begun, and freedom usually scares people because it is responsibility" (June 10, 1944).

"What is this value for which the colored American fights two battles—one to gain it within his own country, the other to preserve his country which holds his only hope of gaining it?" After this, she quoted the part in the Declaration of Independence about "life, liberty, and the pursuit of happiness" (April 17, 1943).

Rose Wilder Lane the *Courier* columnist admitted candidly her ignorance of the mistreatment and oppression of black Americans. And she somewhat ignorantly or blithely stated in one column that the "race distinction" in America was just a leftover from the "old English feudal class distinction" and that race and class distinctions meant nothing (February 20, 1943). But her linking of the equality of all races with her emerging libertarian ideas worked for her audience. In a probing article for the *Independent Review* in 2010, historians David and Linda Beito wrote, "No libertarian has ever more creatively weaved together laissez-faire and antiracism than Lane. Her columns favored the centrality of the individual over artificial collective constructs such as race and class."

In the early 1940s, at the same time Rose and Laura were finishing up *These Happy Golden Years*, Rose had been laboring on a political science book. It would be, she believed, her magnum opus. *The Discovery of Freedom* was published in January of 1943. In it Rose extolled American capitalism, arguing that it alone provided the best quality of life on earth. In the opening chapter, she wrote:

Why did workers walk barefoot, in rags, with lousy hair and unwashed teeth,

247

and workingmen wear no pants, for six thousand years, and here, in less than a century—silk stockings, lip sticks, permanent waves, sweaters, overcoats, shaving cream, safety razors? It's incredible. . . . The plain fact is that human energy operates more effectively in these United States than it has ever operated before, and more effectively than it operates today anywhere else on the planet.

In a later chapter, she linked her opposition to communism with a celebration of property rights. Owning property, she wrote, is essential to people's ability to live fully. Property rights would protect people of all incomes, including poor people. American Indians were communists because they owned no land. The men who started the American Revolution thought they were fighting a *moral* war, but the outcome was economic. America's standard of living had risen to the highest in history because Americans were free to use energy in new ways and create an industrial complex free of controls.

"The true revolutionary course which must be followed toward a free world," she wrote in the chapter "The Third Attempt," "is a cautious, experimental process of further decreasing the uses of force which individuals permit to Government; of increasing the prohibitions of

Government's action, and thus decreasing the use of brute force in human affairs."

When *These Happy Golden Years* was published, it was met with the fans' joy as well as their laments that it was to be the last of the Little House books. When *The Discovery of Freedom* was published the same year, it received almost no notice. Rose argued to herself in her diary that the publisher, John Day Company, had handled it badly. She sent a copy to Herbert Hoover, who wrote to Rose, "A most difficult book to appraise. Basic ideas superb, but treated somewhat in effective fashion. Some chapters brilliant. . . . Because of author's method do not see how anything can be said but 'God bless you.'"

On January 26, despite that tepid response, Rose wrote to Hoover, asking for an endorsement. "The very fact that New York reviewers are killing it," she wrote, "is proof that they regard it as dangerously American." Hoover replied four days later, promising to send copies to friends and to do what he could to promote the book. Rose replied: "Your note overwhelms me." If Hoover would "say a few words about it for publication," publishers would use those words to promote it.

Hoover wrote back that if Rose would draft him the comment, he would "try to turn it into my own expression and send it back." Using his previous remarks, Rose sent this, adding ellipses: "The basic idea is superb. . . . Its optimism is a tonic for the soul. . . . I wish everyone would read it." Hoover sent that blurb verbatim on to the publisher.

Although Rose was angry the publisher hadn't promoted *The Discovery of Freedom*, she herself wasn't satisfied with what she had achieved in the book and intended to revise it. Businessman and radio personality Robert LeFevre, an early champion of libertarian ideas who would later found the Freedom School, asked Rose for reprint rights soon after it came out. In a celebration of the book years later, the Cato Institute reported that LeFevre congratulated Rose by telephone, in response to which she said, "It's a very bad book." LeFevre protested, "It's a very good book. I ought to know. I just read it," and Rose supposedly replied, "It's a very bad book. I ought to know. I wrote it." According to the Cato Institute's article, Rose was dissatisfied with factual errors in her account of recent history. I haven't been able to find any catalog of the errors, even in the writings of libertarian thinkers who admire the book, but they all acknowledge that there were errors, and any close reading will raise questions about Rose's interpretation of historic events in the later chapters in the book. For example, over a few pages she summarizes several centuries' worth of revolutions in Europe, attributing to the United States the power to free countries like Cuba and China. She compares Hitler (then waging war in Europe) to Napoleon. Her brief history of the steamboat suggests leaders in many coastal states tried to stop its progress. She likens compulsory education funded by taxes to the authoritarian policies of a police state. These are just a few examples, but every page of the book fairly quivers with sweeping statements about the potential of individual energy to stop oppression.

Albert Jay Nock, the author of *Our Enemy, the State*, argued that the public should overlook the factual errors in *The Discovery of Freedom* when he reviewed the book for the *National Economic Council Review of Books*. "When it comes to anything fundamental, Mrs. Lane never makes a mistake. She is always right." Like Nock, whom Rose admired as one of the early thinkers in the nascent libertarian movement, Robert LeFevre was gentle on her because he liked the fundamental ideas in her book. He called it "one of the most influential books of the twentieth century." Henry Grady Weaver, the director of customer research for General Motors, obtained Rose's permission to rework major sections into his own book, *The Mainspring of Human Progress*, published in 1947. He admitted that his was both a "condensation" and "amplification" of Rose's work, adding, "Inspired by her thesis and with her gracious consent, I've tried to retell her story in my own way, making liberal use of her material." His book was reported to have sold four hundred thousand copies, compared to Rose's initial one thousand.

Around this time, Rose's relationship with the Turner brothers, her "adopted sons," had deteriorated to the point where she no longer had any contact with them. John had cut off communication after dropping out of Lehigh University a few years earlier. But in 1943, an unexpected turn of events introduced Rose to a teenage boy who would embrace the ideals of independence and the spirit of the Little House books as a basic American right. His name was Roger Lea MacBride. His father, Burt MacBride, was an editor at *Reader's Digest* in nearby Pleasantville, New York. The elder MacBride was editing a condensed version of Rose's 1932 novel, *Let the Hurricane Roar*, a book his wife had recommended to him. One night during the editing phase, Rose invited the MacBride family out to dinner at the White Turkey Inn in Danbury. Roger was away at Exeter, but his two sisters went along and told Rose how proud they were of their brother. Rose began corresponding with Roger, who later wrote, "I was fascinated by her mind, and jumped at the offer to correspond. . . . Over a period, Rose unfolded for me the meaning of personal liberty, and of freedom as part of our nature."

Roger hitchhiked to Rose's house when he was back from school and very soon was calling her "Gramma." Rose felt a mission to correspond with and to mentor younger thinkers about politics. Around this time, she also began corresponding about the importance of strictly following the United States Constitution and limiting the size of government with William F. Buckley—a fact that he revealed years later on his television show, *Firing Line*.

Like many journalists, Rose seems to have generally resisted any urge to take to the streets to advance her causes; she didn't even write letters for publication in the "Letters to the Editor" column. Yet, one Sunday night in March 1943, she heard liberal *New Republic* writer Samuel Grafton recommend on a radio broadcast that American teachers go to Germany after the war and teach children about democracy. Grafton asked listeners for their viewpoints. Rose decided to send a postcard but didn't sign her full name, just "Mrs. C. G. Lane." She wrote: "If schoolteachers say to German children, 'We believe in social security' the children will ask, 'Then why did you fight Germany?' All these 'social security' laws are German, instituted by Bismark and expanded by Hitler. Americans believe in freedom, not in being taxed for their own good and bossed by bureaucrats."

Most of her contemporary anticollectivist

thinkers had already compared Roosevelt's Social Security and other programs to social programs in Germany. Rose's note caught the attention of someone identified only as "a private citizen of excellent reputation"—perhaps a postman—who read it and reported it to the Federal Bureau of Investigation. The person misread the signature, reporting a Mrs. C. G. *Lang* rather than *Lane*, so the FBI set out to find Mrs. Lang. Rose would later write about the incident for the National Economic Council. According to her, a state police officer appeared at her house where she was busy digging up dandelions. The policeman presented a card on which were typed the lines from her postcard and asked if she had written them. She said yes, and added, "What have the State Police to do with any opinion that an American citizen wants to express?"

He replied, "I do not like your attitude."

At this, she and the police officer engaged in a heated back-and-forth. Rose asked, "What is this, the Gestapo?" She took some time to educate the trooper on why she did not like Social Security. The trooper told her that if she had signed her full name, the one she uses as a writer, he would not have bothered her. This, not surprisingly, rankled her. What sort of country targets ordinary citizens for expressing their views?

"Who put him up to this?" Rose wrote. It's easy to imagine her enjoying this analysis. "Is there a censorship of American mail within our borders? . . . Did Samuel Grafton ever receive that postcard? If not, who is obstructing the delivery of American mail?" The FBI dropped the matter after the American Civil Liberties Union inquired. The way Rose crowed about this incident in a public forum can make one wonder whether she envied the general adulation for Laura and the Little House books while her own work slid into obscurity.

Around this time, Rose and Laura achieved a true role reversal. Laura was enjoying a comfortable routine in Mansfield. She'd announced that she would write no more books, and her income from the series provided well for her and Almanzo in retirement. Rose now set herself up as a homesteader in Connecticut. She would not accept a ration card, and starting in the spring of 1943, she gave up her right to buy the rationed foods: sugar, coffee, processed foods, meat, or cheese. She redoubled her gardening efforts. Rose's food-growing enterprise that year was more than a Victory Garden, which Americans had been urged to plant since 1940. This was subsistence farming specifically to prove a point—that she didn't need help and could feed herself. She wrote to Charlie Clark—who had tutored the Turner boys when she'd sent them to Europe in 1937—that the publicity around the

Grafton postcard had cut into her harvest. "I have been submerged in reporters, photographers, long distance calls and a flood of mail (including waves of furious postcards calling me Nazi and Fascist) ever since." This took place while she and a devoted young friend and hanger-on, Virginia Manor, canned beans, beets, squash, blackberries, raspberries, and green applesauce. They dug a sixty-foot ditch, Rose wrote to Clark, "with pick and shovel and my own startled biceps, to keep rainwater out of my kitchen. I wouldn't register for a ration card, so this is the pioneer life with telephone-bells on."

Laura, the actual pioneer, was back in Missouri doing research into one of the saddest losses of her homesteading life. She wrote to the De Smet, South Dakota, Cemetery Association asking if they could locate the grave of the infant son Laura and Almanzo had buried when Rose was two years old. It seems very likely that Laura had her lost son on her mind now because she was writing again, working on a book that she was calling "The First Three Years and a Year of Grace," the story of her and Almanzo's early struggles farming in the Dakotas. It was during those years that the son had died. The cemetery association secretary wrote back to Laura saying that no record of a burial deed existed for the unnamed boy.

Laura wrote George Bye that she had another

book in mind. "I don't know what to say about my writing more," she wrote. "I have thought that 'Golden Years' was my last; that I would spend what is left of my life in living, not writing about it, but a story keeps stirring around in my mind and if it pesters me enough I may write it down and send it to you sometime in the future." We know that she first started thinking about, or working on, "The First Three Years and a Year of Grace" at least as early as 1937, because she'd disclosed to her editor at *Harper's* that she was working on a book for adults. It would be discovered in her papers only after her death and would be published as *The First Four Years* in 1971.

Bye had just congratulated her on the success of *These Happy Golden Years* and encouraged her to write more. He specifically asked if she could produce a short fictional story "about the relationship between a woman of your age and experience and a girl of today, say a munitions worker boarding with you and revealing problems and doubts that you would resolve, so that in the end the girl and her young man would face the future with bright hope." He was sure he could sell it immediately.

Laura declined, "as I have no contact with the working girls in industry today," she wrote. She had no first-hand experience, she said. But she suggested that he ask Rose, who was "familiar with the old-fashioned, homely philosophy of the Little House books."

This letter shows that Laura knew Bye was accustomed to thinking of her and Rose as partners, even though discretion seemed to guide him. Bye wrote Rose immediately, simply quoting what Laura had written to him, but it appears that Rose never answered. Presumably, the venture didn't interest her.

But Laura did work on "The First Three Years and a Year of Grace" at some point, and when she died, a fairly clean handwritten copy of it remained. Historians have puzzled over the timing of this last manuscript, and most seem to agree that Rose did not know about it in the 1930s or 1940s. That question should be revisited. Laura talked to Rose at least once, we know, and she could have written her about it in the 1940s, when Rose wasn't saving letters.

Consider this: Rose, too, was thinking about her own lost infant son at the same time Laura was remembering hers. A few months later, in early February 1944, a young child of Charles Clark and his wife, Joan, died. Rose wrote a condolence letter on February 8 that mentioned she had given birth to a baby who had also died. She wrote, "My own baby son died thirty-five years ago. It isn't true, what people say, that you will ever forget, but in time you do learn that unhappiness and loss are part of living, and that the sum-total of living, as it *is,* really is better than the happiness we imagine, want, and rebel against not having." In all her diary keeping, Rose had never recorded this great loss. Laura must have known about it, but pioneer stoicism evidently had guided them both away from this painful territory. Their lack of communication (as far as we know) over these tragedies further underscores that for all their mutual interdependence, Laura and Rose were not confidantes.

Rose relearned in middle age what she had watched her parents struggle with in the 1880s and 1890s. A farm thrives with many hands, and without them, it's a struggle. During 1944 and 1945, Rose let Virginia earn her keep by over-seeing the back-to-the-land enterprise. Rose no longer recorded summaries of radio broadcasts on the war. Instead, her five-year diary recorded weather, temperature, and crops. Many of the entries are in another person's handwriting—probably Virginia's. In the spring of 1944, Virginia planted lettuce, cabbage, cauliflower, blueberry plants, and potato sprouts. The two women likely together planted ten dwarf apple and pear trees. Later followed sweet potatoes, onions, and tomatoes. Garden notes continued through June. One night late in the month, Rose and Virginia canned five pint-jars of chicken. They worked until two in the morning. The next day, Virginia picked currants. They ate black raspberries for supper.

This subsistence life went on into the summer of 1945. On August 14, 1945, Rose wrote: "War officially ends." It seems that Rose's farming experiments ended around that time, too. Her weather and plant observations slowed.

She focused on writing essays and commentary. Rose became editor of the *National Economic Council Review of Books*, taking over for its first editor, Nock, who had died just weeks before. In the *Review*, she championed free will through her analyses of economic and political books. The publication gave her a platform to debate the pros and cons of collectivism versus capitalism. In the first issue she edited, in October 1945, she was introduced as "one of the keenest in her understanding of the meaning of freedom," and in that issue she praised Ayn Rand's *The Fountainhead* as "a dramatic assertion of the values of individualism."

Today, Libertarian Party histories group Ayn Rand with Rose Wilder Lane and Isabel Paterson as the three founding mothers of the movement. Rose appreciated Rand's writing, but at a distance. Years later, she wrote to Joan Clark: "I think she is useful. She is making a cult of pseudo-individualism, drawing the pseudo 'intellectuals' away from the cult of collectivism. You might say she is leading the lunatic fringe of the growing 'conservative'—i.e., blundering anti-'liberal'—movement. And no movement succeeds without a lunatic fringe."

In another issue of the NEC's book review, Rose asked whether the Walter Lippmanns and Charles Beards (referring respectively to the liberal newspaper commentator and progressive historian, both influential writers) "have the sense to raise a hill of beans." She praised Ludwig von Mises's book *Omnipotent Government: The Rise of the Total State and Total War* and his statement that America's choice as World War II ended was "not between two economic systems. It is between capitalism and chaos."

From her editorial platform, Rose exerted a powerful influence on the postwar American dialogue on economics. In August 1947 in the *Review of Books*, Rose heaved her intellectual weight against a new economics textbook by Lorie Tarshis, an economics professor at Stanford University, calling the book propaganda for Keynesian theories that claimed government intervention could stabilize the economy. After her review appeared, major universities around the United States canceled plans to require the textbook, which left room for another work, one by Paul Samuelson published in 1948, to become the major introductory textbook to Keynesian theories. Because of Rose Wilder Lane's harsh criticism, Tarshis himself became a martyr in his profession, according to economist David Levy, who is studying the public's response to economists in this period. Rose also criticized writing by Joseph Alois Schumpeter, a Connecticut resident who'd been born in Moravia and whose economic theories were widely admired.

After the last Little House books were published, Rose never worked on fiction again that we know of. Even if Laura had insisted that they revise that last manuscript, it seems impossible that Rose, as the war drew to a close, would have traveled in her mind back to simple tales about pioneers. By the mid-1940s she had taken those values deeper. She molded the theme of independence in her writing to an end that the Little House books had hinted at. Rose believed the solution to contemporary problems lay in wholesale policy changes. No more tales of what farmers were doing in the fields. Now Rose's efforts went toward persuading readers that the leaders of the country had lost sight of their root principles.

Though World War II was over, times were still perilous, Rose felt. Communism continued to spread, and she was appalled by the public's apathy about its dangers. Her friend Don Levine started an anticommunist magazine, *Plain Talk*, in the fall of 1946. It reported on atrocities in the Soviet Union, the suicides of Russian refugees forced to return home after the war, the murder of Polish refugees, and other such stories. Rose felt the magazine provided critical information not found in the mainstream press. Levine wasn't publishing it for the money, exactly; he wanted to influence teachers and ministers. Rose supported his efforts, and started promoting the publication to friends at least a month before its official release.

Rose worked out her political ideas through letter writing. Her most frequent correspondent for this, from the late 1930s through much of the 1940s, was Jasper Crane, a retired Du Pont executive. Crane was part of a business leaders' movement against Roosevelt's policies. He became a trustee to the new Foundation for Economic Education, which published handouts on the principles of laissez-faire, hoping to turn back the so-called socialist tenets of the New Deal. Rose debated many aspects of early conservative thought with Crane, but especially whether religion should be part of government. (Crane, an observant Christian, thought it should. Rose did not.) From this correspondence, Rose realized that she believed communists were strong and those opposing it were acting weakly. "Our weakness is that we have no organization at all; I feel that each one of us simply MUST exceed the communist's terrific unremitting energy and fighting spirit—which, in themselves, are wholly admirable," Rose wrote. "As opposition to Lenin's 'professional revolutionists' I am becoming a professional fanatic."

She also turned away from religion—not that she'd been an observant churchgoer to begin with.

One has to agree that Rose had become a bit of a zealot, when one reads her proclamations that the entire country was falling apart. In another letter, Rose warned, "These are the most dangerous times in history and I am convinced they will get much worse before they are better in any obvious or concrete terms. Since 1933 I have not been able to see anything in the near future but a terrific political, economic, social crash and chaos, with violence." She went on to quote Thomas Fuller via "Little Orphan Annie," then a popular Broadway play: "The darkest hour is not the time to despair of dawn. And since then, though the hour grows darker, I see so many indications of dawn that my optimism—which has doggedly been an evidence of things unseen, since the early 1920s—becomes confident, sometimes exuberantly so." To a Little House fan, the passage may be familiar, for Rose had cited it in her revision of *On the Banks of Plum Creek* for Laura. The chapter title in *Plum Creek* is, "The Darkest Hour Is Just Before Dawn."

Eventually, Roger Lea MacBride would collect Rose's letters to and from Crane in a book he titled *The Lady and the Tycoon*. These letters reveal Rose's intensity and preoccupations as a woman who framed the American frontier experience through the lens of libertarianism. Weary from her work with her mother on the Little House books, she could now turn fully to what mattered to her. She hadn't visited Missouri in a decade. She had practically no evident relationship with her old hometown, Laura, or Almanzo.

But her natural inclination to edit and encourage other writers persisted. She told Crane and J. Howard Pew, a Sun Oil executive, that they should write a book about free economies. Ever the advice-giver, Rose wrote Crane on January 22, 1947: "You seem to believe that you have nothing to put into a book, that you can only spend money. Money doesn't write books. *Persons* write books." The remark is revealing because Rose had done so much behind-the-scenes writing for Laura and others (Frederick O'Brien and Lowell Thomas, for example) but would not recommend that Crane trust anyone else to get his knowledge across. "I do know something about writing, and I tell you that you are attempting the impossible," she wrote. "Every person must live his own life, think his own thoughts, reach his own conclusions from his own experience and knowledge, and if he wants a book written he must write it. No one else can write it; anyone else will write *his own* book."

Reading that, one can only wonder about what in her own experience she was referring to. Half of Rose's working life had gone to helping others write their books. Maybe she was tired. The Little House collaboration was one example, though it remained under wraps, of course. Rose's name did come up in an article entitled "Laura Ingalls Wilder" in the *Wilson Library Bulletin* in April 1948, however. Maria Cimino reported, perhaps for the first time, that Laura had written the Little House books "at the insistence of her daughter, Rose Wilder Lane, herself an author, who was eager to preserve a record of her mother's early life." As we've seen, "eager" does not do justice to what probably guided Rose to urge more family stories out of her mother after the stock market crash. Laura had obliged and—a reader of that article might conclude—quickly and easily became famous for her pioneer novels.

Laura was now left with the joyous problem of responding to fan letters and welcoming visitors. No longer working with her mother on the Little House books and having extricated herself from a smothering life with her, Rose would redirect her considerable energies away from Laura and Almanzo for the rest of her life. Articles like the one in the *Wilson Library Bulletin* papered over what had really occurred, but neither woman would have wanted the full story of their partnership to come out. Perhaps Rose felt invisible. She'd watched Laura, whom she'd coached and guided for thirteen intense years, achieve singular prestige as a beloved writer and heroine of her books. *On the Banks of Plum Creek*, *By the Shores of Silver Lake*, *The Long Winter*, *Little Town on the Prairie*, and *These Happy Golden Years* were named Newbery Honor Books in 1939, 1940, 1941, 1942, and 1944. We know that Laura, although not naturally demonstrative about it, did feel gratitude for her daughter's guidance. But I think she minimized what Rose had done. Rose herself had not confided how much of a toll it had taken, and watching the fame and admiration Laura received thanks to her unacknowledged help could only have added to it.

Of Laura, Cimino wrote, "Her sympathetic insight into the urgent unrest that impelled men like her father to take part in the westward expansion and into the courageous patience of women like her mother who accompanied them, are but part of the sense of values and sense of fact that fill this record with the vital breath of full living."

In July 1949, Almanzo suffered a heart attack. He was ninety-two and very frail, but he rallied while Laura cared for him at home. Rose did not visit. Rose felt that "her parents' marriage was complete in itself and she was an appendage," recalled Carol Giffen Mayfield, who would become close to Rose in her later years.

At this time, something prompted Laura to consider what she might owe Rose. The same month, she wrote to George Bye that she would assign ten percent of the royalties from the Little House books to Rose. "I owe Rose, for helping me, at first, in selling my books and for the publicity she gave them," she said. In an attached note, she said, "If anything more is necessary please let me know. This arrangement should have been made long ago. I wonder if you were as surprised as I by the naming of Detroit Branch Library for me. You and I as well as the Little House Books seem to be getting quite a bit of publicity."

Almanzo died in his chair, with Laura embracing him, on October 23. Rose finally returned to Mansfield for his funeral and would have a kind of reconciliation with her old hometown.

10

TWO LEGACIES

In 1949, Laura's income had surpassed Rose's for many years. Laura was the famous writer; her accounts of pioneer life connected deeply with Americans' imaginations, and her fierce attachment to Rocky Ridge Farm in Missouri added to her authenticity. The last years of their lives found Laura and Rose living in different orbits, with different priorities. The drafts and diaries and manuscript pages in each woman's possession from the period when they collaborated on the Little House books went into storage in their respective attics.

Their joint legacy, the work they'd done together to fashion Laura's life story, split in two—one part in Missouri with Laura and the other with Rose in Connecticut. Their two legacies never would rejoin, and part of the reason they didn't was that they both apparently thought that Rose's part in the legacy should not matter.

After Almanzo's death in October 1949, Rose returned to Mansfield for the first time since more than a decade before. Laura and Rose reconciled on what must have been the weakest threads of familial love. Rose began spending winters with Laura at Rocky Ridge. People she'd known around Mansfield remembered her as the cigarette-smoking novelist who'd built the county's first modern home, hosted all those friends, hired servants, and written romantic stories about farmers and hillbillies. The woman who returned was white-haired, overweight, stridently political, and somewhat paranoid. She told them that her anticommunist views had endangered her life and that she would not sit in a public place with her back to the door.

Could she really have feared violence over politics from her former neighbors? Rose's anticommunist views—along with her strong belief in self-reliance and individual liberty—seem to have changed her very personality. In encounters with others, she responded with little emotion now, as illustrated by an odd episode. One night in the early 1950s, Laura, Rose, and friends went out for dinner in a Mansfield restaurant. On the way in, Laura slipped on the steps and fell. Flustered and apologizing, she slowly picked herself up. (Remember, she was in her eighties.) Rose simply stood on the steps watching. Her biographer, William Holtz, who heard this story from witnesses, interpreted Rose's cool response as evidence of her belief that she shouldn't indulge Laura (or perhaps anyone) with extra help.

Laura and Rose shared some affection—they went out for dinner, after all—but at arm's length. Many years later, a Mansfield native told William Anderson that Rose and Laura had felt "blood love" but that they'd lived more happily in separate houses. That observation could explain their relationship going back to the 1920s. And now, living together when Rose visited in the farmhouse (the Rock House had long since been sold) must have seemed close.

Even so, two major stressors had evaporated. They weren't writing together, and they no longer had to scramble for, or argue about, money. They were still linked financially, for as we've seen, by now both of them received income from the Little House books. Laura understood the value of her copyrights. She made her will in February 1952, bequeathing Rose "all my Copyrighted Literary property and the income from same during her natural life and at her death I direct that said Copyrighted Literary property and the income from same be given to the Laura Ingalls Wilder Library of Mansfield, Missouri." The previous year, the little public library had rededicated itself in Laura's name. The wording of the will matters. We remember it because Rose later will make some decisions about the copyrights of the books that fall outside of that document's scope.

Irene Lichty was not one of Laura's close friends, but she took an interest in her. In October

1952 Mrs. Lichty drove Laura sixty miles to Springfield, Missouri, where she met children, signed books, and posed for a photograph. In the photograph, Irene stands shyly behind Laura, who is seated at a table holding open one of her books, pen in hand. Laura smiles at a little girl in an embroidered collared dress. The girl looks stunned, in awe. Irene has pursed lips, a shy, knowing half-smile, and is looking at the camera while everyone but one girl is looking at Laura. Irene wears a dark suit jacket and white shirt with a ribbon tie at her neck. Her brown hair is swept back. It's a sweet picture, even if the children look supremely awkward, the way children made to pose always appear. Irene appears pleased. She seems proud to be ushering her famous friend around, and one wonders why she was in the photo at all. Probably the newspaper photographer encouraged her to stand next to the other woman in back, who was likely the bookstore owner.

In the late 1940s, Ursula Nordstrom, Laura's last editor at *Harper's*, had initiated the huge project of reissuing all the Little House books in a uniform size with completely new illustrations. The artist was Garth Williams, who in 1952 would bring *Charlotte's Web* by E. B. White to life. In 1947, Williams made a trip across the Midwest to all the settings of the little houses, and he stopped in Mansfield to visit with Laura and Almanzo. Williams might not have realized this, but he broke new ground by stopping at Rocky Ridge. Neither of the previous two artists, nor Laura's agent, nor her three editors had ever gone to Missouri. And Laura had never visited New York. All considered, her agent and editors didn't have to write many letters back and forth regarding her manuscripts. They didn't change her copy. It seems somehow that Laura remained in a protective bubble.

One wonders if any of the professionals who handled the Little House manuscripts suspected that Laura relied so heavily on her daughter. What could Virginia Kirkus, her first editor, have thought about the condition of the manuscript she received? She told English professor Rosa Ann Moore years later that the Little House manuscripts "required singularly little editing. . . . I felt that the writing had a distinctive folk flavor; was honestly conceived on the basis of her own childhood experiences." Ursula Nordstrom, too, marveled that the books had never needed editing; she had sent them straight to typesetting. Anyone who's tried writing a book knows how amazing that is.

The new editions of the Little House books, with their soft-pencil sketches by Williams and their homey yellow flyleaves, went out to reviewers in 1953. The reviewer for the *New*

York Herald Tribune, Ernestine Evans, Rose's old friend, remembered Laura's name, though she and Rose had drifted apart. During the Depression, Ernestine worked for the Works Project Administration, editing writers of its state guidebook series. During World War II, she had held another government job. She and Rose probably would have become enemies had they stayed in touch.

Ernestine Evans, though, was one of two people who knew something firsthand about Rose's collaboration. In 1931, after Laura's contract with Knopf was canceled on the closing of its children's department, Rose had rushed Laura's first book manuscript to Ernestine. Now, twenty-two years later, on August 3, 1953, Evans rolled a sheet into her typewriter and wrote a page-and-a-half query to their mutual friend Berta Hader—the other person who knew something about Rose's involvement.

"I'm supposed to do an article about all those eight children's books by Laura Ingalls Wilder—Rose's mother, who must be some terrific age now . . . yes?" she wrote, continuing:

> Did you ever meet her? They really are evocation of the prairie days, and middle of the country standards, simplified, of course. . . .
> I had always imagined Rose had written

or edited them, that they weren't wholly the elder's work; but I may be quite wrong; and in any case would not disturb the publisher's assurance, nor upset any of Rose's own reasons . . . and of course I may be all wrong anyway, and should treat the little collection as from-a-stranger. But in the fifteen years since I have laid eyes on Rose, and during which I fancied her floating between sanity and a bedlam of hates and sort of Whittaker Chambers save the world notions, I never cease to be curious and very puzzled. . . . Do you ever hear anything at all?

I searched in Ernestine Evans's papers for a reply from Berta, but found nothing. Evans seems to have saved everything: solicitations for money from the University of Chicago, publishers' publicity notes, rejection letters of all sorts—from Doubleday, where she worked as a book scout; Reader's Digest, where she tried to place her literary clients' work; and a host of other periodicals. Evans kept letters from her agent saying how worried everyone was about her, and would she please come back from Norway, and he would send her the fare. I believe Berta Hader never replied to Ernestine Evans's query out of deference to Rose and Laura—and because, if she had, word of Rose's role would have been out. It is true that Berta could have called her on the phone. But if they spoke, they must have talked about keeping Rose's part as quiet as Rose wanted.

Laura's fame endured. The Little House books inspired the imaginations and devotion of young and old. Laura's fierce attachment to Rocky Ridge Farm and her simple rural lifestyle only added to her aura and status as a symbol of authentic American values. Adoring fans stopped by regularly. Sometimes Laura couldn't greet them because she didn't feel well. In 1951, a newspaper reporter described the eighty-four-year-old Laura in this way: "Mrs. Almanzo Wilder, with silvery white hair, sits and plays solitaire or crochets in her Ozark mountain home, daintily dressed in a black dress with white lace collar. . . . She looks fragile, and even in her prime must have been delicately built. Yet she had led a life of hard labor, felling trees, tilling soil, tending poultry and livestock." Eight years before, Laura and Almanzo had sold Rocky Ridge Farm to a buyer who as part of the deal granted life tenancy in the farmhouse and paid them a stipend of $50 a month. (The Rock House had been sold earlier.) Now that Almanzo was gone, she was living there alone. She still walked the quarter-mile down to her mailbox. She usually found the box stuffed with fan letters.

She kept close to home but ventured out once a week to town, in a car she'd bought a few years earlier. Jim Hartley drove her. She'd hired him as an occasional chauffeur.

Rose rarely mentioned her mother's books. Certainly, she felt some relief and satisfaction that the Little House books had done so well and felt relief that her mother was financially secure. For herself, living in Danbury, she seems to have found a degree of contentedness. Her happiness amounted, in part, to a decline in resentment and worry. Her days had grown placid. She'd largely stopped keeping a diary back in the late 1930s, but on January 14, 1949, at age sixty-two, she checked in with her notebook. It was the first time she'd made an entry in eight years: "Here I sit alone and contented in my new-made house with the two Maltese, David & Junior," she wrote. She detailed an ongoing renovation that included two new fireplaces, a new porch upstairs, a breakfast room, and new kitchen. "It is all paid for, I can't think how. I feel fine, though now I can't see without glasses, wear an upper plate, have only 6 lower front teeth left, and pains, maybe arthritic, in my knees." Gone was striving for story sales, money, security for her parents. It seems that Rose had become more detached—an observer, perhaps even a somewhat serene one, of her own life.

If Laura and Rose wrote to each other, those

letters have disappeared. They probably talked on the phone. In February 1954, as William Anderson reported in *Laura Ingalls Wilder: A Biography*, Mansfield friends held two parties for Laura's eighty-seventh birthday, and later that year Rose arrived in Missouri for a long visit with her. Then the two of them took an airplane back to Connecticut. So close in age, both of them elderly by now, both were also still independent and capable. The next year, at eighty-eight, Laura told the *Kansas City Star* that she kept her pistol by the screen door and a shotgun in her bedroom. "I know how to use them both," she said.

Such spunk and mettle lasted two more years. Rose arrived in Mansfield just before Thanksgiving, 1956, ready to spend the holidays and winter with Laura. She found her mother acting strangely, "physically active and raving," as she wrote to Jasper Crane. "Against her violent resistance, I got her into an ambulance and sixty miles to the nearest decent hospital," she wrote. Laura spent the holidays at St. John's Hospital, where doctors diagnosed diabetes and put her on insulin and a special diet. For a few weeks Laura seemed to improve, and she went home in late December. Rose felt "frantically busy." She cleaned the house, nursed Laura, and could not even read a book unless Laura was asleep. She was hoping Laura would go with her to live in Danbury, she told Crane, "but of course I understand her attachment to her home." Laura lay in bed on her ninetieth birthday, on February 7, 1957. "I often say, not without smugness, that I come from the nineteenth century," Rose wrote. "My mother, who lived much longer there, refuses to budge from it; she will have NO truck with the twentieth, she detests it."

Laura's decline in health had probably prompted Rose to think about her own advancing age. A few days after Thanksgiving, Rose signed her own will at a banker's office in Mansfield. She left everything to Roger Lea MacBride, who would also be her executor. "I intentionally make no provision in this Will for my mother . . . as I know that she has means ample for her support and welfare." Laura died at Rocky Ridge on February 10, three days after her ninetieth birthday. She was buried in Mansfield next to Almanzo.

Immediately after Laura's death, Rose rummaged through some of her mother's belongings, but apparently she couldn't bring herself to do much tending to Laura's affairs. Townspeople remembered that Rose did burn some family letters and some of Laura's papers. She returned to Connecticut, leaving most of Rocky Ridge untouched.

She felt grief, that's clear, but the fact that Rose left to no one in particular the huge job of sorting through sixty years of Laura's papers shows, I think, the degree of estrangement between mother and daughter. Rose must have found and read Laura's last letter to her, left in a desk in 1952, full of rather terse instructions about what to do with her jewelry and a few items she'd promised to friends, and signed, "my love will be with you always."

Both women had continued to keep secret the facts of their collaboration. This secrecy, and their estrangement, set up the situation that led to another schism: between Laura's and Rose's literary legacies. One set of manuscript drafts and revisions continued to reside at Laura's house after her death. Rose might have taken everything back with her to Danbury, Connecticut, and placed it in her own house with the rest of the papers in her possession, but she apparently could not do it. She could not look at those papers.

At Rose's request, an ad hoc group of men took Laura's revolver and some other things. Harland Shorter and his family, who had bought Rocky Ridge, had access to the house and the Lichtys seemed eager, unlike Rose, to tame the disarray in Laura's house as a way to honor her. Lewis Lichty immediately spearheaded a campaign to open a Laura Ingalls Wilder museum in the house and gathered townspeople who supported the idea. The group formed the Laura Ingalls Wilder Home Association. To Rose, it must have seemed sudden, but again, she probably felt inclined to let the fans and Laura's friends do what they wanted to do rather than inject an opinion that could have brought up questions of her work on the books.

Years later, in 1979, Irene Lichty would tell a reporter that the idea of opening Rocky Ridge to the public had been her husband's but that in her last months Laura had been interested in the idea when the Lichtys brought it up. Irene had thus felt that they had Laura's blessing. And so the Lichtys moved quickly and with fervor and fortitude. First, they told Rose of the movement. Rose agreed to buy back the farmhouse. The Shorter family, to whom Laura had sold it, had been paying the purchase price in installments for several years. Rose may have acceded to this plan because she didn't want to be part of it or because she had no particular objection. She also agreed to donate several thousand dollars toward a museum and curators' house next door, where the Lichtys would live rent-free.

And so, a shrine came to be. By May 1957, three months after Laura died in the house, members of the garden club had cleaned it and left it set up as it had looked in Laura's last days, with her rocking chair covered by her favorite pillow on the porch, the calendar turned to February 1957, and the living room neat with its chairs and books. They held an open house for five hundred visitors.

Soon after, the Lichtys and others began assembling display cases of the Wilder family's photos, mementos, and scrapbooks. They bought secondhand cases for displays. They chose some things for display and left many other things in storage upstairs. The association's swift work gave an eager public direct access to Laura's effects and home at a time when a whole new crop of Wilder devotees wanted to know Laura better, hear more about her, and honor her life.

New fans were moving into the fold every year. A Michigan woman, Julie Davis, the Lichtys, and others worked on a movement for Laura to appear on a postage stamp. (In 1993, a stamp with a sun-bonneted girl and the words "Little House on the Prairie" was in fact issued.)

Rose, who originally hadn't wanted a museum, felt that the Lichtys were in the best position to organize Laura's effects. Yet, think what must have gone through her mind: the Lichtys would display parts of Laura's manuscripts, and some of what Laura had there in Missouri would suggest the other parts of their story, which Rose had no interest in telling.

But the Lichtys had met Laura only after she had finished with her writing; they had helped her in old age. They probably knew little or nothing of what manuscripts sat in boxes at

Rocky Ridge until they began to sort. And they would not know for twenty-three years—not until 1979, when Holtz explained it in a letter to Irene, who had been widowed and remarried and was now known as Irene Lichty LeCount—that Rose's papers in boxes a thousand miles away, in Roger MacBride's house in Virginia, held later manuscripts that revealed Laura and Rose's secret that Rose had collaborated with Laura on the books.

Holtz had contacted Mrs. Lichty LeCount to ask if he could read Laura's "memoir," a word that Laura's first biographer Donald Zochert had used to describe Laura's original version of her life story, "Pioneer Girl." Mrs. Lichty LeCount responded with surprise. First, on the question of a memoir, she said she had seen nothing like a memoir. One wonders why she was shrugging off the "Pioneer Girl" tablets. Someone (I believe one of the Lichtys) did read those notes and label the tablets with which of the fictional Little House books each tablet applied to. Those labels have since been removed.

The matter of manuscripts found with Rose's papers landed in the curator's consciousness like a bomb. She wrote to Holtz that she believed that Rose would have been "very angry" if she could have known that scholars were beginning to postulate that Rose had a role in the books.

What is it about a secret that invests the

information kept secret with such power? If Rose's part in the project had always been known, it would not have shocked anyone. It's the fact that the two women hadn't talked about it that makes it so strong.

To Mrs. Lichty LeCount, the version of events Bill Holtz relayed may have sounded as if scholars were pitting one woman against the other, and Irene certainly did not want that. "Both Mrs. Wilder and Rose were friends of mine," she wrote to Holtz. "I was *very* fond of them. My anxiety stems from the fact I do not want to see the faith of readers (devotees) destroyed. It will be if they are caused to feel that 'Laura' did not write the Little House books."

Of course, all Irene knew of Rose's part was what Rose had written to her in 1963. Rose's description did not include her part at all. "If you take one of the tablets—original manuscripts—remember that it is the first draft," Rose said in the letter. "After more or less cutting it up and pinning it together again, my mother made a typed copy from it which she sent to her agent in New York, who sent it to the publisher, and that was the end of that."

In the time right after Laura's death, Lewis Lichty found several of Laura's handwritten drafts of the Little House books, the diary of the trip from Dakota to Mansfield in 1894, and—here's the treasure—a handwritten manuscript titled "The First Three Years and a Year of Grace." On a trip east a few years later, the Lichtys carried all of these papers to Rose's Connecticut house. "Rose put the manuscripts and little diary back in the carton we took them in, and said to me, 'You may take this back with you and use them however you see fit,' " Irene wrote in a 1986 letter to Holtz. "Perhaps you could use the unpublished one to make some money for the Home." Irene's letter continued:

> We brought them back but before I could plan how to use the unpublished book as a money maker for the Home, a telegram came from Rose requesting that I return all the manuscripts to her, which we did, including the diary.
>
> She sent back to us all of the tablets except the unpublished one and the diary. It was the diary on which she based *On the Way Home*.
>
> She told me she would never have "First Three Years and a Year of Grace" published as it was not up to her mother's writings. It was some time after Rose's death that Roger MacBride published it.

"Not up to her mother's writings." This was the manuscript Laura had mentioned to George Bye that she was working on in the 1940s. Rose asked the Lichtys for it because she did not want them to publish it themselves. She hadn't seen it before, or she had last seen it many years back and wondered how Laura had completed it. Not long after the Lichtys' visit to Rose, Rose did edit and write an introduction and epilogue for Laura's trip diary from 1894, when they'd ridden the wagon from South Dakota to Missouri. But she must have realized that she could not edit "The First Three Years and a Year of Grace" at that point because, if she did, her editing of the other Little House books might become known. This is all conjecture, of course, because whatever Rose thought or wrote about this manuscript, she did not share those thoughts with anyone or posterity.

Back in Missouri, the Lichtys worked hard bringing Rocky Ridge alive for its visitors. They published pamphlets, took photographs, and led tours, but they were not naturally gregarious hosts. About a decade after the Laura Ingalls Wilder Home and Museum had opened to tourists, Larry Dennis, a longtime editor of the local newspaper, the *Mansfield Mirror*, drove the mile out of town on Highway 60 for an interview with Irene. Dennis chatted with her as they stood in the driveway that curved up from the road. A busload of children pulled in. Irene turned to him and complained, "Don't tell anyone about the place—then we'll get more kids."

Perhaps she'd been trying to make a light-hearted, even self-deprecating, joke. But the quip is surprising, coming from the woman representing America's optimistic prairie heroine who had gone to the trouble to answer most of the letters children wrote to her.

Rose's activities with the public found expression in a very different place. The businessman and champion of laissez-faire government and property rights, Robert LeFevre, who had written to Rose about *The Discovery of Freedom*, began holding classes on an idyllic tract with rustic buildings north of Colorado Springs in the late 1950s. He called the place the Freedom School. Small groups of students visited for two weeks at a time, listening to lectures by LeFevre and others on the theory of "nonarchism" (or "stateless capitalism," a form of government that is hardly government at all) and other libertarian concepts that were then very new. LeFevre named a log building Rose Wilder Lane Hall in 1962, honoring Rose, who donated badly needed funds. Rose attended the dedication ceremony.

Because she disliked the cold and snow of Connecticut, Rose in the early 1960s began spending winters in southern climes. By January 1965 she'd bought a house in a subdivision in Harlingen, Texas, and relocated there. She left behind a couple of unlikely caretakers in

Danbury: Joseph Kamp—a "self-taught historian and theorist," according to Holtz—and his wife, Mildred. Kamp was vice chairman of the Constitutional Educational League and shared many views with Rose.

MacBride would say later that Kamp "emerged in the days when there were very few anti-Communists in the intellectual/literary world. [Kamp] used to give seminars back in the fifties on various subjects; some of them were anti-Communist and some of them related to his own intellectual or religious hobby horses." MacBride considered Kamp "a very unreliable individual. He became something of a scrounge, I gather, in the late fifties and solicited funds from private individuals to subsidize him in the work he was doing investigating and reporting on Communist activities."

MacBride believed that Kamp was responsible for Rose's support of the Vietnam War. "Of course Gramma needed somebody to babysit her house while she wasn't there, and so she invited the Kamps to do so and they were there for three or four years before her death."

Rose had mostly given up writing for money; she didn't want to pay income tax. But she realized in 1962 that she could still write all the essays she wanted and simply refuse pay. She wrote Jasper Crane that year, "There's nothing courageous or useful about this, and I'm the opposite of proud of it, but legally—at present—I can keep out of what's called 'Social Security' and write for publication if I give away the *manuscripts,* truly give them away and receive no money whatever from them."

Rose labored on a new edition, apparently to be greatly expanded, of *The Discovery of Freedom.* Her many years' worth of articles about American needlework in *Woman's Day* finally were gathered into *The Woman's Day Book of American Needlework.* (Rose was the author, but the copyright was held by her publisher.) Rose's text interpreted needlepoint as an expression of American freedom. "The first thing that American needlework tells you is that Americans live in the only classless society," Rose wrote in the introduction. "This republic is the only country that has no peasant needlework." She argued that American women expressed their independence without articulating it in words— they did it by inventing new stitches and designs. Rose's analysis was that American needlework is a hybrid, whereas in the rest of the world, poor people and rich people worked very different patterns. She connected needlework to attitude. "As Americans were the first to know and to declare that a person is the unit of human life on earth, that each human being is a self-governing source of the life-energy that creates, controls, and changes societies, institutions, governments, so American women were the first to reverse the old meaning in needlework design."

Many times in this large, beautifully illustrated book, Rose's narrative strays far from the subject at hand—stitchery—and connects America's farm roots to individual freedom. In this segment she praises her forbears' pluck: "Struggling for bare life itself, against the forests, the grudging soil, the weather, the sea, they learned that differences between human beings are superficial. . . . In sharing danger and hardship, they learned that every person is self-controlling, responsible for his acts; that each one makes his own life what it is and that all alike must struggle to survive and to make human living better than it is."

Subtle though it is, Rose's connections to her more famous mother Laura are evident in photographs of crocheting on page 147, where samples of popcorn stitch and hairpin lace come from the Laura Ingalls Wilder Home and Museum, and where the book includes a photo of "one of a pair of cuffs made and worn by the writer's grandmother, Caroline Quiner Ingalls, about 1870."

Such connections to Laura remained very quiet. Rose's adopted family now consisted of MacBride, his wife Susan (called Susie), and her neighbors the Giffens in her winter home of Harlingen, Texas. Rose no longer cooked for her friends—she asked them for rides and took them out to restaurants. The MacBrides were in the process of moving from their rural house in Vermont to an estate in Virginia. They discussed with Rose their plans to move Rose's books from Vermont to a guest house in Virginia. They had for some years readied themselves to care for Rose's belongings and provide her with another home.

Rose meanwhile was trying to sever the last ties she had to Rocky Ridge Farm in Missouri. The Lichtys and the board of directors there were asking if Rose would pay the rest of the mortgage on the curators' house that she had mostly financed. Rose sent what she called her final payment of $4,000 toward the Lichtys' mortgage in August 1968, but the Lichtys wanted her to pay off the shortfall of several thousand more dollars. Roger wrote Rose: "Mrs. Lichty seems to feel that you have assured her 'many times that she would pay for the house'. I know that your intentions were different. Unless you for some reason have changed your mind, I will go ahead and tactfully but firmly break the news to the Lichtys."

As of 1965, Rose was living most of the year in her Texas house. In the close-knit subdivision, she socialized often with her neighbors, the Giffens, and was host to a young Vietnamese friend she'd taken under her wing. Carol Giffen

Mayfield, who was a teenager in those years, said in an interview that her mother sewed Rose a few loose-fitting dresses to help her handle the intense heat of southern Texas. Rose became close to Mayfield and her brother, Don Giffen, talking about her travels and politics around their dinner table with a dry delivery that reminded the Giffens of Alfred Hitchcock.

Harlingen's charms weren't enough for Rose, though. She became restless that summer and started preparing for a three-year-long trip abroad. Rose wrote Roger, reminding him that her will resided in a safety deposit box in Danbury to which he had official access. She had kept the Connecticut house as her legal residence.

She got the required shots for "smallpox, anthrax, cholera, plague, yellow fever, typhoid, paratyphoid, polio," and suffered reactions. She complained in a September 2 letter to Roger, "I run high fevers, my arms are swollen, ruddy and screaming, I can't sleep nor really wake up. I liked this country better when it wasn't so damned healthy."

Rose knew she'd need a companion and driver on the world trip, so she hired Don Giffen, who was twenty-two and a talkative college graduate who adored Rose. "He leapt at the opportunity," Giffen's sister Carol remembered. "He and Rose were very close." Rose told the family that, while traveling, she would tell everyone he was her grandson, a term she'd usually reserved for Roger MacBride.

In fact, things seemed strained with Roger then, but Rose arranged to stop at Roger's new house in Virginia on the drive up to Connecticut. Once back in Danbury, they'd spend one night there with Joseph Kamp. She and Don wanted to leave Texas on October 7 but apparently stayed several days more, while Rose waited for her royalty check to arrive. Rose and Giffen would sail on November 9 on the Dutch line Bremen.

At the MacBrides, Roger and Susie had Rose and Don stay in a guesthouse on their property, which upset Rose, according to John Bass, who interviewed Giffen a few years ago, before Giffen's illness made this impossible. Rose already was upset, Giffen recalled, because Roger had supposedly spent money in her accounts on real estate, and she argued with him about money. During the ride north from Virginia to Connecticut, Rose complained to Giffen that she was rethinking her decision to leave all of her assets to Roger. Rose and Giffen arrived in Danbury on October 30 for a short stay—one or two nights, until they could get on their ship for Europe.

Don stopped with Rose for groceries on the way into town, and she bought herself a large container of vanilla ice cream. When they got to the King Street house, only a few years earlier the subject of a glowing article about her new renovations, they found it was a wreck. Joseph Kamp, then alone because his wife had recently died, was no housekeeper.

The trip had tired her out, but Rose baked a loaf or two of her famous bread for the group that included Kamp, Giffen, and herself. After dinner, they all stayed up late talking and, no doubt, telling stories. Rose was cranky, Giffen recalled, and fussed that she wanted her favorite couch moved downstairs. This appeared to be difficult, so she eventually climbed upstairs to the couch. Much later that night, she got up and retrieved the ice cream and some other snacks, which she took upstairs to her bed. Eating in bed was a long habit of hers that dated at least to the 1920s. She'd sometimes complained to her journal that she was making herself sick eating crackers and butter in bed on the sleeping porch of Rocky Ridge.

On the morning of October 31, Giffen went downstairs and wondered why Rose wasn't up. He climbed back up to look for her, and found her, dead in her bed. She'd eaten the entire container of ice cream. Rose had told Roger only weeks earlier that she was sure she had diabetes as Laura had had late in life—but she was not going to see a doctor. MacBride wrote the details of the next day in a letter to Rose's biographer Holtz. "Apparently her heart just stopped in the night," Roger remembered. The MacBrides chartered a plane to LaGuardia and drove to Danbury in a rental car. Susie "had to do a lot of the work on details because I was inconsolably grief-stricken and prone to burst into tears every five or ten minutes," MacBride wrote.

Rose had been stilled, in a sense, mid-sentence. She would not take her trip, although she had told Roger that if anything happened, she wanted Don Giffen to go, which he did, for most of a year. She would not revise her libertarian treatise *The Discovery of Freedom.* And the secret she'd kept for four decades, her role in the Little House books, remained undiscovered in boxes of diaries and manuscripts in her Danbury house. Susie had a slice of Rose's homemade bread encased in plastic as a memento. By the mid-1970s, the MacBrides had moved Rose's papers to Virginia. And it would be several years before anyone had the time or courage to look at them. Roger's grief centered on the loss of his personal and political mentor. He was deeply sad. He believed that he would devote himself to her ideals of limited government. And soon he would realize he had another huge task ahead of him: preserving the story of Rose's parents and ancestors.

PART IV
LITERATURE AS POLITICS

11

ROGER, ROSE'S LIBERTARIAN LEGACY

The story of the Little House books and their influence on American beliefs and life would not be complete without attention to Roger Lea MacBride, Rose's heir. Just as Rose's personal philosophy of individual freedom shaped the Little House books, so too did this ethic guide Roger, as he propagated the Little House legacy after her death. In both his career and his personal life, Roger reflected and perpetuated Rose's politics and worldview. His influence over the Little House enterprise would be enormous, helping to increase the books' impact on conservative thought. Roger managed to both embody the values he learned from Rose and to affect how they were shared with the fascinated public, who hungered for more Little House wisdom.

In taking on the mantle of Wilder family representative, Roger might have felt an ease and freedom in promoting the stories that Rose, tied by blood and emotion, couldn't. Even after Laura's death, Rose had kept her distance from the Little House fans. She chose not to be the public face of the books she had worked hard to create. Fans did write to her, hoping that Rose might respond as kindly as Laura had, but she answered with curt letters of a few sentences directing them to the Laura Ingalls Wilder Home in Mansfield. "She had a form letter in her head that she wrote back to people," William Anderson, the foremost expert on the history of the Ingalls and Wilder families, told me in an interview. Rose would say she could not answer their questions, and "the last paragraph was PR for Mansfield. I realized she was bluffing." In fact, Anderson said, Rose remembered a lot about her family, as proven by her detailed story "Grandpa's Fiddle," which I described in Chapter 2.

Anderson first wrote to Rose in 1967, when he was only thirteen, showing her a draft of his first historical booklet about Laura's family, *The Story of the Ingalls*. He reported in the manuscript that the family had settled in Dakota Territory "through the mild winter of 1879–1880 with a few settlers as neighbors." Rose responded angrily, "I object to your publishing a statement that my mother was a liar. The Ingalls family spent their first winter in Dakota Territory approximately sixty miles from any neighbor. This is a formal protest against your proposal to publish a statement that my mother was a liar." In a later letter, Rose told Anderson, "If my mother's books are not absolutely accurate, she will be discredited as a person and a writer." As Susan Wittig Albert, author of the novel about Rose, *A Wilder Rose*, has noted, Laura herself would have disagreed with Rose on this point. In "Pioneer Girl" Laura had reported that the Ingalls family took in a boarder.

Anderson notes in his article, "The Literary Apprenticeship of Laura Ingalls Wilder," that admirers of the books wanted desperately to see Rose. "She refused most visits from 'Little House' fans, and when she did allow visits from her mother's readers, the conversation steered clear of the Wilder writings," he wrote. He went on to say that Rose "maintained this form of devotion to the life and work of Laura Ingalls Wilder until her own death in 1968."

Roger's devotion to Laura's legacy after Rose died was very different. He held high the Little House light. He believed deeply in the values of self-sufficiency, and he admired Rose's metamorphosis from farmer's daughter to self-taught woman of letters. And he said so, publicly and often. Roger MacBride also understood the financial value of Laura and Rose's stories. His actions between 1968, when Rose died, and his own death in 1995, transformed one beloved book series into an enterprise: television show, spinoff titles, and countless other products.

In his first act as torchbearer, Roger published

Laura's last manuscript, the "adult novel" she had discussed with Rose but apparently never shown to her, "The First Three Years and a Year of Grace." *Harper's* editor Ursula Nordstrom rejoiced when MacBride told her about the manuscript. Nordstrom excitedly wrote another editor, calling the newly discovered pages "a voice from the grave." She decided she would change not a word of the story, even though it overlapped with the previous *These Happy Golden Years*—and did so with details and interpretations that contradicted the earlier book.

Nordstrom and Roger MacBride did make a few key changes. They gave the book a new title, *The First Four Years*. And before Roger sent off the handwritten manuscript to be typeset, he removed the last lines, the poem about asking God to be merciful toward "me, a fool."

I am not the first to note that this manuscript finally revealed the differences between Laura's rough drafts and the polished final drafts. This manuscript intimated the secret that Rose had kept to her death. Fans caught some of the differences right away: In both books, Laura and Almanzo took an unexpected weekday buggy ride for a big talk about their wedding plans. They decided they must get married quickly to head off Almanzo's mother and sister's plans for an expensive celebration.

In *The First Four Years*, the pre-wedding talk

lasts longer, and it is not a pleasant chat. Laura tells Almanzo that she does not want to marry a farmer, and Almanzo bargains with her. If she will try farming for three years and, at the end of that time, they aren't successful, he'll do something else. Laura complains to him that "a farmer never has any money. He can never make any because the people in towns tell him what they will pay for what he has to sell and then they charge him what they please for what he has to buy. It is not fair."

Almanzo replies, "But you've got it all wrong. Farmers are the only ones who are independent." This introduces the book's theme. Their debate over whether farmers are slaves or masters continues bravely, and darkly, through the chapters. Laura and Almanzo watch their crops fail in hail and drought. They suffer through barn and house fires. Events match real life quite closely: Rose is born and thrives, but their second child dies almost immediately. Then they become deathly ill with diphtheria. At the end of three years, Laura agrees to try one more year. By the book's end, the character Laura adds a quick few sentences of optimism. She says, as she contemplates the difficulty of paying their debts, "It would be a fight to win out in this business of farming, but strangely she felt her spirit rising for the struggle." This note of optimism stands out because it was a rare one in the book.

It's easy to imagine why the two women did not move forward with this text. In all eight previous books, farming is a noble goal. No one doubts farming's worth. But now Laura had moved into adult territory. Her new book echoed, through the tragic events in its chapters, the theme of Rose's adult novel *Free Land*, which concludes that no land is free and farmers pay for it with their lives.

Roger felt no hesitation about publishing the final manuscript. He and Rose had probably talked about the struggles of her family and the importance of American quests for better lives. He might even have seen no lack of consistency between *The First Four Years* and the previous Little House books. He certainly yearned for readers to meet Rose, who is born in this volume.

And so Roger went ahead with publication. He wrote an explanatory introduction to the book, in which he skirted the truth with two near-truths. First, he perpetuated Rose's secret, never mentioning the fact that she and Laura had worked together on Laura's story in the previous books of the series. Roger might not have heard from Rose that she had done so much on the Little House books, but at the very least, he had to have sensed it. Second, Roger avoided talking about Laura and Almanzo's farming failures, about which readers would shortly read. His introduction joins this very different last manuscript to the rest of the Little House books as if *The First Four Years* were merely a sequel that Laura had not had time to polish up.

"My own guess is that she wrote this one in the late 1940s and that after Almanzo died, she lost interest in revising and completing it for publication," he surmised in his original introduction. "Because she didn't do so, there is a difference from the earlier books in the way the story is told." That sounds a fair enough guess, from his point of view. Roger probably had not yet read any of the old letters (still in boxes on his property) from the early 1940s, when Laura had told Rose she was working on an adult novel. Roger might not have heard much from Rose about the Little House books at all, since by the time he met her that work was finished. By this point, he knew mostly Rose's frustrations over the building of the curators' house at Rocky Ridge Farm.

Roger went on in his introduction to say that Rose had been his close friend, a famous writer "who carried on Laura's pioneer spirit by having many adventures in America and abroad." He wrote that the reason *The First Four Years* had not appeared before was that: "Rose grew up in a time when ladies did not consciously seek fame. She chose to shed light on the lives of others instead of her own, and so this book about her mother, father and herself had to wait until after her death to be published." The statement, of course, strains credulity. Rose's life—from her first-person writing about her Balkan travels to her opinion pieces about avoiding taxes, making a home, and exploring—belies it. She often sought attention to her own life. By the time Roger met her, in her later years, Rose had retreated from certain kinds of public statements and writing, but she had told Roger all about her doings with the likes of Herbert Hoover, Henry Ford, Jack London, Dorothy Thompson, Sinclair Lewis, and many more.

Roger's words imply that Rose's only motivation in suppressing publication of her mother's last manuscript was social convention. He, probably innocently, sidesteps her larger reason and dilemma, that Rose didn't publish "The First Three Years and a Year of Grace" because she'd had enough of editing and rewriting her mother's stories. And yet, to publish it without revising it might shed light on Rose's earlier role. Most important, the themes Laura explored in what would became *The First Four Years* did not fit the values of pioneer optimism advanced by the Little House books. If Rose had seen the manuscript in the early 1940s, she would have found it so lacking in the correct message as to be unsalvageable.

The First Four Years established itself as the series sequel. It's a compelling glimpse into Laura's own, authentic take on her last years in

Dakota. Roger invited readers to seek out the traces of Laura's life in Missouri. "If you go, the curators, who loved and knew the Wilders personally, will take you around and tell you details that may not be in the 'Little House' books, to help you better to know Laura, Almanzo, and Rose." In this way, Roger created on the page an atmosphere of warmth.

He had good reason to—it fit the brand. He sought to extend the reach of the Little House series even further, granting rights for a television show, *Little House on the Prairie*, starring Michael Landon as a beardless Pa and Melissa Gilbert as Laura. The show was set in Walnut Grove, Minnesota, the background for *On the Banks of Plum Creek*. The first episode aired in 1974. Roger and a business partner, Edwin Friendly, also made Rose's first pioneer book, *Let the Hurricane Roar*, into a television movie called "Young Pioneers." He also oversaw the book's re-release as a paperback with this new title and with new names for the main characters: Charles and Caroline were now David and Molly, matching the fictional names Rose used later in *Free Land*, a decision that apparently avoided confusion with the Little House books.

In later years, Roger continued his devotion to Rose's legacy and wanted to share it. In the 1980s and 1990s, eight books about Rose's childhood and early adulthood appeared with his byline.

They begin with *Little House on Rocky Ridge* and concluded with *Bachelor Girl*, titled after a nickname Rose and her contemporaries used for one another during her days as a telegrapher.

Driven, as he said, by the beliefs Rose had instilled in him, Roger pushed his political career forward. He had faltered in his quest for elected office in Vermont, where he'd served just one term in the state legislature and failed to get the Republican nomination for governor. But in Virginia, where he and his wife moved in 1968, he made history as a Republican member of the Electoral College. In the 1972 election, he cast his electoral vote not for the Nixon ticket, to which he'd pledged, but for John Hospers, the Libertarian Party's first ever presidential candidate. Roger's choice to act as a "faithless elector" gave the first Libertarian in history and the first woman candidate (Hospers's running mate, Toni Nathan) electoral votes.

Roger stepped into a national spotlight just when his private life teetered on the edge of collapse. He and Susie had adopted a daughter, Abigail, but by 1972, when Abigail was not yet two, Roger asked Susie to leave and move to Nevada for a quick divorce. Susie, whose name now is Susan Ford Hammaker, said in an interview that she did so because she had always done what Roger asked.

Susie had shared a warm rapport with Rose, who had sent letters about cooking and writing (she urged Susie to fictionalize her college trip to Europe). Susie recalled a dramatic meeting with Rose on her patio in Harlingen, Texas, not long before Rose died. She advised Susie to stand up for herself more, to be strong. Susie would always consider her friendship with Rose an early tutoring in pioneer life. After Susie went west, where for a time she farmed in a rural area, her absence apparently figured into a court's decision to award Roger custody. Roger hired graduate student couples to help raise their daughter.

Roger took Abigail with him on his campaign for president as the new Libertarian Party's candidate in 1976. He traveled the country widely during the campaign, flying in a plane painted with the words: LIBERTARIAN PRESIDENTIAL CAMPAIGN.

The party's official biography of Roger connected him to Rose and to the new television show he had created with producer Ed Friendly (who had produced *Rowan and Martin's Laugh-In*). The biography played up Roger's connection to the Little House books: "As an admirer and close friend of Rose Wilder Lane, he was instrumental in the creation of the NBC-TV series, 'Little House on the Prairie,' based upon books by Rose Lane's mother, Laura Ingalls Wilder."

After he was formally nominated on June 26, 1976, MacBride promised in his speech: "We together will wage a presidential campaign the likes of which this nation hasn't seen since the Jefferson–Adams campaign of 1800, when Jefferson carried the day for libertarian ideas, ousted the federalist Adams to become the third president of the United States." Roger campaigned on ending marijuana laws, censorship, and the war in Vietnam. "We want to make massive cuts in that legalized theft called taxation."

The very next day, Roger spoke to fifteen thousand motorcyclists in the capitol square in Madison, Wisconsin, where the members of the Wisconsin Better Bikers' Association had gone to demonstrate against helmet laws. Roger put a note in his handwritten speech, "SMASH"— presumably what he would do to the helmet he held. He promised that the Libertarian Party was there to stay and that it agreed with their slogan, "Let those who ride decide!" The WBBA arranged for a motorcycle escort to the airport.

Two of Roger's supporters were two of the most enthusiastic early members of the Libertarian Party, who also had been influenced by Rose Wilder Lane. Charles G. Koch, chairman and CEO of Koch Industries, and his brother, David Koch, who shares control and runs its chemical technology business, became libertarians in their twenties to fight government controls on their family's energy and engineering companies.

Charles Koch worked for Roger's campaign, writing to leaders in the western oil industry. "Dear Rocky Mountain Oilman," one letter began, "I have been a supporter of libertarian activities since the early 1960s and have found them to be the only effective way to combat the rapidly increasing governmental control over all aspects of our lives. . . . For nearly ten years, Roger MacBride and I have worked together attempting to advance ideas of liberty and free enterprise." When Charles Koch wrote that he'd been a "supporter of libertarian activities" since the 1960s, he meant that he had attended classes at the Freedom School in Colorado, the very school Rose Wilder Lane had financially supported and on the campus of which now stood Rose Wilder Lane Hall.

In 1977 Charles Koch helped found the libertarian think tank the Cato Institute. It was named after "Cato's Letters," essays against government power published in the 1700s in England and which the institute says inspired the Founding Fathers.

Libertarian presidential bids have never done well, but the early ones got the public's attention. Roger hoped to receive a million votes but ended up with 172,557—two-tenths of one percent of the popular vote—and no electoral votes. His best single-state showing was in Alaska, where he earned 5.5 percent of the popular vote. Despite this rather meager result, Libertarian historians count his effort as a vital first step to establish the anti-big-government movement. Jeff Riggenbach wrote for the Von Mises Institute that, "For, at a time when he was in a position to do a lot for the public image of the libertarian movement, Roger MacBride came forward and did it."

David Koch became the Libertarian Party's 1980 vice-presidential candidate. After that campaign, as Nicholas Confessore has written in the *New York Times*, the Koch brothers turned away from overt political action, instead forming a nonprofit that evolved into Americans for Prosperity and which raises enormous amounts of money to oppose Democratic candidates.

Although the ties to Rose's libertarian ideas are clear in history, the lines between libertarianism (which historically could be socially liberal, favoring legalization of prostitution and drugs, for example) and right-wing conservatism (which tends to be socially conservative) have become blurred. The public's interest in libertarianism rises and falls, perhaps with the presidential election cycles, but it does remain a viable movement.

The Koch family provides the filiation that helps understand the power of libertarian ideas as expressed in the Little House books. They bridge Rose's early libertarian thought and today's conservative appropriation of some of those ideas. Therefore, a brief review of the Koch brothers' political activities since 1980 is instructive.

As I've shown especially in Chapters 7 and 8 and will buttress in the appendices, Rose wrote some scenes touting free-market principles in the last three Little House books, *The Long Winter*, *Little Town on the Prairie*, and *These Happy Golden Years*. It's likely, I've argued, that Laura ceded more control to Rose over these books, for which the earliest drafts are missing, unlike for the earlier books. Laura had to have reworked the completed drafts that Rose sent her as she penciled her near-final drafts, which consist of handwritten tablets that Laura later donated to the Detroit Public Library and the Pomona Library. During the period when Rose was adding scenes about independence and free-market interactions to Laura's books, she was also deep into composing her libertarian manifesto, *The Discovery of Freedom*. Rose was also simultaneously writing letters to friends and book reviews about limited government, taxation, and the problems of communism. There is a temporal and personal link between the making of the Little House books, which helped shape Rose's evolving values, and Rose's contribution to the Libertarian Party, as one its three "founding mothers." That link is made manifest in the last three books of the series.

In the years since Rose's heir Roger Lea MacBride and Freedom School alumnus David Koch helped found the Libertarian Party, its ideas about individual and economic freedoms have seemed to move like an undulating wave from outside mainstream politics to inside the Republican Party. In presidential campaign years, the Libertarian Party tends to gain more members and its platform becomes more mainstream. The two biggest symbols of this trend are former Senator Ron Paul and his son, Senator Rand Paul. The elder Paul ran for president as a Libertarian in 1988 and as an outlier Republican in 2008 and 2012; Rand Paul rose to national prominence with some decidedly libertarian ideas like non-interventionist foreign policy, and he ran for president as a Republican in 2016. The elder Paul raised his children on the ideas of Friedrich von Hayek, Ayn Rand, and Ludwig von Mises and worked on Ronald Reagan's first campaign for president in 1976.

Both of the Pauls—like Rose Wilder Lane—have opposed military spending, and this put them at odds with Republican leaders. But many of their ideas—ending Social Security, cutting taxes, and privatizing Welfare—have connected them.

The Koch brothers have moved more to the right at the same time that certain Little House fan groups have publicly linked conservative beliefs to the books. Writer Caroline Fraser has argued that conservatives have appropriated Laura Ingalls Wilder's books and made them political symbols. I would argue that what actually happened is the opposite: the books have inspired conservative thinkers because those thinkers found in them libertarian ideas about limited government.

The Koch brothers have remained sympathetic to libertarian ideals. Speaking in the 1990s about the influence the Freedom School and its ideas had on his life, Charles Koch acknowledged that the school was "where I began developing a passionate commitment to liberty as the form of social organization most in harmony with reality and man's nature, because it's where I was first exposed to in-depth thinkers such as Mises and Hayek."

He went on: "in short, market principles have changed my life and guide everything I do." Such ideas have expanded their reach into Republican Party and Tea Party causes. Over the last nearly four decades, the Kochs have formed an immensely influential political donors' organization that, early in the 2016 presidential campaign, sent a reported $889 million to conservative candidates via super

PACs and advocacy groups. The Koch family runs a reported $50 million statistics organization that gathers data on Americans for its clients that some analysts say is more powerful than the analytics for the Republican Party—about how people vote, interact online, choose cars, and more. Socially conservative though the influential Koch brothers may be, their political activism began a half-century ago in sync with Rose Wilder Lane's principles of economic freedom.

After 1980, Roger's involvement in the Libertarian Party waned. By the 1980s he had returned to the Republicans, putting his efforts into the Liberty Caucus, a conservative branch. He remained a visible and involved spokesman for the Little House books and related projects, but he did not run for office again.

During the years Roger expanded the reach of Laura's stories to wider audiences and received their substantial income, a small public library in Mansfield to which Laura had tried to leave royalty income struggled. The details of this discrepancy have remained mostly private, but some facts emerged in 1999, when those who ran the little library realized that Laura had intended to leave them money. She'd stipulated in her will that Rose would inherit the Little House book copyrights but that after Rose's death the library would get them. But neither Laura nor the drafter of her will had considered that the copyrights might expire before Rose died, and that copyright law took precedence over a will. Rose authorized the renewal of the Little House book copyrights as each expired, because they otherwise would have expired during her lifetime. At that time, the law required authors to renew copyright after twenty-eight years or lose the rights. The first book, *Little House in the Big Woods*, hit the twenty-eight-year mark in 1960. The copyrights for *Farmer Boy*, *Little House on the Prairie*, *On the Banks of Plum Creek*, *By the Shores of Silver Lake*, and *The Long Winter* were similarly renewed in 1961, 1963, 1965, 1967, and 1968, respectively. When Rose died at the end of October 1968, Roger inherited the copyrights. In 1969 and 1970, he renewed the copyrights for the two remaining books, *Little Town on the Prairie* and *These Happy Golden Years*. He had to hire a Missouri lawyer to represent him in reopening Laura's estate for this purpose. He wrote to a probate judge that Rose's death "gives rise under a federal law to a power in Mrs. Wilder's estate which should be exercised in order satisfactorily to conclude my responsibilities with respect to Mrs. Lane's affairs." Within a few years, the lawyer assigned to Laura's estate in the matter turned over the last copyrights to Roger.

The library then received royalty payments

covering ten months (for *Little Town on the Prairie*) and twenty months (for *These Happy Golden Years*) to represent the period of time between Rose's death and when the copyrights were turned over to Roger. The payment totaled $28,011. That amount offers a clue to the extraordinary value of the other Little House books. One expert estimated the literary and media business of the Little House books, spin-off books, television show, and other enterprises and products to be worth $100 million. In 1999, the library sued Roger's estate and his daughter, Abigail, claiming that income due to the library had been diverted away from it starting in 1968 with Rose's death. A judge assigned a mediator to settle the question of claims to the copyrights of the last two books, which had been assigned to Roger during the settling of Rose's estate. Even for two books, the royalties probably would yield a significant income. The library agreed to renounce claims to the last two books and it received a sum from the MacBride estate and HarperCollins. The final amount was not made public; the *Kansas City Star* reported during negotiations that the amount was $875,000.

Roger had created a Little House brand with the spin-off books and the television show. Fans responded to his efforts. They wanted to hear, over and over, Laura's simple messages, and he had obliged by reproducing and offering them through every medium he could. One might observe that creating such a large media network collided some with the values of the Little House books themselves: that the simple things are best, and that the value of life is not money but freedom.

12

WHAT WE WANT

I wandered through waving grasses and wild-
flowers near what used to be the southwestern
edge of Silver Lake in De Smet, South Dakota.
A woman ambling on the path ahead of me pulled
a handful of the tough blades of grass and began
twisting them into a figure-eight. I knew what
she was doing—she was seeing if the grass would
form a hay stick like those the early settlers
burned for fuel during the harsh winters. As we
passed each other, I smiled and nodded at her
handiwork—both of us understood. She left, and
I turned my face into the warm wind, watching
the pink light suffuse milkweed blossoms. The
goldenrod and thigh-high grasses rustled this
way and that.

A half mile or so north of where I stood, one
remaining portion of Silver Lake still holds water
and flows into the marsh called the Big Slough.
In the 1920s, officials had drained a big part of
the lake into a series of ditches to create more
farmland. Plans have emerged for restoring the
original lake.

I imagined Laura standing near here in the
predawn, pausing on her way to the well. Birds

would have screamed above the once-rippling waters. I asked myself what it was that inspired me about this flat, mostly treeless, incessantly windy, hot-in-summer, deadly-cold-in-winter land.

Later that afternoon, history consultant Roland Rydstrom drove me (and a man who was studying Wilder-era buildings) three miles north of De Smet to the site of Laura and Almanzo's former tree claim. It is now the municipal airport. Rydstrom, an enthusiastic and talkative native of Indiana, parked his sedan on the side of Route 25. We stood across the pavement from a ragged row of twisted box elders. Almanzo Wilder planted these circa 1885. They're all that's left of the grove he tried to save on this tree claim. They amazed me. I ran around with my smartphone, videoing the two men striding up to the fence, trying to get as close as they could to the trees.

In these gnarled trees, we all perceived the very resilience Almanzo and Laura had found on their first failed farm. What's important is not that they had failed but that they'd tried. Many fans of Laura Ingalls Wilder understand that, in adoring her, they love a myth: in surviving extremes, people build themselves, and they build America.

Rose and Laura together created this myth— the frontier as a place for optimistic courage, the pioneers as heroes. "Everything came at us out of the west—storms, blizzards, grasshoppers, burning hot winds, and fire—yet it seemed that we wanted nothing so much as we wanted to keep on going west." This sentence, almost certainly written by Rose, appeared in the last known revision of Laura's life story "Pioneer Girl." It prefigured the Little House frontier legend. The family could handle all adversity, in part because they could always choose to shed their troubles and move on. The American frontier offered a promise of unfettered opportunity.

Rose and Laura created an idealized story of the American West, built on their beliefs that people should make their own destinies and be strong.

Rose knew that stark truths about the drudgery and hardships of pioneer life would not appeal to young readers. So she applied her narrative skills to making Laura's experiences into adventures. Rose edited and rewrote scrupulously and without asking Laura. Over time, Laura adjusted to these rewrites. Of course, she watched over them and read the late proofs and, when some detail was wrong, Laura corrected it. Vernacular from the wrong era, overdramatization, and missed details—all these irritated Laura. One can see this irritation at the Detroit Library, in marks she made on the late manuscripts of "The Long Winter" and "These Happy Golden Years." Laura ran her pencil like an angry zigzag through lines Rose had crafted describing two boys on mules caught in a tornado. Laura didn't want the boys to yell, "Run, run!" as Rose had written; she crossed that part out. She also crossed out a bit Rose had crafted that said the mules were still "wildly running in the air" as the storm lifted them up.

Reading Laura's penciled changes—her efforts to tamp down Rose's tendency to overdramatize— as I sat in the Burton Historical Collection reading room holding the manuscript in my hands, I could sense her frustration.

Their joint efforts led, as we've seen, to huge success. One mark of that success is that the American Library Association created the Laura Ingalls Wilder award, of which Laura was the first recipient. Another is that Laura appeared on a US postage stamp in 1993 after her devotees' decades-long campaigns. She's an icon. Rose's and Laura's efforts over the thirteen years they collaborated on the Little House books created heroes and heroines out of pioneers where none had been before.

But they paid a price for their triumph. The myth creation severed Rose and Laura's relationship. It happened slowly. Rose had pulled away from Laura gradually from age sixteen onward, and we've seen that, when they tried to live together in the 1920s and 1930s, during the period when they worked on most of the Little House books, their strong personalities clashed. They sustained a strained détente for a while, but Rose withdrew under the stress of shaping and revising her mother's writing.

• • •

The books have transformed how we view pioneers and, therefore, how we view what it means to be an American. Laura's life has become an example not just of western migration but of virtues associated with that migration: courage, perseverance, even triumph.

As early as 1937, Laura became aware of the possible symbolism she as a pioneer could have in American culture. This attention shows in the speech she handwrote and delivered at the Book Week event in Detroit in 1937. This was the only time Laura spoke publicly about the historical significance of her life story. She portrayed her life as representative of a quintessentially American experience, as I quoted earlier: "I realized that I had seen and lived it all—all the successive phases of the frontier, first the frontiersman then the pioneer, then the farmers, and the towns. Then I understood that in my own life I represented a whole period of American history," she said. Her goal, she noted, was to tell children "what it is that made America as they know it."

Laura was telling her fans that she herself helped make the unique American spirit because she had grown up as a pioneer. She would not have reflected on her life in this way without the hindsight she and her daughter had perfected as Depression-era writers newly appreciating the hard years between 1870 and 1885. As I discussed, such a perspective rode on the work of popular historians like Frederick Jackson Turner, who wrote that settling the frontier uniquely formed Americans' imagination and identity. He said this happened because citizens made their ways west into primitive lands, built crude homesteads, and established prosperous farms and settlements. In his seminal 1893 essay, "The Significance of the Frontier in American History," Turner claimed that the "perennial rebirth, [the] fluidity of American life, [the] expansion westward with its new opportunities, its continuous touch with the simplicity of primitive society, *furnish the forces dominating American character*" (emphasis mine). In her speech in Detroit, Laura was saying that she, through her books, was a living example of how the migration did that.

She did not comment on another possible theme that her life, through the books, might have suggested: to influence our political leanings. I've questioned, in the years since I began studying the making of the Little House books, whether the books quietly caused me to admire libertarian ideas. The answer is: not often. The Little House books do not automatically convert readers to libertarian or individualist or antitax points of view. People who already think in such ways might be drawn to the books more than they would otherwise. And people who do *not* espouse libertarian ideals have found in the books appealing messages about wilderness, self-sufficiency, and pluck. The books speak universally, somehow, to Americans who consider courage in harsh landscapes part of the national character. But it is also fair to say that the books bolster values prized by libertarians and other antitax conservatives.

For myself, I'm aware that the ideas the books celebrate may have influenced me in a general way. I dislike chaff in organizations, for example, can't stand red tape and ponderous debate that seems to lead nowhere. The Little House books offered early lessons that influenced these attitudes. They also instilled in me attitudes of the more "rugged individualist" libertarians: Where did I learn to appreciate wild animals and respect their need to go on their ways? When did I first think that the government went too far in slaughtering so many bison? I find in myself a few personal standards about self-sufficiency that have nothing to do with politics, and probably much to do with having internalized values conveyed by these books. Where did I get the idea that doing work myself is superior to getting someone else to do it? Or the idea that I was born in the wrong century? It's likely that Rose Wilder Lane put those ideas in my head.

Why Rose, and not Laura? Because they took different approaches to politics. We've seen that Laura and Rose, in the time they wrote the Little House series, considered the public ready for this pioneer story. Yet Laura wrote her stories to honor her father foremost and incidentally to counter the weakness and whining that she felt Americans had succumbed to in the 1930s. Rose, on the other hand, fully recast the pioneer story. Rose's work pushed readers to think for ourselves. She created an ideology of individual freedom and limited government in opposition to communism, the New Deal, and the buildup to a world war. While Laura was a storyteller in the folk tradition, Rose, a modern writer, was a public philosopher.

Rose's libertarian ideology shapes the Little House books not because Rose hoped to sneak in political lessons but because to her this interpretation of her mother's life was one that captured their achievement in being pioneers. She realized and reinforced this interpretation by inserting fictional, overtly political scenes. I mentioned a few of these scenes in this book's introduction. Here are three more:

- In the last scene of the final version of *Farmer Boy*, a wagon maker, Mr. Paddock, has invited Almanzo to become an apprentice wheelwright. Almanzo's parents are fighting over the offer. He listens as his mother declares that she and her husband will have failed if their children work for other people instead of for themselves. He realizes that he knows exactly what he wants. He believes that only farmers, working for themselves on their own land, can be free.

- As I've discussed earlier, the character Laura has an epiphany about being responsible for herself during the Fourth of July ceremony in *Little Town on the Prairie.*

- Laura witnesses a rant by Mrs. McKee, the dressmaker Laura works for in *These Happy Golden Years.* The scene occurs in the McKees' empty homestead claim shanty, where Laura has come to keep her company while her husband works in town. The law requires that Mrs. McKee and her husband's land be occupied for six months a year if they want to "prove up" after five years and own the 160 acres. But they don't have the money to leave their jobs and buy farm supplies yet. Mrs. McKee complains, as the hot summer winds blow outside the window: "If he hasn't got money, he's got to earn it, so why do they make a law that he's got to stay on a claim, when he can't? . . . I could be earning something, dressmaking, to help buy tools and seeds, if somebody didn't have to sit on this claim." It's a complaint against government meddling. Laura's telling of this episode in her "Pioneer Girl" manuscript had not included any discussion of the government's rules or how they made Mrs. McKee feel.

If these scenes Rose added underscore themes of American freedom, her removal of others during the drafting and revisions underscores Rose's interest in advancing individual liberty even more powerfully. Here are a few examples of episodes in Laura's life that, if included in the Little House books, would have muddied the simplicity of a family standing alone in a new and awesome land.

- In most of the books, the Ingalls family is portrayed as living alone and far from neighbors. But in reality, the family was alone on the prairies only when traveling by wagon along a barely discernible track through the grass. The rest of the time, they lived near others in camps and houses. The first historian to realize this was Anderson, as I've said. In "Pioneer Girl," Laura had reported that the family took in a man named Walter Ogden to spend the winter with them in the surveyor's house. One wonders if Rose, late in life, began to believe her own revisions as facts—such as Pa's remark, which Rose had inserted into the final book, that the family would be living sixty miles from anyone else.

- In *The Long Winter*, as we've seen, the Ingalls family retreats for warmth to the back room of Pa's new store building in De Smet. They ration their last potatoes, take turns grinding seed wheat in the coffee mill, and share the meager loaves Ma bakes from these last provisions. They truly did ration food in this way, but the social life inside the house included a couple, George and Maggie Masters, who had been boarding with them all winter. Laura herself told Rose she thought the couple should be removed from the story during their early discussions. We've seen that in "Pioneer Girl" Laura wrote of George's greed and laziness and that Ma delivered Maggie's baby upstairs in the house. Putting George and Maggie into the book would have complicated the fictionalized story, but especially would have obscured the survival theme. The Masters couple were pioneers in Dakota, too, but their attitude didn't exemplify the pioneer spirit.
- The Ingallses traveled west because their farm in Minnesota had failed them in the locust-plague years. Further west, they "filed on" homesteads, meaning they applied at land offices for government-issued land.

And, again, once they had the claim, they had to live on it half the year. Although the Homestead Act's offers of free land for anyone who can live on it figures fairly heavily in the plot of *By the Shores of Silver Lake*, it appears there as a sort of backdrop to courage. Pa tells the family, "Well, girls, I've bet Uncle Sam fourteen dollars against a hundred and sixty acres of land, that we can make out to live on the claim for five years. Going to help me win the bet?" And Laura promises, but "soberly," because her character wants to keep on moving west, to "fly with the birds."

- Laura's sister, Mary, attended a school for the blind in Vinton, Iowa. In the books, her family works hard to pay her way, and Laura contributes by teaching school. The books do not mention that the Ingalls family benefited from the government: Dakota Territory paid the cost of tuition for the seven-year program. This fact was omitted, though Laura did mention it in her original memoir, "Pioneer Girl."

- Rose revised Laura's original picture of the costs and risks of isolation and constant migration. These details didn't make it into the final drafts: A baby brother, Freddie, who died at nine months when the Ingallses were on the road. A miserable year living and working in an Iowa hotel. Unpleasant encounters in the Dakotas with the American Indians, including a grim tale of a doctor who stole an Indian baby being prepared for burial, sending the corpse to Chicago for study, thus causing a near-war at a railroad camp. Such stories would only have detracted from the Little House books' portrayal of pioneer integrity and courage.

Rose exerted a quiet power when she added or removed episodes in Laura's frontier stories. Sometimes, under immense deadline pressure, Rose rewrote or edited scenes in the way that seemed to her truest and resonated the most. She did not necessarily do so with a plan to share her political views. Rose felt so strongly about individual freedom that it was inevitable these views would inhabit rewritten sections.

The nature of their collaboration on the early books, like *Little House in the Big Woods*, *Farmer Boy*, *Little House on the Prairie*, and *On the Banks of Plum Creek* resembled that of a teacher, Rose, tutoring a student, her mother Laura. The collaboration evolved after 1936. Other scholars and writers have concluded that Laura did more of her own writing in the later books, after she had benefitted from Rose's teaching and guidance in the earlier books. I believe that, although Laura had become more skillful at putting together narratives as the years went by, she did not advance in her ability to structure her narratives around a theme and continued to rely on Rose for that contribution.

During their work on the first four of the Little House books, Rose enlivened and simplified Laura's prose and built structure. After 1936, working on the last four original Little House books, Rose inserted ideas that she also wrote in her libertarian treatise *The Discovery of Freedom*. By then, Rose was inserting political principles into everything she wrote—magazine articles for *Woman's Day*, letters to Jasper Crane and others, and the Little House books. It's my opinion that she didn't think to herself, "I am going to sneak ideas into my mother's books and create a story that will become a text for the next political movement." No, she was just being herself.

Rose developed as a writer over two distinct periods, and the Little House books also reflect her own growth: Rose's book-length profiles of famous people like Henry Ford and Herbert Hoover show that she believed all accomplished people were products of their early years, and she wrote about them through what had happened to them as children. She often didn't interview the subjects themselves. That's why she imagined Hoover trading a handmade sled for a "boughten" one and why in 1940, assigned to write a story for *Woman's Day* about the young Minnesota governor Harold Stassen, Rose didn't talk to Stassen but drove to Stassen's parents' farm and asked them what their son had been like as a child. One sees evidence of hard work on farms as the ideal life in the first four Little House books.

After 1938, Rose's writing changed. She stopped writing fiction and her journalism comprised mostly political opinion. She had decided that America was the best country on earth but was still tremendously flawed, and that, to get it right before everything fell apart, Americans needed to go back to the Founding Fathers, and particularly to the Declaration of Independence, for political, social, and moral guidance. After 1938, Rose believed that democracy itself was a flawed construct because majority rule took away the power of the individual. Rose was working with Laura on the last four of the original Little House books during those years, and in these books, as we've seen, political themes emerge in dialogue and action. The Little House books after 1938, starting with *By the Shores of Silver Lake*, incorporated Rose's political thinking in manifest ways. Some of the scenes became fables for the power of the individual.

The result was a set of stories that I and a few million others can't get enough of. The result was a multimillion-dollar cultural phenomenon.

• • •

Roughly sixty million Little House books have sold. The character who felt sorry for wolves, loved horses, and helped her father twist hay sticks for the stove has inspired millions of fans, many of them children but many of them adults too, around the world. Devoted amateur researchers still seek new details about the lives behind the Little House characters. After the television show first aired, a new wave of enthusiasts, including President Ronald Reagan, took the stories to heart. But this large group has only slowly turned its eyes toward Rose, the quiet and important shaper of the Little House myth, who molded it in response to national problems.

Because Rose and Laura never talked about their writing partnership, some Laura fans seem to believe that shedding light on the collaboration constitutes a kind of betrayal.

Rose's biographer William Holtz was not the first to bring the collaboration to light. Rosa Ann Moore, a children's literature scholar, documented Rose's influence on and editing of the Little House books in her 1977 paper, "The Little House Books: Rose-Colored Classics," which she delivered at a conference that year. Moore had spent three months that summer in the Virginia office of Roger Lea MacBride, going through the papers he'd inherited from Rose. Earlier she'd faced the crucial question that had occurred to me and probably many others, but which I had repressed: how could Laura, who until she was sixty-five had written only terse farming columns, have composed books so wonderful, with characters so clearly drawn and events so cohesive?

Moore felt that Rose was like Martha of the Bible laboring in the kitchen while Laura was Mary in the living room sharing "the outpouring of feeling and memory" with visitors. In other words, the books needed both women to make a complete picture, but Rose had the thankless role.

The Wilder historian, Bill Anderson, was the next to study the family papers. He published two well-researched articles in the academic journal *South Dakota History*. The articles detailed Laura's early writing career and her work with Rose in drafting the first two Little House books. Anderson argued that Rose trained Laura and that over time Laura did more of her own writing. Anderson decided not to continue writing scholarly articles after this groundbreaking start; he wrote and edited several popular books about Laura and Rose, Mark Twain, and the von Trapp family.

I began studying Laura's collaboration with her daughter after I read William Holtz's biography of Rose. I believe fans may have criticized or rejected this work because of its unfortunate title, *The Ghost in the Little House*. Nowhere does he say that Rose wrote the whole series as a true ghostwriter. Of course, the truth—that Rose was a very important quiet partner in the writing—still can offend.

Holtz told me that he was unprepared for the anger and betrayal fans expressed after reading his biography. His task, writing about Rose's life, presented her collaboration with Laura as an accepted fact—it had, after all, come up in detail in articles by Anderson and Moore as early as the late 1970s, although those articles were in scholarly journals. Holtz's book received wider attention after the school paper at the University of Missouri interviewed him and the story went out on one of the newspaper wire services. Then it became national news, and from the public's point of view, it might have seemed as if Laura's and Rose's collaboration had never before been revealed.

Holtz received anonymous calls from upset Little House book fans who seemed to suggest that he had gained some kind of pleasure from shocking people with his research: "Are you happy *now?*" Or, "Laura wouldn't have done that." Roger Lea MacBride withdrew his permission for Holtz to compile a book of letters between Rose and Rexh Meta, her Albanian ward. Some of the Little House sites would not sell Holtz's book. The reaction, Holtz said, suggested that many of us had blurred Laura the actual person with Laura the fictional character. He said later he realized that "the whole issue of sole authorship or corporate authorship" underpinned scholarship on both women. He later wrote a separate article touching on the points I'm considering in this book, and he told me that he realized dealing with Rose's political principles in her mother's books would be the next step. He said, "I wasn't sure I wanted to be that smart."

I would not respond to any implication that this quest of mine was smart. It did seem necessary. Yet my understanding of the collaboration, and of the political ideas that reveal themselves in the products of that collaboration, could not dampen my enthusiasm for the literary value of the Little House books. They remain evocative tales of a strong-willed girl who loved wild animals in untamed lands. The strength of an ordinary girl living in extraordinary circumstances remains true to something elemental in who the real Laura was.

Who—one might ask—owns the Little House story? Why do the Little House books particularly inspire political conservatives, on the one hand—Tea Party members, and homeschoolers—people who hold up the self-sufficient simplicity of the stories as evidence that America's unique soul comes from frontier hardships? On the other, why do the Little House books inspire progressive left-wing advocates of back-to-the-land independence in the wilderness?

The answer may lie in the evolving ideas of the Libertarian Party itself. Founded on the idea of individual freedom and small government, the movement has (to this observer's mind) wavered from an ultraconservative party standing against taxes and government programs to a radically progressive one that wants to end drug laws. I don't think it's clear to many people what being a libertarian, small "l," means today.

The real Laura was complex—less conservative than the Right would like to believe and less idealistic about pioneer life than readers can tell from her books. And Rose's beliefs ran radical on political principle but neutral on the subject of her mother's history.

Somehow these two women, mother and daughter, overcame their fraught personal dynamic, came together, and made the Little House books. They built a children's series that built loyalty for the ideas of the Founding Fathers, and for wilderness and wildlife. The books have represented the pioneer allegory's triumphant side. Many of those pioneer home-steaders failed, and many were made miserable in failing. But all of us admire those who tried.

ACKNOWLEDGMENTS

I would like to thank all the colleagues and friends whose interest in this project goes back many years.

I owe the greatest indebtedness to editors and colleagues whose perspective enabled me to understand what I knew, especially Nell Lake, who patiently guided my drafts during spring and summer 2015; Cal Barksdale, my thoughtful editor at Arcade Publishing, who urged me deeper into my argument; my colleague Farah Stockman, who helped me realize the importance of the politics and pushed me to get my idea out there early; and former *Boston Globe* ideas editor Stephen Heuser, who helped me write this book's premise as a feature article in 2013.

Continuing with the above category, I thank Mark Kramer's Kitchen Workshop in Newton Lower Falls, Massachusetts, who read and commented on drafts for four years: Mark Kramer, who patiently taught me how to write a book and stayed with it; Dan Grossman, who brought me to the workshop; Farah Stockman and Nell Lake (again), whose own work taught and inspired me; Karen Weintraub, who gave me a plan for getting my draft done; and six insightful readers and friends: Michael Fitzgerald, Robert

Weiss, Catherine Buni, Jon Palfremon, Beth Schwartzapfel, and Kathleen Burge.

Thanks to my agent, Craig Kayser, who persisted for months until we found the right publisher, and thanks to LinkedIn (of all things), where he "met" me.

I recognize the many who offered bed and board and transformed research and writing trips into reunions: Cay and Phil Lodine, who for years have provided family-level support and a second home in the Boston area; Julie and Mike Rogers in Zionsville, Indiana; Mark Ruggeberg, Bob Brooks, and Daissy Owen, innkeepers in Iowa City; and Doug Mayer, Edith Tucker, and John Phinney in Randolph, New Hampshire.

Thanks to the archivists and staffers at the Herbert Hoover Presidential Library in West Branch, Iowa, especially archivist Matthew Schaefer and archives technician Spencer Howard. Thanks to Dwight M. Miller, former archivist at Hoover, who became part of the story as he improved scholarship for all. Thanks to Jean Coday and the staff at the Laura Ingalls Wilder Home and Museum for hosting two days of tours; and museum curator Kathy Short in Mansfield for offering local perspective on farming and the Wilders.

Gratitude to the Herbert Hoover Presidential Library Association for their generous research grant.

I built my understanding of my subject on writers, scholars, and researchers who went before, especially those who spent much time talking with me. Thanks especially to William Holtz, author of the first biography of Rose Wilder Lane. He pieced together Rose's collaboration with Laura in letters and other information from many sources years before most of us started. Thanks also to his wife, Lora, who hosted me and my husband during our meeting in 2014. Thanks to writer, editor, and historian William Anderson, a colleague and supporter of my work who has been an expert on the lives of Laura Ingalls Wilder and her family since the 1960s. And thanks to: researcher Gina Terrana of Seattle; writer Susan Wittig Albert, who shared her perspective and her typed file of Rose Wilder Lane's diaries; historian and writer John Miller; researcher John Bass; historical consultant Roland Rydstrom, who took me around De Smet and Walnut Grove; author Barbara Walker, who offered perspective on the Ingalls family's poverty, and who read and improved sections; writer and editor Pamela Smith Hill; and researcher Nansie Cleaveland. Your dedication and perspective served me well. I thank all those I met at the LauraPalooza conference in Brookings, South Dakota, in July 2015. And thanks to Josh Katz for outlining the history of the Libertarian Party.

Thanks to Susan Ford Hammaker, the former wife of Roger Lea MacBride, for telling her memories of Roger and Rose and for hosting me in Key Largo. I extend appreciation to Larry Dennis, editor and publisher of the *Mansfield Mirror-Republican*, and his staffers, for sharing memories of Irene Lichty.

Thanks to lawyer Sean Ploen for his navigation through the world of contracts, Tim Good and the staff at Good Design, for expert marketing help; and James "Mac" McComas III for research in the Hader Papers.

For early support of my project, I thank writers Paul Kramer, Wendy McClure, and Laura Waterman, and editor Jennifer Huget of *Connecticut Explored* magazine.

My parents, Gloria N. Woodside and the late Robert H. Woodside, gave me Laura Ingalls Wilder's books, and my brother, John T. Woodside, shared a keen interest in them from the early years.

Thanks to my husband, Nat Eddy, for loyalty, companionship, and occasional research help; and to our daughters, Elizabeth T. Eddy and Annie S. Eddy, who traveled with this story their entire lives but remained enthusiastic with me.

My good friends taught me that motivation means doing the work. Sincere thanks to them, especially Lynn Cochrane and Ted Potter, Dody Cox, Noelle Crombie, Jan Cronan, Mags

DePetris, the Rev. Jonathan Folts, Martha H. Lyon, Traci Marando, Priscilla Martel, Jenifer McShane, John B. Paulson, my friends in the Society of Environmental Journalists, Joann Sweasy, and JoAnn Walden.

APPENDIX I

PAPER MOVEMENTS: TRACING TWO SETS OF DOCUMENTS

Laura and Rose worked together for nine years in Missouri, but for most of their collaboration they lived apart. After Laura died in 1957, Rose stayed at the farmhouse on Rocky Ridge Farm for a few weeks, when she almost certainly burned or discarded some of the drafts and correspondence of her parents, as Wilder historian William Anderson has determined. Several boxes remained upstairs, though, so many pages of handwritten and typed notes and drafts were left intact in Missouri.

Rose's death in 1968 was sudden. She probably had not organized (or discarded) the boxes of old papers for several years. Rose had, though, been throwing away correspondence from most people as she received it for about twenty-five years.

This list below explains which papers each woman held when she died, and where the papers ended up. The paper movements prove that the Little House book creation story is one of two legacies, not one.

1. A box of papers in Laura's possession from her death until 1982, when they joined Rose's collection at the Herbert Hoover Presidential Library

The following list of papers were found upstairs at Rocky Ridge Farm in 1957 and were kept there for twenty-five years. In May 1982, Rose's heir, Roger Lea MacBride, went to Rocky Ridge with Herbert Hoover Presidential Library archivist Dwight Miller. They met Irene Lichty LeCount (who had remarried after the death of her husband) and visited the upstairs. Miller said in an interview that he was very excited to open boxes and find typed manuscripts with Laura's handwriting on them. With Roger's approval, the following papers were transferred to the Hoover Library:

- Typescript drafts of several Little House books
- Drafts of articles by Rose
- Hundreds of negatives of photos of Middle East Relief, from Rose's travels
- Early prints of the Wilder family
- Letters between Laura and Harper and Row

Miller wrote to William Anderson, who was then doing graduate work at South Dakota State University in Brookings. He said they "reviewed the materials in storage in the home and I selected a carton of Little House book gallies [sic], and typed drafts with handwritten corrections" plus the other materials listed above.

In an interview, Anderson wryly called this paper transfer "the raid" because it came with no warning to the Wilder home's board of directors, and because it removed so many papers from the place where they had been last used. Note that Anderson was instrumental in Rose's collection moving from MacBride's house in Virginia to the Hoover Library, in preserving artifacts for a museum in De Smet (the setting of the last four books), and in preserving the properties on Rocky Ridge Farm in Missouri. He could not be said to favor one property over another.

From the point of view of a researcher, the raid served a purpose. These papers had not been on display at the museum in Mansfield, nor were they open for research. At the Hoover Library, these papers became available to scholars and the public.

2. Papers found in Mansfield, and still in Mansfield

Final handwritten manuscripts—not all of them complete—of several of the Little House books were with Laura's papers when she died. These occasionally go on display under glass at the Laura Ingalls Wilder Historic Home and Museum. When not on display, these tablets reside in a bank vault in Mansfield. These manuscripts could represent Laura's last handwritten drafts, which she would have copied from earlier drafts that Rose had worked on using a typewriter.

- Final handwritten manuscripts for:
  - *Little House in the Big Woods*
  - *Little House on the Prairie*
  - *Farmer Boy*
  - *On the Banks of Plum Creek*
  - *By the Shores of Silver Lake*
- Various letters, periodicals, and memorabilia

3. Papers Laura donated to the Detroit Public Library

- *These Happy Golden Years* handwritten final manuscript
- *These Happy Golden Years* typed final manuscript with some edits inserted by Laura, particularly of the storm story after page 240
- *The Long Winter* handwritten final manuscript
- *The Long Winter* typescript final manuscript

4. Papers Laura donated to the Pomona, California, Library

Laura corresponded with a children's librarian, Clara Webber, from the late 1940s. She donated some manuscripts to the library in 1950:

- *By the Shores of Silver Lake* typescript final
- *Little Town on the Prairie* handwritten final

5. Papers at Rose's house in Danbury, Connecticut, when she died, now at the Hoover Library

Roger Lea MacBride allowed some scholars to read Rose's papers in his office in Charlottesville, Virginia, in the late 1970s. Donald Zochert, Rosa Ann Moore, William Anderson, and William Holtz all reviewed the papers this way. At Anderson's suggestion, Roger donated Rose's papers to the Herbert Hoover Presidential Library in 1980. Some of these papers could have been already transferred to Roger Lea MacBride's house in Virginia at the time of Rose's death, but most of them he had moved out of her house in Connecticut after her death on October 30, 1968. The Hoover Library was interested in the collection because of Rose's biography of Hoover and her correspondence with him.

- Rose's diaries
- Rose's journals
- Drafts of letters from Rose to publishers and friends
- Carbons of letters from Rose to publishers and friends
- Letters from friends pre-1939
- Letters from Laura pre-1939
- Tax returns from the 1930s

- Garden notebook
- "Books read" notebook
- Miscellaneous photos
- Miscellaneous clippings
- Various articles and books by Rose

6. Missing documents

The following documents have been thrown away or lost:

- Letters to Rose after 1939, when she stopped saving correspondence
- Most intermediate drafts of these six Little House books:
  - *Little House in the Big Woods*
  - *Little House on the Prairie*
  - *Farmer Boy*
  - *The Long Winter*
  - *Little Town on the Prairie*
  - *These Happy Golden Years*
- Tax returns and personal correspondence of Laura Ingalls Wilder

7. Documents in other collections

Although Rose herself threw out most correspondence after 1939, some letters sent to her were copied by the senders. Letters from Rose to her agent and friends can be found in other collections, as noted in the Notes.

APPENDIX II

NOTES ON THE DRAFTING OF THE LITTLE HOUSE BOOKS

All but one of the Little House books were drafted, one by one, out of Laura's memoir, "Pioneer Girl." (*Farmer Boy* Laura drafted and Rose revised based on interviews with Almanzo Wilder.) Laura finished "Pioneer Girl" in May 1930. Rose typed and revised it and peddled it to magazines in New York that fall for serialization. Rose revised "Pioneer Girl" twice more between then and late 1931. Rose drafted the first Little House book out of "Pioneer Girl" in 1931. The two women continued work on the series from then until 1943. They always began with pages from various versions of the revised "Pioneer Girl" and proceeded to Rose's typed revisions, which Laura then copied over as she further revised, sending the handwritten drafts back to Rose for typing, after which Rose returned the handwritten drafts to Laura.

In the catalog below, I have made my best guess at the timing of versions. The location in bold type at the end of each entry is where this document was first found after the women died.

In several cases, what I call "version 1" begins

with pages pulled out of the revised "Pioneer Girl" manuscripts. "Pioneer Girl" went through four versions, beginning with Laura's handwritten memoir on tablets, which were found in Missouri after she died. The later versions of "Pioneer Girl," all of them typed drafts, were: Rose's first revision of 160 pages, which she sent to her first agent, Carl Brandt (and which researchers often call the first "Brandt version"); Rose's revised 123-page draft, which was probably also sent to Brandt (the second Brandt version); and Rose's final revision of 203 pages, which she sent to her new agent, George Bye.

Little House in the Big Woods

Version 1. Although not conceived yet as a separate book, the earliest draft of the story appears in "Pioneer Girl" in both Laura's handwritten version and in the first of the typed revisions by Rose, on pages 7–23. **Handwritten pages found in Missouri with Laura's papers. Typed draft of the first "Brandt version" found in Connecticut with Rose's papers.**

Version 2. "When Grandma Was a Little Girl," twenty-two pages long, double-spaced typed. Rose made this version in November 1930, after magazines had rejected her first round of submissions of the full "Pioneer Girl" memoir. This typed manuscript is told from Laura's point of view and in the third person; but she's called "Grandma." Rose mailed a version of this manuscript to her friends Berta and Elmer Hader, children's book writers and illustrators who lived in Nyack, New York, who then passed it on to Marion Fiery at Knopf. **Found in Connecticut with Rose's papers.**

Version 3. Wisconsin segment from "Pioneer Girl," which Rose revised again in a new draft of the entire "Pioneer Girl." This section measures six pages long (pages 8–14). On page 11, Rose notes in pen in the margin: "take something from juvenile." That is proof that this draft came later than "When Grandma Was a Little Girl," which Rose always called "the juvenile." **Connecticut.**

Version 4. The next revision of the Wisconsin segment, still not conceived as a separate book, appeared on pages 12–21 in Rose's revision of "Pioneer Girl" for her new agent, George Bye. This draft of the full "Pioneer Girl," known as the Bye version, is the one fans of the books have most often photocopied. **Connecticut.**

Version 5. After Knopf children's editor Marion Fiery saw "When Grandma Was a Little Girl" and asked Laura to expand it into a chapter book, Laura worked on pages to add to the story. No complete version of this draft—if indeed she did redraft everything at this stage—seems to exist. For this work to expand the story, Laura referred to the twenty-two "Grandma" pages and an earlier version of "Pioneer Girl" for those Wisconsin stories that Rose had taken out of "Grandma": the story of cousin Charley getting stung by bees and the stories of Pa Ingalls when he was young. She also added scenes describing how Pa Ingalls cleaned his gun. In this draft, Laura added more descriptions to a paragraph Rose had used in the setting, "There were only trees where wild animals had their homes." Laura also added this line to the early paragraphs: "A wagon track ran before the little house, turning and twisting among the trees of the Big Woods where wild animals lived." **Missouri.**

Version 6. Some pages of a typed draft preceding the next draft were found in Missouri with Laura's papers. **Missouri.**

Version 7. Laura produced a full draft, inserting and attaching typed scenes, certainly taken out of the previous typed draft. This appears to be the draft from which Rose produced a final typed draft. **Missouri.**

Version 8. Final typescript. There must have been one, but it has been lost or destroyed. **Location uncertain.**

Farmer Boy

Version 1. Laura drafted this in the Rock House, the house Rose built for her, in 1932. This draft is probably not extant. Early notes sketching scenes were left behind in the Rocky Ridge farmhouse when Laura died. **Missouri.**

Version 2. Between early March and mid-August 1932, Rose edited and revised the book into a typed draft she sent to *Harper's*. **This draft is missing.**

Version 3. After *Harper's* rejected the manuscript in September 1932, Laura worked on it again. The handwritten draft of the book—which includes many scenes not in the final book and whose ending differs greatly because it ends with the family leaving for Minnesota—probably is Laura's revision. **Missouri.**

Version 4. Final typescript. In January 1933, after the publisher asked how it was coming, Rose worked on it again. The typescript, 226 pages long, was in Missouri but was taken to the Hoover Library in 1980. **Missouri.**

Little House on the Prairie

Version 1. Laura started drafting using the handwritten opening pages of "Pioneer Girl," which cover her earliest memories and the period when the Ingalls family lived in the

Osage Diminished Reserve, which they called Indian Territory. These pages are now published on pages 1–22 of *Pioneer Girl: The Annotated Autobiography* (South Dakota Historical Society Press, 2014). The originals are stored at the Laura Ingalls Wilder Home and Museum but are not open to the public. They are available on microfilm at the University of Missouri and at the Herbert Hoover Presidential Library. **Missouri.**

Versions 2 and 3. Laura might also have referred to pages from the typed "Pioneer Girl" (the two Brandt versions) or the last "Pioneer Girl" (the Bye version). **Connecticut.**

Version 4 and 5. Handwritten draft pages, rough portions of chapters 2, 3, 5–19, 25, and 26, and a tablet covering Chapter 15 through the end, both were found at Rocky Ridge. Those are also on microfilm. **Missouri.**

Version 6. A later draft of the book was found at Rocky Ridge. **Missouri.**

Version 7. Final typescript was found with Rose's papers. **Connecticut.**

On the Banks of Plum Creek
Version 1. The earliest version of many of the episodes in this book was in Laura's first draft of

"Pioneer Girl" and can be read in the published *Pioneer Girl* on pages 64–96.

Version 2. Presumably Laura handwrote a first draft and gave it to Rose around the time Rose left Rocky Ridge Farm to live in Columbia, Missouri. **Draft missing.**

Version 3. "Draft A," a typed version. Portions of this were in Missouri and moved to the Hoover Library in 1982. **Missouri.**

Version 3. "Draft B," a typed version. Again, only portions of it survived and traveled from Missouri to the Hoover Library in 1982. **Missouri.**

Version 4. The final typed copy was duplicated with carbon paper, which Rose did (or had hired typists do) as a standard practice. Rose would have mailed this to Laura to look over. The carbon was found with Laura's papers and moved to the Hoover in 1982. **Missouri.**

By the Shores of Silver Lake
Version 1. The handwritten version of "Pioneer Girl" (*Pioneer Girl*, pages 151–199).

Version 2. Notes plus pages from "Pioneer Girl." **Connecticut.**

Version 3. Handwritten manuscript by Laura. **Missouri.**

Version 4. Various intermediate drafts. **Connecticut.**

Version 5. The final typed manuscript was sent to Laura, who made changes in pencil. She donated this manuscript to the Pomona Library in 1950. **Missouri.**

The Long Winter
Version 1. Referring to sections in "Pioneer Girl" about the Hard Winter of 1880–81, Laura worked on this in 1938 and 1939.

The early sections were:
- A seventeen-page story that is part of the second typed draft of "Pioneer Girl," also sent to Brandt. It begins partway down page 92: "The fall rains began on the 25th of September."
- The section on the Hard Winter in the last "Pioneer Girl" draft, the one sent to Rose's new agent George Bye, began on page 115 and ended on page 134.

Laura penciled a first draft and sent the pages to Rose in Connecticut in May 1939. **Draft is missing.**

Version 2 and other intermediate drafts. Rose typed an intermediate draft (or drafts) in Connecticut. Some typed manuscript pages with changes in Laura's handwriting were with Rose's papers when she died. **Most intermediate drafts missing; some pages were in Connecticut.**

Version 3. Laura took the intermediate drafts and handwrote a near-final draft. Laura donated this to the Detroit Library late in life. **Missouri.**

Version 4. Rose worked on it again, and the final version was typed in the East. It was at this stage that the title was changed from "The Hard Winter" to *The Long Winter*, done with a cross-out and a handwritten change on the cover. Laura and Rose objected to the title change. Rose wrote to their agent, George Bye, who quoted the letter to editor Ursula Nordstrom on July 3, 1940: "My mother wrote me about the suggested change in title. She is strongly opposed to a change and I agree with her attitude. . . . My mother has written a book about the Hard Winter, and I think an attempt to conceal that fact from the book's reader is worse than futile. . . . I would suggest to *Harper's*, as a selling scheme, honesty. The jacket is their opportunity to tell the truth that the book is NOT depressing." This typed manuscript was sent to Laura for final review. She donated it to the Detroit Library. **Missouri.**

Final version. It seems a reasonable guess, because several episodes in Version 4 were omitted from the final book, that another version went to the publisher. **This version is missing.**

Little Town on the Prairie and *These Happy Golden Years*

Version 1. In 1939 Laura sketched a list of episodes and mailed them to Rose only about a month after she'd sent Rose a draft of *The Long Winter*. Laura called the volume "Prairie Girl." I think it unlikely that Laura drafted a whole manuscript to send Rose at this stage. Laura was 72 and Almanzo, 82; they were going on a long car trip to South Dakota, and Laura wanted Rose to finish the series if something happened to them (that is, if Laura died on the trip).

Laura, in my opinion, assumed Rose would use the ample material available in "Pioneer Girl" to create early drafts. Laura had written many pages about those early years in the memoir. Pages 227–260 in the published *Pioneer Girl* correspond to *Little Town on the Prairie*; pages 260–324 cover the episodes in *These Happy Golden Years*.

Version 2 and perhaps other intermediate versions. Rose certainly created an intermediate draft. She sent these to Laura, who made changes as she revised Rose's drafts, writing by hand on tablets. Laura donated her late "fair copy" handwritten tablets of *Little Town on the Prairie* to the Pomona Library and those of *These Happy Golden Years* to the Detroit Public Library. These manuscripts contain scenes that did not end up in the published books. **California and Michigan.**

Final versions. The last typed version of *Little Town on the Prairie* is missing. Galley proofs were found in Mansfield, suggesting Laura did not see a typed manuscript before typesetting but reviewed Rose's changes on the galley proofs.

The final version of *These Happy Golden Years* Laura donated to the Detroit Library. She made changes and marks on this that suggest she was seeing some of Rose's wording for the first time. See Chapter 8, "Libertarians in Connecticut." **Mansfield, but whereabouts of some pages unknown.**

Notes

A word about two of the sources cited below:

- I have quoted brief passages from Laura's unedited memoir, "Pioneer Girl." In 2014, the South Dakota Historical Society Press published this narrative, with annotations by Pamela Smith Hill, as *Pioneer Girl: The Annotated Autobiography.* Here I will reference pages in the published version. I did my research for this book by reading Laura's handwriting on microfilm impressions of the original pages. The Laura Ingalls Wilder Historic Home and Museum in Mansfield, Missouri, owns the original pages. The microfilm version is available from the University of Missouri-Columbia.

- I have quoted several letters, diaries, and other papers housed in the Rose Wilder Lane Papers at the Herbert Hoover Presidential Library. I cite this collection as "Hoover." Rose's heir, Roger Lea MacBride, donated many of Rose and Laura's papers to the Hoover Library because Rose wrote a biography of Hoover in 1920 and corresponded with him for many years. Letters between Rose and Laura come from Box 13. Rose's diaries and journals

I quote are from Boxes 19, 20, 21, 22, 23, and 24. Other sources I list by box number. Many of these documents I quote have been previously published in pamphlets, scholarly articles, or books. When possible, I cite those publications, too.

Introduction: Irene Lichty Turns Me Down

22 **"I wish I could explain how I mean about the stoicism of the people"**: Laura to Rose, March 7, 1938, Hoover, box 13. (Letters between Laura and Rose come from this box, and hereafter will be noted by date only.)

22 **And the then wildly popular Western novels of Zane Grey**: Zane Grey (1872–1939) was an Ohio native and dentist who wrote sixty popular Western novels. Laura read Zane Grey before she wrote her books (interview with Kathy Short, Mansfield, Missouri, 2008). Zane Grey often wrote of an unwritten "code" of the West that guided cowboys (honesty, kindness, hospitality, generosity, loyalty, integrity, respect for the land). Dr. Joe Wheeler and Marian Kester Coombs, Zane Grey's West Society, zgws. org.

23 **Laura thought people were complaining too much**: Laura to Rose, March 12, 1937.

28 **Some of Rose's friends guessed but they,**

too, kept silent: The friends were all writers or editors who knew Rose well: Helen "Troub" Boylston; Ernestine Evans; Norma Lee Browning and her husband, Russell Ogg; Berta Hader and her husband Elmer Hader. All of them will come up later.

28 **"You work hard, but you work as you please, and no man can tell you to go or come"**: See Laura Ingalls Wilder, *Farmer Boy*, uniform edition (New York: Harper & Row, 1953), 371.

29 **"This is a free country and every man's got a right to do as he pleases"**: Laura Ingalls Wilder, *The Long Winter* (Harper & Row, uniform edition, 1953), 305.

30 **They say that "we'll weather the blast" and come out happy**: "We'll weather the blast" is a line from an old song: "Let the hurricane roar!/ It will the sooner be o'er!/ We'll weather the blast and land at last,/ On Canaan's happy shore!" Laura's sister Carrie Ingalls Swanzey sent the words to Laura. Rose was the first of the family to use this in a book—she used it in her 1932 novel, *Let the Hurricane Roar*, and it appears again in the Little House books.

30 **the full extent of Laura's revision process was unknown**: In an appendix to his biography *Laura*, Donald Zochert wrote, "The artistic gulf between the draft manuscript,

such as those which Laura donated to the Detroit Public Library, and the final version as it was submitted to the publisher, clean and without requiring any editing, is too large to allow for anything less than an intermediate manuscript. . . . These intermediate drafts, as I say, are missing; should they ever come to light they will measurably illuminate the process by which a true children's classic was created." Donald Zochert, *Laura* (Chicago: Henry Regnery Company, 1976), 247. I interpret what happened differently. I believe that Laura's "draft manuscripts," like those she donated to the Detroit library, had to have been late drafts made by reviewing intermediate (typed) revisions Rose had done, and that, therefore, what's also missing for several of the books are rough early drafts from Laura.

31 a National Public Radio host interviewing William Holtz: The interview took place on May 31, 1993.

Part I: Outsiders
Chapter 1: Laura (1867–1885)
35 "We were on our way again and going in the direction which always brought the happiest changes": The full quotation is: "This was my first ride on a train and was all too short for leaving Walnut Grove in

the morning we were at Tracy by noon, but short as it was I enjoyed it, while I helped Ma with Grace and the satchels and told Mary about every thing I saw, for we were on our way again and going in the direction which always brought the happiest changes." *Pioneer Girl: The Annotated Autobiography*, ed. Pamela Smith Hill (Pierre, SD: South Dakota Historical Society Press, 2014), 145.

38 "The crops were ruined again, and Pa said he'd had enough. He wouldn't stay in such 'a blasted country!' ": *Pioneer Girl*, 94.

39 "Little Brother was not well and the Dr. came": *Pioneer Girl*, 97.

39 "She was dilierous [sic] with an awful fever": *Pioneer Girl*, 141–142.

42 "at least a half dozen railroad companies built tracks west through the upper Midwest": *Dakota: The Story of the Northern Plains*, by Norman K. Risjord (Lincoln: University of Nebraska Press, 2012), 116–118.

44 "Potatoes do hold the heat!": *Pioneer Girl*, 215.

47 "The driving civilization of the country has banished the loom": *The Kansas Farmer*, Wednesday, January 27, 1875, 4.

49 "The storm had lasted only twenty

minutes but it left a desolate, rain-drenched and hail-battered world": Laura Ingalls Wilder, *The First Four Years* (Harper and Row, 1971), 55.

Chapter 2: Rose and Laura (1886–1920)

51 "Laura thought the trouble was all over now": *The First Four Years*, 89.

53 "But for our blunders, Lord in shame": Laura Ingalls Wilder, "The First Three Years and a Year of Grace," handwritten manuscript, Rose Wilder Lane Papers, Hoover, box 16.

55 "The prairies were dust" and "We were camping, my mother said": Rose Wilder Lane in setting for *On the Way Home* (New York: Harper and Row, 1962), 1 and 4.

56 "It sounds to tell it, as if they'd known nothing but calamities": Rose Wilder Lane, "Grandpa's Fiddle" manuscript, Hoover, box 34.

61 "It appears that Laura was a bit pedantic": Teresa Lynn, *Little Lodge on the Prairie: Freemasonry & Laura Ingalls Wilder* (Austin, TX: Tranquility Press, 2014).

62 Years later, Rose called herself a "malnutrition child": William Holtz, *The Ghost in the Little House: A Life of Rose Wilder Lane* (Columbia: University of Missouri Press, 1993), 154. The citation is of a letter

Rose wrote to her boyfriend, Guy Moyston, in the 1920s.

62 "No one can tell me anything about the reasons young people leave farms": Rose, "A Place in the Country" *Country Gentleman* Vol. XC no. 11, March 14, 1925, 26.

63 After school, as Rose reminisced: Rose to Norma Lee Browning, May 17, 1964, Hoover, box 10.

64 "It's a perfect little horror story": Rose Wilder Lane, "Faces at the Window," Hoover, box 32. This was also published in 1989 in William Anderson, *A Little House Sampler* (New York: Harper and Row, 1989).

64 A surviving postcard from a friend mentions "Mr. Lane," and says, "It's your move now": Postcard from Julian Bucher to Rose, September 3, 1907, quoted in *The Ghost in the Little House*, 49.

65 Rose was pregnant soon after the wedding: *The Ghost in the Little House*, 51.

65 she gave birth three months early: The death certificate found by researchers a few years ago lists the cause of death as "stillborn," and the contributory cause as "premature birth (6 months)." Scan of the certificate accessed on April 6, 2016, at http://archives.utah.gov/indexes/data/81448 /2229322/2229322_0000278.jpg

65 Thompson was expecting a baby; Rose

advised her against visiting: Rose to Dorothy Thompson, March 8, 1930, Hoover, box 11.

66 **she clipped a newspaper article about a young woman who was challenging doctors' apparent view**: "Writer Opposes Theory Suffering is a Virtue; Would Reveal Facts to Check Maternity Deaths: Helena Smith Holds Anaesthetic and Medical Skill Can Prevent Pain," by Marguerite Young, *World-Telegram* Staff Writer. Undated clipping probably saved in 1933. Hoover, box 2.

66 **"if there are any country women who are wasting their time envying their sisters"**: Mrs. A. J. Wilder, "Favors the Small Farm Home," *Missouri Ruralist*, February 1911. Also published in *A Little House Sampler*, 99–103.

67 **Rose wrote a confessional article for *Cosmopolitan* harkening back to this period**: Rose Wilder Lane, "I, Rose Wilder Lane, Am the Only Truly Happy Person I Know, and I Discovered the Secret of Happiness on the Day I Tried to Kill Myself," *Cosmopolitan*, June 1926, Hoover, box 35.

68 **Laura stayed long enough to cover the exposition for the *Ruralist*, an assignment Rose had urged her to request**: This

summary comes from Laura Ingalls Wilder, *West From Home*, edited by Roger Lea MacBride (New York: Harper and Row, 1974).

69 "Whom Will You Marry?" opens with a scene in the kitchen: Laura Ingalls Wilder, "Whom Will You Marry?," *McCall's*, 49 (June 1919), 8.

70 "The method used in handling this biographical material": Rose Wilder Lane, *The Making of Herbert Hoover* (New York: The Century, 1920), v.

72 where, she later wrote, she attended an early meeting of communists: Rose Wilder Lane, "Credo." *Saturday Evening Post*, March 7, 1936. Also published as a booklet, *Give Me Liberty* (New York: Longmans, Green, 1936).

Part II: The Family Business
Chapter 3: The Albanian Inspiration

77 "This life is almost intolerable": Rose diary, January 10, 1926. The quotation also appears on page 37.

79 "Forty miles behind and below us Lake Scutari lay flat": Rose Wilder Lane, *The Peaks of Shala* (New York: Harper, 1923).

80 Only one guide, a fifteen-year-old named Rexh Meta: Ibid.

82 "Eighteen months gone. . . . The Albanian

373

book sold in England and America": Rose idea journal, July 11, 1922, Hoover, box 20.

83 "I DON'T WANT TO BE CLUTCHED": Rose to Guy Moyston, January 17, 1925, Hoover, box 9.

83 "Mama Bess [Laura] said 'come' and Rose went": William Anderson, "The Literary Apprenticeship of Laura Ingalls Wilder," *South Dakota History*, 16, no. 2 (Summer 1986), 91–92. Anderson is quoting an interview he conducted with Helen Boylston in 1981.

83 "Papa and Mama quarreling as usual about the farm": Rose diary, February 11, 1924.

84 "I am on Rocky Ridge, where Guy is visiting": Rose diary, May 4, 1924.

84 "I told her many years ago that I would give her five hundred a year": Rose to Guy Moyston, July 27, 1925, Hoover, box 9.

86 "an ordinary rewrite job": Rose to Laura, undated letter from circa November 1924, box 13 quoted in John E. Miller, *Laura Ingalls Wilder and Rose Wilder Lane: Authorship, Place, Time, and Culture* (Columbia, Missouri: University of Missouri Press, 2008), 50.

87 "There was something I wanted the girls to do for me, but they never got around to it and Mother herself was not able":

Laura to "Aunt" Martha Carpenter, June 22, 1925, Hoover, box 14. Most of this extract was published in Anderson, "The Literary Apprenticeship of Laura Ingalls Wilder," *South Dakota History*, 13, no. 4 (Winter 1983), 316.

88 It's unfortunate that the original of this letter is not available for research: Pamela Smith Hill and William Anderson both have written about the likelihood that Laura for a time owned a typewriter that she'd bought around 1910 or 1911 at Rose's urging: " 'Why don't you go to Springfield and look for a good Underwood, rebuilt?' Lane advised her mother to give the typewriter a one-month trial, then pay no more than fifty dollars for it in five-dollar installments." Pamela Smith Hill, *Laura Ingalls Wilder: A Writer's Life* (Pierre: South Dakota State Historical Society Press, 2007), 100. The letter she quotes is an undated one from Rose to Laura between 1908–1914, also available at Hoover.

Anderson wrote, "With some of her early earnings, she purchased a typewriter and thereafter submitted her work [to the *Missouri Ruralist*] typed, on half-sheets of yellow paper." Introduction to William Anderson, editor, *A Little House Reader: A Collection of Writings by Laura Ingalls*

Wilder (New York: HarperCollins, 1998), 70.

No evidence exists that Laura used a typewriter for any of her Little House book drafts.

88 **"In any case, it is certain that Laura did appeal to her aunt"** and **"The wolves would howl first at the North then the East the South and at last to the West"**: Martha Carpenter to Laura, September 2, 1925, Hoover, box 14, page 7. The letter of at least nineteen pages appears to be in several installments, and not all pages are numbered.

89 **this daughter "who roams around the world, borrowing money here and being shot at there"**: Rose to Moyston, July 27, 1925, Hoover, box 9.

91 **"I try to be at the typewriter, in its established place"**: Rose to Moyston, February 10, 1927, Hoover, box 9.

91 **"Old Ibraim, the gardener, putters around all day in this garden"**: Rose to Dorothy Thompson, undated, sometime in 1927, Hoover, box 11.

93 **"I don't like The States because I don't like The States"**: Rose to Moyston, February 16, 1927, Hoover, box 9.

94 **"Her agent said that the big magazines were disgusted by the snakes"**: Rose quotes a telegram from her agent Carl Brandt. "Sorry Yarbwoman refused stop they say

too many snakes stop cheer up am trying Harpers," at the end of her article, "How I Wrote 'Yarbwoman,' " *The Writer* 40, no. 5 (May 1928), 145. Hoover, box 35.

94 "If I can't—*and I can't*—be Shakespeare or Goethe, I'd rather raise good cabbages": Rose to Guy Moyston, July 10, 1927, Hoover, box 9. The passage is also published in Holtz, *The Ghost in the Little House*, 179.

94 "So you see, your critical judgment is again confirmed": Rose to Moyston, September 2, 1927, Hoover, box 9.

95 "Real stories come out of the subconscious, eventually": Rose, "How I Wrote 'Yarbwoman,' " 144.

95 "Going to Albania might have been a mistake": Rose to Clarence Day, September 3, 1927, Hoover, box 5.

96 "Idea/A series of pioneer stories, featuring the woman": Rose, story ideas and notes, February 6, 1928, Hoover, box 20.

97 Then came an excuse in the form of a cable from Laura: Rose diary, January 23, 1928. It says only, "Suddenly, the cable from my mother." Holtz also interprets this as one key reason Rose and Troub left Albania: see *Ghost in the Little House*, page 184.

99 "one serial and a few short stories": Rose, notebook, February 6, 1928.

102 "Here is my wants is to borrou one thousand dollars on my property": April 8, 1928, Rose to Clarence Day. Hoover, box 5.

104 "Aug. 1, 1928, the day after saying I will build a $4,000 house": Rose, diary, August 1, 1928, Hoover, box 20.

105 "Certainly I should have thrilled all over when my mother walked into the new house": Rose to Fremont Older, January 23, 1929, Hoover, box 10.

105 "I look forward with eagerness to the starting of your new Lodge": Eugene F. Johnson to Rose, December 28, 1928, Hoover, box 53.

106 "Took a little drive with both dogs in the afternoon to Cedar Gap": Rose diary, Monday, February 11, 1929.

107 "Joyous day, of discovering via Corinne what Mrs. Young thinks": Rose diary, April 8, 1929.

107 "I find that I have a conscience": Rose to Floyd Dell, July 1928, Hoover, box 5.

107 The "bank account's draining rapidly away to nothing": Rose to Fremont Older, October 7, 1929, Hoover, box 10.

108 "This was the day of the Great Crash—the

evening I said to T": Rose diary, Wednesday, October 23, 1934.

109 **"Once upon a time years and years ago"**: Laura Ingalls Wilder, *Pioneer Girl*, 1.

112 **"no word from Carl about my mother's story"**: Rose diary, June 4, 1930.

112 **"I am a failure and a fool"**: Rose diary, July 29, 1930.

112 **"At typewriter till 4 pm rewriting my mother's story"**: Rose diary, July 31, 1930.

113 **"Bad night, smothering and very much depressed"**: Rose diary, August 4, 1930.

114 **"God! I need money"**: Rose diary, August 14, 1930.

115 **"stupidly, for will it come to anything?"**: Rose diary, August 19, 1930.

116 **"gave him a sales talk on Pioneer Girl"**: Rose diary, October 28, 1930.

116 **"I'm awfully sorry"**: Rose to Laura, November 12, 1930.

117 **"I think I must stay in America and write American stuff"**: Rose diary, memoranda, January 1931.

117 **"I have read it with the greatest interest"**: Marion Fiery to Laura, February 12, 1931, Hoover, box 13.

118 **"Dearest Mama Bess, Marian Fiery (if that's the way she spells it?) said she had written to you"**: Rose to Laura, February 16, 1931.

121 "In reply to your letter of the 12th, I have many more memories": Laura to Fiery, drafted on back of Fiery's February 12 letter.

121 "Our interest in having this book is very definite": March 3, 1931, Fiery to Laura, Hoover, box 13.

122 "This kind of work is called 'ghosting' and no writer of my reputation does it": Rose to Rexh Meta, March 23, 1931, Hoover, box 8.

122 Laura and Rose spent May 21 together: Rose diary, May 21, 1931.

122 "My mother is just sending you the revised manuscript of those tales of her childhood in the Big Woods": Letter draft, Rose to Fiery, May 27, 1931, Hoover, box 13.

123 "Laura Ingalls Wilder, Mansfield, Missouri, Suggested titles: Trundle-bed Tales": Undated, typed list, Hoover, box 13.

123 "Everything still and parching. The locusts are loud and near": Rose journal/notebook, summer 1931.

Chapter 5: The Big American Novel

127 "If ever I write my beautiful great novel and no one cares, I will be so hurt": Rose journal, June 25, 1933.

127 "She took it very well, considering": Rose diary, December 10, 1931.

128 "to get me to answer Harper's Letter": Rose diary, December 11, 1931.

128 "My own stuff is no good": Rose's diary, January 10, 1932.

130 "I am so upset by hope that I can't work": Rose's notebook, August 1932, box 22.

132 "There's a curious half-angry reluctance in my writing for other people": Rose journal, January 25, 1933.

133 " 'Why do they place it in the Dakotas?' ": Rose journal, January 25, 1933.

134 she drafted notes for a multivolume novel about America: Rose's notes for an American novel, Hoover, box 23.

137 "All these days and weeks I am trying to work out my novel": Rose journal, June 25, 1933.

137 "Yesterday I worked out the basic plan of the novel—ten books": Rose journal, June 26, 1933.

142 "He's gone just as I will go, everything lovely in us wasted, uncared for, lost and forgotten": Rose date book, 1933, Hoover, box 23.

144 "I must have known, without knowing, what was coming": Rose journal, April 10, 1933.

147 "Wild hullabaloo because the Morgan firm handled big stock flotations": Rose journal, undated entry probably June 3 or 4, 1933.

147 "There's room for a movement of American

writers, loving the American scene": Rose journal, June 2, 1933.

148 "The dust storms, the dry, harsh winds, the sudden reversions to low temperatures": "Wheat and the Great American Desert," by "A Grain Trader" (Rose), *Saturday Evening Post*, 206, no. 13 (September 23, 1933), 10.

149 "On an impulse I put him to work. Weeded border in the rain": Rose diary, September 25, 1933.

150 Rose corresponded with Grant Forman of Muskogee, Oklahoma: Grant Forman to Rose, March 27, 1933, Hoover, box 14.

151 "In reply to your letter, I will say that the chief of the Osages at that time was named Le Soldat-du-Chene": R. B. Selvidge to Laura, July 5, 1933, Hoover, box 13.

152 Laura used this name in the book, as we know. It was the best she could do drawing on memories from very early childhood. But the chief the Ingallses might have met could not have been Le Soldat-du-Chene, an Osage reported to have lived in the early 1800s. See Frances W. Kaye, "Little Squatter on the Osage Diminished Reserve: Reading Laura Ingalls Wilder's Kansas Indians," *Great Plains Quarterly* 20, no. 2 (Spring 2000), 123–140. Another helpful article on the making of the book and how it departs from history is Penny T. Linsenmayer, "Kansas

Settlers on the Osage Diminished Reserve: A Study of Laura Ingalls Wilder's *Little House on the Prairie*." (*Kansas History* 24, no. 3, 169–185.)

Chapter 6: The Break-Up

155 "It is none of my business but I would suggest": Almanzo to Rose, a note he added at the end of a questionnaire he filled out at her request, about his early farming life, undated in 1937, Hoover, box 33. The quotation also appears on page 97.

158 "As she attempted to draw these together in a single volume": Holtz, *The Ghost in the Little House*, 255.

159 "Now some of us seem to see, in our country's most recent experiences": Rose, *Old Home Town* (New York: Longmans, Green, 1935), 24–25.

162 "My mother was happy because there were trees": "The Name is Mizzoury," typed draft of Rose's book on Missouri, 1–2, Hoover, box 38.

164 "Corinne tired and Jack suddenly yelled at her at dinner": Rose diary, January 27, 1935.

164 "Gosh! Rose your [sic] such a sweet person": Corinne Murray to Rose, October 24, 1935, Hoover, box 52.

165 she wrote to former president Herbert

Hoover: Rose to Herbert Hoover, April 12, 1936. Hoover to Rose, April 16, 1936. Letters from the Herbert Hoover post-presidential collection of Hoover Library, reviewed as assembled in William Holtz Collection, Hoover, box 3.

167 **"We raised our faces and looked straight into the sun"**: *Pioneer Girl*, 79.

168 **"A cloud was coming from the northwest, moving swiftly over the sun"**: Rose Wilder Lane, *Let the Hurricane Roar*, 42.

168 **"A cloud was over the sun. It was not like any cloud they had ever seen before"**: Laura Ingalls Wilder, *On the Banks of Plum Creek* (New York: HarperCollins, 1937, revised edition 1953), 194.

169 **'I don't know. . . . but I do know this, Caroline!"**: *On the Banks of Plum Creek*, 209.

170 **Laura had been going for a doctor**: *Pioneer Girl*, 85. A note there refers readers to page 85 of Laura's early draft of the "Plum Creek" story. That draft is at the Laura Ingalls Wilder Home and Museum in Mansfield, Missouri.

171 **"Look, Mama Bess, If the grasshoppers eat all the tops off the garden vegetables"**: Rose to Laura, undated letter circa 1935, Laura Ingalls Wilder Papers, microfilm of letters from Laura Ingalls Wilder Historic

Home and Museum, State Historical Society of Missouri, Reel 2.

171 **"This week all shot to hell by my mother's yowls"**: Rose diary, July 15, 1936.

172 **Rose recorded that woeful news**: Rose diary, August 10, 1940.

173 **Rose published an essay**: Rose Wilder Lane, "Credo." *Saturday Evening Post*, March 7, 1936. Also published as a booklet, *Give Me Liberty*. New York: Longmans, Green, 1936.

174 **it "has great possibilities for a long time sale"**: Maxwell Aley to Rose, August 28, 1936, Hoover, box 36.

174 **"I meant to send you at least a note"**: Rose to Laura, September 21, 1936.

174 **"I think you are quite right in saying we have not sufficiently stressed the fact that these stories are true"**: Ida Louise Raymond to Laura, December 22, 1936, Hoover, box 13.

176 **"Be deeply, fundamentally, wholly feminine"**: "Woman's Place is in the Home," *Ladies' Home Journal*, October 1936, page 96, clipping in Hoover, box 44.

178 **"if Rose needs money badly, I'll break all the rules"**: Wesley Winans Stout to George Bye, February 24, 1937.

179 **"Farming there was like the chicken business"**: Laura to Rose, March 23, 1937.

179 **"Did folks generally feel that free land,**

homesteading, was a new thing?'": Question-naire from Rose to Almanzo, undated 1937, Hoover, box 33.

180 "People drive me wild. They as a whole are getting just what they deserve": Laura to Rose, March 12, 1937.

181 "Even if we move to the other place, you can still be head of the household": Laura to Rose, March 12, 1937.

181 "Some time ago Rose sent you some of my children's verses and some of hers": Laura to Berta Hader, September 11, 1937, 1–3. Berta and Elmer Hader papers, Ax 441, Special Collections & University Archives, University of Oregon Libraries, Eugene, Oregon. A copy of this letter is also available in the Holtz Collection, Hoover, box 3.

182 "Welcome to Detroit! Remain calm, darling": Rose to Laura, October 11, 1937.

184 "When to my surprise the book made such a success": Laura, Detroit Book Week speech, Hoover, box 13.

185 She told the crowd: Ibid.

185 "Every story in this novel, all the circum-stances, each incident are true": Ibid.

187 "The spirit of the frontier": Ibid.

188 "Thanks for the pages from Pioneer Girl": Laura to Rose, "Monday P.M.," believed to be March 21, 1937 (because it is attached to a letter from Almanzo Wilder with that date).

189 "There were no jobs lying around to go begging": Laura to Rose, March 23, 1937.

190 "I am using a mob scene at the land office": Laura to Rose, undated 1937, probably March 21 or 22.

191 "Like a fool, I paid up all my debts": Rose to Mary Paxton Keely, February 14, 1938. Holtz, box 3.

Part III: The Estrangement
Chapter 7: The Hard Winter

195 "we knew we could expect no help from outside. We must depend on ourselves": *Pioneer Girl*, 212.

196 "You don't know how much good your letter did me and I can't tell you": Laura to Rose, February 19, 1938.

196 The day she moved in, she had one ton of nut coal delivered: Receipt from Union Coal Company of Danbury, April 1938, Hoover, box 3.

197 "For the first time a normal happy feeling of coming home": Rose diary, April 14, 1938.

198 "As you may have guessed, I am again asking you": Ida Louise Raymond to Laura, January 23, 1939, Hoover, box 13.

198 "I have used up all my excuses etc.": Laura to Rose, on back of January 23, 1939 letter from Ida Louise Raymond, Hoover, box 13.

198 "Without your help I would not have the royalties from my books in the bank to draw on": Laura to Rose, January 27, 1939.

199 "And we are living within our income in spite of your advice": Laura to Rose, February 20, 1939.

199 "Hitler's word is about as good as Roosevelt's, isn't it": Laura to Rose, "No. 2 Letter," February 20, 1939.

199 "You will see by this that we have a little more time on Silver Lake": Laura to Rose, April 2, 1939.

202 "I might have known you would fix things!"; "You see, if we are by ourselves, we will be independent"; and "I expect you will find lots of fult [sic] in it": Laura to Rose, May 23, 1939.

203 "You could write the last book from them and finish the series": Laura to Rose, June 13, 1939.

203 "steadily lifts himself by the bootstraps": Rose, note to editor of *Saturday Evening Post*, summer 1939.

203 "SEP turns down serial because it is propaganda": Rose diary, September 14, 1939.

204 "Halgar says this is my unluckiest day. Feels like it. Began typing from tablets Hard Winter": Rose diary, Nov. 12, 1939.

207 "The famous 'October Blizzard' stopped

the trains": Rose to George Bye, July 30, 1932, Hoover, box 1.

208 "Really they took the whole experience": Ibid.

209 "Check for $500 received from mother. Working on Hard Winter": Rose diary, March 9, 1940.

210 "The book . . . is the first candid exposition of the Underground": Rose, book proposal, undated and assumed to be 1940, Hoover, box 1; and rejection letter, Angus Cameron of Little, Brown to George Bye, February 15, 1940, Hoover, box 1.

211 "I can't seem to find a plot, or pattern as you call it": Laura to Rose, February 19, 1938.

213 "I would suggest to Harpers, as a selling scheme, honesty": Rose to George Bye, quoted in George Bye to "Miss Nordstrom," July 3, 1940, James O. Brown Associates records, box 402, Rare Book and Manuscript Library, Columbia University Library.

Chapter 8: Libertarians in Connecticut

225 "Something must be done to enable me to write fiction": Rose diary, May 9, 1940.

226 "Couldn't you work less and pay less and get by just as well": Laura to Rose, March 15, 1938.

227 "Of course (for she has no fear of the

truth) his wife sees him as he is": Rose, "All Men Are Liars," *Woman's Day* (March 1940), Hoover, box 26.

230 **except to say that it included "speeches and singing"**: *Pioneer Girl*, 236.

231 **"Then another speaker talked about 'our glorious country' "**: Holtz, *The Ghost in the Little House*, 384.

231 **"We revolt against the murderous insanity of war"**: Rose, apparent last version of unpublished manuscript, "Don't Marry for Love," Hoover, box 41.

232 **"Don and Ruth *want* this country in the war *now*"**: Rose, journal, May 11, 1940. Also quoted in William Holtz, *The Ghost in the Little House*, 299.

234 **idea for a novel . . . about "a woman hated all her life . . ."** and notes about Churchill: Rose, notebook, Hoover, box 24.

235 **"I.M.P. says the Allies have not fought"**: Rose, notebook, Hoover, box 24.

236 **Early on May 23, she wrote**: Rose, notebook, May 24, Hoover, box 24.

237 **"Dear George," Rose wrote to Bye**: Rose to George Bye, September 11, 1942, James O. Brown Associates Records, box 224, Rare Book and Manuscript Library, Columbia University Library.

238 **"Fact! . . . It is what you might call laconic"**: Laura's outline, "Prairie Girl,"

which became the last two Little House books, 4.

239 "It is a beautiful ring": Laura Ingalls Wilder, *These Happy Golden Years* (New York: Harper and Row, uniform edition, 1953), 215.

241 "Then one morning they heard, far off": *These Happy Golden Years*, 108–110.

242 "One requirement is that my mother *must* have a set of proofs by air mail": Rose to George Bye, September 11, 1942, James Oliver Brown Papers, Columbia, box 224.

Chapter 9: Freedom

245 The *Pittsburgh Courier* had a circulation of about a quarter million: For a thorough analysis of Rose's writing for the *Courier*, see David T. Beito and Linda Royster Beito, "Selling Laissez-faire Antiracism to the Black Masses: Rose Wilder Lane and the *Pittsburgh Courier.*" *The Independent Review* 15 no. 2 (Fall 2010), 279–294.

246 "Here, at least, is a place where I belong": October 31, 1942 column in *The Pittsburgh Courier* quoted in David T. Beito and Linda Royster Beito, Ibid, 283.

246 "Tyrants will always reappear": "ROSE LANE SAYS: America Will Be Saved When the Masses Critically Examine the Spoken

246 **"The effort to create a free economy"**: "ROSE LANE SAYS: Do Americans Intend To Go on Acting As Free Persons?" June 10, 1944, 6.

246 **"What is this value for which the colored American fights two battles"**: "ROSE LANE SAYS: Every Colored American's Insistence on Equality Has Historic Importance," April 17, 1943, 6. Columns accessed from ProQuest Historical Newspapers.

247 **the "race distinction" in America was just a leftover**: February 20, 1943 column in *Pittsburgh Courier*, quoted in David T. Beito and Linda Royster Beito, "Selling Laissez-faire Antiracism," 283.

247 **"No libertarian has ever more creatively weaved"**: David T. and Linda Royster Beito, "Selling Laissez-Faire Antiracism to the Black Masses," *Independent Review* 15, no. 2 (Fall 2010), 283.

247 **"Why did workers walk barefoot, in rags"**: Rose Wilder Lane, *The Discovery of Freedom: Man's Struggle for Authority, Fiftieth Anniversary Edition* (San Francisco: Fox & Wilkes, 1993; the book was originally published in 1943), ix.

248 **"The true revolutionary course which must be followed"**: *The Discovery of Freedom*, 190.

249 **"A most difficult book to appraise"**: Herbert Hoover to Rose, Herbert Hoover Papers, Post-Presidential Individual Correspondence, Herbert Hoover Presidential Library, box 119.

249 **"The very fact that New York reviewers are killing it"**: Rose to Hoover, January 26, 1943, Hoover Papers, Post-Presidential Individual Correspondence, box 119.

250 **For example, over a few pages she summarizes several centuries' worth of revolutions**: *The Discovery of Freedom*, 248–259.

251 **"When it comes to anything fundamental"**: Albert Jay Nock, review of *The Discovery of Freedom* in *National Economic Council Review of Books*, quoted in Ronald Hamoway, editor, *The Encyclopedia of Libertarianism* (Los Angeles: SAGE Reference Publications, 2008), 282.

251 **He admitted that his was both a "condensation" and "amplification" of Rose's work**: Henry Grady Weaver, *The Mainspring of Human Progress*, (originally published in 1947; I quote introduction by Leonard E. Reed, edition published in 1953 by Foundation for Economic Education), 8.

253 **"If schoolteachers say to German children"**: Rose, "What Is This—The Gestapo?" Pamphlet published by the

National Economic Council in New York, August 1943. Hoover, Holtz papers, box 16.

256 **"I have been submerged in reporters, photographers, long distance calls"**: Rose to Charlie Clark, August 11, 1943, Hoover, box 2.

256 **The cemetery association secretary wrote back to Laura**: Mary A. Green to Laura, September 10, 1943, Hoover, box 13.

257 **"I don't know what to say about my writing more"**: Laura to George Bye, May 10, 1943, James Oliver Brown papers, Columbia, box 380.

257 **she first started thinking about, or working on, "The First Three Years and a Year of Grace" at least as early as 1937**: William Anderson has argued that Laura could have started the adult book as early as 1932 or 1933 because she did some drafting on the backs of other papers dated that early. I do not agree that this is proof, because old papers can get mixed up. See Anderson, "The Literary Apprenticeship of Laura Ingalls Wilder," 299.

257 **"about the relationship between a woman of your age and experience and a girl"**: George Bye to Laura, May 5, 1943, James Oliver Brown papers, Columbia, box 380.

257 **"as I have no contact with the working girls"**: Laura to George Bye, James Oliver

Brown papers, Columbia, box 380.

258 Bye wrote Rose immediately: George Bye to Rose, May 14, 1943, James Oliver Brown papers, Columbia, box 224.

258 "My own baby son died thirty-five years ago": Rose to Charlie and Joan Clark, February 8, 1944.

260 "I think she is useful. She is making a cult of pseudo individualism": Rose to Joan Clark, December 29, 1963, Hoover, box 2.

261 Tarshis himself became a martyr in his profession: Email exchange with David Levy, July 28, 2015.

263 "Our weakness is that we have no organization at all": Rose to Jasper Crane, September 11, 1946, Hoover, box 3.

264 "These are the most dangerous times in history": Rose to Crane, September 22, 1946, Hoover, box 3.

264 "The darkest hour is not the time to despair of dawn": Ibid. Rose tells Crane she's quoting her own letter to Herbert Hoover. I have concluded that Rose appropriated this line—"The darkest hour is not the time to despair of dawn"—from "Little Orphan Annie," which was in her time a popular radio drama based on the comic strip of the same name. The earliest use of a very similar phrase that I can find comes from the seventeenth-century theologian Thomas

Fuller in *A Pisgah Sight of Palestine*, "It is always darkest just before the Day dawneth." (She's also quoting the fourth Little House book, *On the Banks of Plum Creek*, which has a chapter entitled, "The Darkest Hour Is Just Before Dawn.")

265 **"You seem to believe that you have nothing to put into a book, that you can only spend money"**: Rose to Crane, January 22, 1947, Hoover, box 3.

266 **"at the insistence of her daughter"**: Maria Cimino, "Laura Ingalls Wilder," *Wilson Library Bulletin* 22 no. 8 (April 1948), 582.

268 **Rose felt that "her parents' marriage was complete in itself"**: Interview with Carol Giffen Mayfield, August 15, 2015.

268 **"I owe Rose, for helping me, at first"**: Laura to George Bye, July 16, 1949. James O. Brown papers, Columbia, box 224. The quotation also appears on page 126.

Chapter 10: Two Legacies

270 **Laura slipped on the steps**: Holtz, *The Ghost in the Little House*, 337. This account is based upon comments made to Holtz by William Anderson and Irene Lichty.

271 **She made her will**: A copy of Laura's will is in the collection at Hoover, box 52.

273 **"required singularly little editing"**: Rosa Ann Moore, "Laura Ingalls Wilder's Orange

Notebooks and the Art of the Little House Books," *Children's Literature* 4 (1975), 118.

274 **"I'm supposed to do an article on all those eight children's books"**: Ernestine Evans to Berta Hader, August 3, 1953, Hoover, box 5 (interfiled from the Berta and Elmer Hader Papers, Special Collections, Knight Library, University of Oregon).

275 **Evans seems to have saved everything**: I reviewed the Ernestine Evans Papers, Rare Book and Manuscript Library, Columbia University.

276 **"Mrs. Almanzo Wilder, with silvery white hair"**: "Mrs. Wilder Led Hard Life In Setting Up Home," *Mansfield Mirror*, May 2, 1957, Hoover, box 17. This article, printed nearly three months after Laura's death, was "a revision of an interview" Laura had given a St. Louis reporter in 1951.

277 **"Here I sit alone and contented in my new-made house"**: Rose diary, January 14, 1949.

278 **she kept her pistol by the screen door**: *Kansas City Star* undated article 1955, quoted in Pamela Smith Hill, *Laura Ingalls Wilder: A Writer's Life* (Pierre: South Dakota State Historical Society, 2007), 186.

278 **"physically active and raving"**: Rose to Jasper Crane, January 5, 1957, Hoover, box 27.

279 **"I often say, not without smugness"**: Rose to Jasper Crane, January 30, 1957, Hoover, box 3.

279 **"I intentionally make no provision in this Will for my mother"**: A copy of Rose's will is at Hoover, box 6.

280 **"My love will be with you always"**: Laura to Rose, undated, 1952, Hoover, box 13.

284 **"If you take one of the tablets"**: Rose to Irene Lichty, August 15, 1963, Hoover, William Holtz Collection, box 3.

285 **"Rose put the manuscripts and little diary back in the carton"**: Irene Lichty Lecount to William Holtz, February 24, 1986, Hoover, William Holtz Collection, box 3.

288 **"There's nothing courageous or useful about this"**: Rose to Jasper Crane, September 5, 1962, Hoover, box 4.

292 **"I run high fevers, my arms are swollen, ruddy and screaming"**: Rose to Roger Lea MacBride, September 2, 1968, Hoover, box 8.

293 **according to John Bass**: He relayed the account of Rose's last days with Don Giffen in a series of emails in 2016.

295 **the MacBrides had moved Rose's papers**: Roger Lea MacBride to William Holtz, January 14, 1991, Hoover, William Holtz Collection, box 3.

300 "**through the mild winter of 1879–1880 with a few settlers as neighbors**": William Anderson tells of his correspondence, at age thirteen, with Rose, who claimed that if he printed that the Ingalls family had had neighbors in 1879 (contrary to *By the Shores of Silver Lake*, which portrays the family alone in the surveyors' house), he would be stating that Laura was a liar. Rose then claimed something that was not true, that the family was sixty miles from a neighbor, in her letter to him: "I object to your publishing a statement that my mother was a liar. The Ingalls family spent their first winter in Dakota Territory approximately sixty miles from any neighbor.

"This is a formal protest against your proposal to publish a statement that my mother was a liar. You will please correct your proposed publication to accord with my mother's published statement in her books." The published booklet, *The Story of the Ingalls* (privately published, 1971 and 1993), does not mention the winter of 1879 specifically. Anderson tells this story in "The Literary Apprenticeship of Laura Ingalls Wilder," 288.

300 **"If my mother's books are not absolutely accurate"**: Ibid, 289.

301 **Laura herself would have disagreed with Rose**: Susan Wittig Albert, *A Reader's Companion to* A Wilder Rose (Bertram, TX: Perservero Press), 40. Albert sums up the point succinctly: "Rose's claim about the Ingalls family's isolation isn't true—and anyway, it was not her mother's representation, it was hers. In 'Pioneer Girl' (in Laura's manuscript and in both the Brandt and Bye versions), the Ingalls family is described as spending the winter of 1880–1881 in the surveyors' house, where they took in a boarder named Walter Ogden."

301 **"She refused most visits from 'Little House' fans"**: Anderson, "The Literary Apprenticeship of Laura Ingalls Wilder," 289.

303 **"a farmer never has any money"**: The quotations on these pages are from Laura Ingalls Wilder, *The First Four Years*, (New York: Harper and Row, 1971), 4, 133.

305 **"My own guess is that she wrote this one in the late 1940s"**: Quotations from Roger's introduction, *The First Four Years*, xiv, xv, xvi.

315 **"In short, market principles have changed my life and guide everything I do"**: Charles Koch's remarks are quoted in *Dark Money*, by Jane Mayer (New York: Doubleday, 2016), Kindle edition.

317 But neither Laura nor the drafter of her will had considered: See Francis M. Nevins, "Little Copyright Dispute on the Prairie: Unbumping the Will of Laura Ingalls Wilder," *St. Louis Law Journal* 44 (Summer 2000), 922–928.

317 Rose's death "gives rise under a federal law to a power in Mrs. Wilder's estate": Roger Lea MacBride to Wright County probate judge Philip Huffman, February 5, 1969, quoted in Complaint, Wright County Library Board and John T. Miller, Personal Representative of the Estate of Laura Ingalls Wilder v. HarperCollins Publishers Inc. and Abigail MacBride Allen and Joe B. Cox, Personal Representative of the Estate of Roger Lea MacBride, October 5, 1999, page 8.

317 The library then received royalty payments: The details of the library's lawsuit are summarized well in Lynda Richardson, "Little Library on the Offensive," *New York Times*, November 23, 1999. The settlement figure of $875,000 came out during negotiations in the *Kansas City Star* story circulated widely by the Associated Press. The final settlement never was made public.

322 **"Everything came at us out of the west—storms, blizzards, grasshoppers"**: "Pioneer Girl" manuscript, version sent to agent George Bye, Hoover, box 14, page 92. Rose probably wrote this sentence, because it does not appear in Laura's original.

323 **Laura ran her pencil like an angry zigzag**: "These Happy Golden Years" typed manuscript, Burton Historical Collection, Detroit Public Library.

325 **"I realized that I had seen and lived it all"**: Laura's Detroit "Book Week" speech, Hoover, box 13. The quotation also appears on page 105.

335 **Rose didn't talk to Stassen but drove to Stassen's parents' farm**: Rose Wilder Lane, "Minnesota Farm Boy," *Woman's Day*, July 1940, Hoover, box 36.

336 **"The Little House Books: Rose-Colored Classics"**: Rosa Ann Moore, typescript of paper delivered at a conference, Hoover, box 17.

338 **Holtz received anonymous calls**: Interview with William Holtz, June 26, 2014.

BIBLIOGRAPHY

The Little House Books
(in chronological order)
Wilder, Laura Ingalls. *Little House in the Big Woods*. New York: Harper and Row, 1932, Uniform Illustrated Edition, 1953.

————. *Farmer Boy*. New York: Harper and Row, 1934, Uniform Illustrated Edition, 1953.

————. *Little House on the Prairie*. New York: Harper and Row, 1935, Uniform Illustrated Edition, 1953.

————. *On the Banks of Plum Creek*. New York: Harper and Row, 1935, Uniform Illustrated Edition, 1953.

————. *By the Shores of Silver Lake*. New York: Harper and Row, 1939, Uniform Illustrated Edition, 1953.

————. *The Long Winter*. New York: Harper and Row, 1940, Uniform Illustrated Edition, 1953.

————. *Little Town on the Prairie*. New York: Harper and Row, 1941, Uniform Illustrated Edition, 1953.

————. *These Happy Golden Years*. New York:

Harper and Row, 1943, Uniform Illustrated Edition, 1953.

―――. *The First Four Years*. New York: Harper and Row, 1971.

Wilder, Laura Ingalls, and Lane, Rose Wilder. *On the Way Home*. New York: Harper and Row, 1962.

Other Works by Laura Ingalls Wilder and/or Rose Wilder Lane

The following strike me as significant to Laura and Rose's thinking and development as writers. This list is by no means exhaustive. I do not list here the few hundred columns Laura wrote about farming life for the *Missouri Ruralist*, for instance, or Rose's huge volume of magazine short stories and essays on individual freedom for the Pittsburgh Courier.

Lane, Rose Wilder. "Credo." *Saturday Evening Post*, March 7, 1936. Also published as a booklet, *Give Me Liberty*. New York: Longmans, Green, 1936.

―――. *The Discovery of Freedom: Man's Struggle Against Authority*. New York: John Day, 1943. Fiftieth Anniversary Edition with new forewords by Roger Lea MacBride and Hans F. Sennholz. San Francisco: Fox & Wilkes, 1993.

―――. Dorothy Thompson and Rose Wilder

Lane: *Forty Years of Friendship. Letters, 1921-1960.* Ed. William Holtz. Columbia: University of Missouri Press, 1991.

———. *Free Land.* New York: Longmans, Green, 1938.

———. *He Was a Man.* Ghostwritten for Jack London. New York: Harper & Brothers, 1925.

———. *Hill-Billy.* New York: Harper & Brothers, 1926.

———. "How I Wrote 'Yarbwoman.'" *The Writer*, May 1928.

———. "I, Rose Wilder Lane, Am the Only Truly Happy Person I Know, and Discovered the Secret of Happiness the Day I Tried to Kill Myself." *Cosmopolitan*, June 1926.

———. *Let the Hurricane Roar.* New York: Longmans, Green, 1933.

———. *The Making of Herbert Hoover.* New York: The Century Co., 1920.

———. "Object: Matrimony." *Saturday Evening Post*, September 1, 1934.

———. *Old Home Town.* New York: Longmans, Green, 1935.

———. *The Peaks of Shala.* New York: Harper & Brothers, 1923.

———. *Travels with Zenobia: Paris to Albania by Model T Ford, A Journal by Rose Wilder Lane and Helen Dore Boylston.* Ed. William Holtz. Columbia, Missouri: University of Missouri Press, 1983.

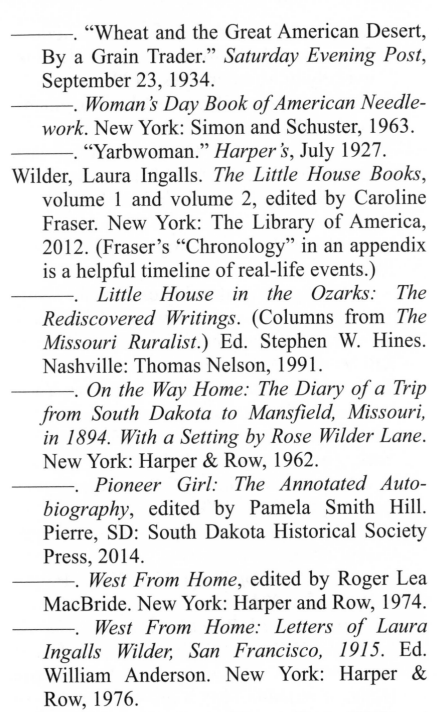

———. "Wheat and the Great American Desert, By a Grain Trader." *Saturday Evening Post*, September 23, 1934.

———. *Woman's Day Book of American Needlework*. New York: Simon and Schuster, 1963.

———. "Yarbwoman." *Harper's*, July 1927.

Wilder, Laura Ingalls. *The Little House Books*, volume 1 and volume 2, edited by Caroline Fraser. New York: The Library of America, 2012. (Fraser's "Chronology" in an appendix is a helpful timeline of real-life events.)

———. *Little House in the Ozarks: The Rediscovered Writings*. (Columns from *The Missouri Ruralist*.) Ed. Stephen W. Hines. Nashville: Thomas Nelson, 1991.

———. *On the Way Home: The Diary of a Trip from South Dakota to Mansfield, Missouri, in 1894. With a Setting by Rose Wilder Lane*. New York: Harper & Row, 1962.

———. *Pioneer Girl: The Annotated Autobiography*, edited by Pamela Smith Hill. Pierre, SD: South Dakota Historical Society Press, 2014.

———. *West From Home*, edited by Roger Lea MacBride. New York: Harper and Row, 1974.

———. *West From Home: Letters of Laura Ingalls Wilder, San Francisco, 1915*. Ed. William Anderson. New York: Harper & Row, 1976.

Wilder, Laura Ingalls and Lane, Rose Wilder. *A*

Little House Reader. Ed. William Anderson. New York: HarperCollins, 1998.

―――. *A Little House Sampler*. Ed. William Anderson. New York: Harper & Row, 1989.

About Laura Ingalls Wilder and Rose Wilder Lane

The following books have contributed to my understanding.

Anderson, William. "Laura Ingalls Wilder and Rose Wilder Lane: The Continuing Collaboration." *South Dakota History*, 16, no. 2 (Summer 1986), 89–143.

―――. *Laura's Album: A Remembrance Scrapbook of Laura Ingalls Wilder*. New York: HarperCollins, 1998.

―――. *Laura's Rose: The Story of Rose Wilder Lane, Daughter of Laura Ingalls Wilder*. De Smet, South Dakota: Laura Ingalls Wilder Memorial Society, 1976.

―――. *Laura Wilder of Mansfield: A Life of the Author of the "Little House" Books*. Privately published, 1968 and 1982.

―――. "The Literary Apprenticeship of Laura Ingalls Wilder." *South Dakota History*, 13, no. 4 (Winter 1983), 285–331.

―――. *The Story of the Ingalls: A Biography of the Family from the "Little House" Books*. Privately published, 1971 and 1993.

————. *The Story of the Wilders: A Biography of Almanzo Wilder and the Family from "Farmer Boy."* Privately published, 1972 and 1983.

Anderson, William, ed. *The Horn Book's Laura Ingalls Wilder: Articles about and by Laura Ingalls Wilder, Garth Williams and the Little House Books.* Privately published for distribution at Ingalls-Wilder home sites, 1987.

Anderson, William, and Kelly, Les. *Laura Ingalls Wilder Country: The People and Places in Laura Ingalls Wilder's Life and Books.* New York: Harper Perennial, 1990.

————. *Little House Country: A Photo Guide to the Home Sites of Laura Ingalls Wilder.* Kansas City, MO: Terrell Publishing, 1989.

Fellman, Anita Clair. *Little House, Long Shadow: Laura Ingalls Wilder's Impact on American Culture.* Columbia: University of Missouri Press, 2008.

Holtz, William. *The Ghost in the Little House: A Life of Rose Wilder Lane.* Columbia: University of Missouri Press, 1993.

Lynn, Teresa. *Little Lodge on the Prairie: Freemasonry & Laura Ingalls Wilder.* Austin, Texas: Tranquility Press, 2014.

Marcus, Leonard S., ed. *Dear Genius: The Letters of Ursula Nordstrom.* New York: HarperCollins, 1998.

Miller, Dwight M. ed. *Laura Ingalls Wilder and the Frontier: Five Perspectives.* Lanham, MD: University Press of America, 2002.

Miller, John E. *Becoming Laura Ingalls Wilder: The Woman Behind the Legend.* Columbia: University of Missouri Press, 1998.

————. *Laura Ingalls Wilder and Rose Wilder Lane: Authorship, Place, Time, and Culture.* Columbia: University of Missouri Press, 2008.

Smith, Dorothy Belle. *The Wilder Family Story.* Malone, NY: Almanzo and Laura Ingalls Wilder Association, 1972.

Spaeth, Janet. *Laura Ingalls Wilder.* Boston: Twayne Publishers, 1987.

Walker, Barbara M. *The Little House Cookbook.* New York: HarperCollins, 1979. (Not only recipes. A history of the hardships of daily life for the Ingalls and Wilder families.)

The Pioneer West: A Brief Bibliography

For years, every time I picked up a history book about the American West, I'd turn to the index and look for "Wilder, Laura Ingalls." Her name was not there, ever. Well, maybe it was a few times, but the references were secondary to Western events. Historians have not found Laura Ingalls Wilder to be a significant figure in the settling of the West. Either her family moved there too late, or their experiences were considered too ordinary, or the interpretation of her experiences in her children's books was not complete enough.

Those who follow her life—such as the dozens of amateur and professional researchers I met in summer 2015 at a conference called the Laurapalooza in Brookings, South Dakota—would disagree. Laura's life, her real life, painstakingly researched, shows us ordinary life in the last years of the transcontinental railroad expansion across the Upper Midwest. The reality of the Ingalls and Wilder families' struggles augment our perceptions of the frontier in their time. Consider the facts those and other historians have dug up: the actual illness that took away sister Mary's sight was not scarlet fever but spiral meningoencephalitis; the reason the grasshoppers that ate every living thing in Minnesota in the mid-1870s no longer exist is that their refuge zone in Colorado was developed; Laura's father acquired his violin while living in Illinois as a teenager; and more. Their search for such details goes beyond simply loving the Little House books and a devotion to its author. They are serious searchers who want the real stories, sad though they might be.

Laura said it herself in her letters to Rose: life on the frontier broke the will, health, and economies of many a farmer who tried. It broke Almanzo and her, who fled Dakota Territory. Of course, the Little House books don't dwell on many of the difficult aspects of the frontier. That they did not begs the question, then: What else *was* going on out there?

Life on the road west was dusty, cramped, and uncomfortable. Children not struck down by illness grew up early.

Settlers clashed with American Indians and their ways of life. (The tribes were moved, lied to, and moved again; settlers tended to view the Indians' reactions as strangely hostile rather than understandably hostile.) Crazy Horse's last battle raged just west of where the Ingalls family settled and only three years before they arrived there.

Shacks, sod houses, and dugouts provided dark quarters. Food was limited and cooking implements very basic. Land they tried to farm was ravaged by various natural forces that included multiyear locust plagues and too little rainfall. The land that became eastern South Dakota is high and arid, unsuitable for farming water-needy crops except in wet years and impossible to irrigate. (South Dakota learned that last lesson in the 1970s, when the federal government put a stop to a massive water-moving project that would have destroyed much land and altered the course of the Jim River.) Food and fuel were limited, and farming the tough sod in the semidry climate was not a long-term living.

Life for women was especially trying. They cooked, cleaned, and tended gardens and livestock in marginal conditions. Education was usually cut short.

Here is a select bibliography of excellent studies and discussions that cover aspects of the American frontier during Laura Ingalls Wilder's time not addressed in her books.

Enss, Chris. *Hearts West: True Stories of Mail-Order Brides*. Guilford, Connecticut: Two Dot, 2005.

Frazier, Ian. *Great Plains*. New York: Picador, 2001. First published 1989 by Farrar, Straus, and Giroux.

Klein, Kerwin Lee. *Frontiers of the Historical Imagination: Narrating the European Conquest of Native America, 1890–1990*. Berkeley: University of California Press, 1997.

Lesy, Michael. *Wisconsin Death Trip*. Albuquerque: University of New Mexico Press, 1973, reprinted 2000.

Lockwood, Jeffrey A. *Locust: The Devastating Rise and Mysterious Disappearance of the Insect That Shaped the American Frontier*. New York: Basic Books, 2004.

McMurtry, Larry. *Crazy Horse*. New York: Penguin, 2001.

Peavy, Linda, and Smith, Ursula. *Pioneer*

Women: The Lives of Women on the Frontier.
Norman, Oklahoma: University of Oklahoma
Press, 1998.

Rolvaag, Ole Edvart. *Giants in the Earth: A Saga
of the Prairie.* New York: Harper Perennial
Modern Classics, 1999.

Slotkin, Richard. *The Fatal Environment: The
Myth of the Frontier in the Age of Indus-
trialization, 1800–1890.* Norman, Oklahoma:
University of Oklahoma Press, 1985.

Stratton, Joanna. *Pioneer Women: Voices of
Women on the Kansas Frontier.* New York:
Touchstone, 1982.

Webb, Water Prescott. *The Great Plains.* New
York: Grosset & Dunlap, 1931.

I have found the following books a great help
in understanding the rhythms of daily life and
suffering going on around them during the years
that Laura Ingalls Wilder and Rose Wilder Lane
were writing together.

Egan, Timothy. *The Worst Hard Time: The
Untold Story of Those Who Survived the
Great American Dust Bowl.* New York:
Mariner Books, 2006.

Kyvig, David E. *Daily Life in the United
States, 1920–1940: How Americans Lived
Through the Roaring Twenties and the Great
Depression.* Chicago: Ivan R. Dee, 2002.

Resources on Anti-New Deal Politics and the Libertarian Movement

Boaz, David. "Key Concepts of Libertarianism," Cato Institute, January 1, 1999. cato.org /publications/commentary/key-concepts -libertarianism.

Boaz, David, ed. *The Libertarian Reader: Classic and Contemporary Writings from Lao-Tsu to Milton Friedman.* New York: Simon and Schuster, 2015.

Mayer, Jane. *Dark Money: The Hidden History of the Billionaires Behind the Rise of the Radical Right.* New York: Doubleday, 2016.

Phillips-Fein, Kim. *Invisible Hands: The Making of the Conservative Movement from the New Deal to Reagan.* New York: W. W. Norton, 2009.

Center Point Large Print
600 Brooks Road / PO Box 1
Thorndike, ME 04986-0001 USA

(207) 568-3717

US & Canada:
1 800 929-9108
www.centerpointlargeprint.com